# Tom Hayden
## on
## Social Movements

# Also by Tom Hayden

*The Other Side* (with Staughton Lynd) (1966)

*Rebellion in Newark: Official Violence and Ghetto Response* (1967)

*Rebellion and Repression: Testimony by Tom Hayden Before the National Commission on the Causes and Prevention of Violence, and the House Un-American Activities Committee* (1969)

*Trial* (1970)

*The Love of Possession Is a Disease with Them* (1972)

*Vietnam: The Struggle for Peace, 1972–1973* (1973)

*The American Future: New Visions Beyond Old Frontiers* (1980, 1999)

*Reunion: A Memoir* (1988)

*The Lost Gospel of the Earth: A Call for Renewing Nature, Spirit, and Politics* (1996)

*Irish Hunger: Personal Reflections on the Legacy of Famine* (1998)

*The Zapatista Reader* (2001)

*Irish on the Inside: In Search of the Soul of Irish America* (2003)

*The Port Huron Statement: The Visionary Call of the 1960s Revolution* (2005)

*Radical Nomad: C. Wright Mills and His Times* (2006)

*Street Wars: Gangs and the Future of Violence* (2006)

*Ending the War in Iraq* (2007)

*Voices of the Chicago 8: A Generation on Trial* (2008)

*Writings for a Democratic Society: The Tom Hayden Reader* (2008)

*The Long Sixties: From 1960 to Barack Obama* (2009)

*Inspiring Participatory Democracy: Student Movements from Port Huron to Today* (2012)

*Listen, Yankee! Why Cuba Matters* (2015)

*Hell No: The Forgotten Power of the Vietnam Peace Movement* (2017)

# Tom Hayden
## on
## Social Movements

Copyright © 2019 by Paul Ryder and Susan Wind Early. All rights reserved. This book may not be reproduced, in whole or in part in any form beyond that copying permitted by Sections 107 and 108 of the U.S. Copyright Law and except by reviewers for the public press, without written permission from the publishers.

| | |
|---|---|
| Editing and publishing: | Paul Ryder and Susan Wind Early |
| | Mariposa, California, pryder888@gmail.com |
| Printing and distribution: | Amazon.com |
| | Seattle, Washington |

Front-cover quotation by Tom Hayden, interview, Washington University in St. Louis, University Libraries, "Interviews with Civil Rights and Peace Movement Activists," 1985.

Back-cover photograph by Vic Condiotty with permission of the *Seattle Times*. All rights reserved.

Chapters 1 and 2 appeared in *Rolling Stone* magazine as an interview by Tim Findley. Copyright © Rolling Stone LLC 1972. All Rights Reserved. Used by permission. Chapters 3 through 6 are in the public domain. All contents are transcripts of talks by and interviews with Tom Hayden, lightly edited for clarity. The chapter introductions, footnotes, chronology, and index are by the editors.

Typeset in Adobe Garamond Pro
Printed in the United States of America
ISBN-13: 978-0-578-40047-1 (Paper)
ISBN-13: 978-0-692-19682-3 (Ebook)

SEBASTIAN.

    I am standing water.

ANTONIO.

    I'll teach you how to flow.

— William Shakespeare, *The Tempest*

# Contents

Chapter 1
    Tom Hayden: The Rolling Stone Interview, Part I    1

Chapter 2
    Tom Hayden: The Rolling Stone Interview, Part II    57

Chapter 3
    The History of the Antiwar Movement    95

Chapter 4
    Indochina and the American Power Structure    151

Chapter 5
    Patterns in the Way People Struggle    179

Chapter 6
    What is the Hardest Question We Face Now?    195

A Vietnam Peace Movement Chronology, 1945–1975    213

Index    229

Acknowledgments    253

*Chapter 1*

# Tom Hayden: The *Rolling Stone* Interview

Through the Sixties with the Principal Author
of The Port Huron Statement
By Tim Findley, *Rolling Stone*
June 22, 1972

## Part I

*This interview took place as Tom Hayden and activist-actress Jane Fonda were preparing to launch the Indochina Peace Campaign with a nationwide speaking tour during the 1972 presidential election. The Democratic Party was about to nominate South Dakota Senator George McGovern to run against incumbent Republican President Richard Nixon. McGovern had pledged to end the Vietnam War. Joining in the questioning was Richard Flacks, a founder of Students for a Democratic Society (SDS).*

ଔ

*Rolling Stone: You were a reporter at the 1960 Democratic Convention in Los Angeles.*

Right. I hitchhiked to Berkeley. Then I went to Los Angeles. I was a college editor, influenced by the Beat Generation. My thing was to hitchhike all over the country in different directions—the Latin Quarter of New Orleans and Miami and New York,

Greenwich Village, so that summer I went to North Beach. My justification for it as an editor was I was going to cover the Democratic convention. I was always divided between being what now you would call a radical and what didn't have a name then because there was no politics.

*You passed for a liberal.*

No, there was no politics. It was unimaginable to me. I'd never heard of or seen a demonstration. There was no sense that there was something like a political form of protest. It was mainly like trying to mimic the life of James Dean. It wasn't political. The other half of me was in the establishment, an ambitious young reporter who wanted to be a famous correspondent. I got to Berkeley and immediately went to the first person who was giving out leaflets. I'd never seen anything like this before, and I told her who I was and what I was interested in. Being political, they took me home and gave me a room to stay in for a few weeks and tried to educate me politically, because I was a student editor. They wanted me to form a campus political party back in Michigan, which I did when I went back in September. But anyway, come August I went to Los Angeles to cover the Democratic Convention for the *Michigan Daily*.

*This at a time when social protest was beginning?*

The people I stayed with in Berkeley were involved. You know what they were doing? They were organizing farmworkers. This guy, Herb Mills, came up to me one day. I had heard he was a leftist, and I didn't know what that was, but he drove me out to Livermore one day and showed me the nuclear reactor, where all the hydrogen bombs were made, with the fence around it, and he described the nuclear weapons and the arms race. Then another day, he drove me out into the fields and valleys, and he told me about the Chicanos and the farmworkers, and the conditions under which they labor. And I went with him and some others to the convention, where he was organizing a demonstration. I believe the demonstration was about civil rights because that's the first time I saw or met Martin Luther King. He was on the picket line. The sit-ins had started in February.

I spent the time during the convention half on the picket line and half inside covering the convention. By the end, the divisions in me had grown further. I was writing articles back to the *Michigan Daily* proclaiming the birth of an American student movement, given what I had seen in California. The university officials were upset in Ann Arbor, because apparently they sensed the danger in this, even though I had no idea of it, and they immediately began a campaign to control me as editor of the newspaper. On the other hand, I was in part tied to the Kennedy image also, in the sense he was younger, he seemed more in touch with reality than Nixon. Now I look back on it, it may have made him a more dangerous person, but the appeal of the New Frontier and the Peace Corps was pretty great.[1]

There was a group in Ann Arbor called the Americans Committed to World Responsibility that now sounds like something Rockefeller would set up. This group conceived of the idea of the Peace Corps, and I was a marginal member of it. During Kennedy's campaign, they took the idea to him, and he said he approved of it and would work it into his speeches and programs, and he did. I recall the excitement of our group that the possibility of doing service for humanity was opening up because of Kennedy, and that was the difference between him and Nixon.

I remember meeting Kennedy in the middle of the night during the campaign. He came to Ann Arbor, and I was standing

---

[1] The "New Frontier" was the theme of Senator John F. Kennedy's 1960 presidential campaign. He meant it to describe all his programs, but the public focused on space exploration. Kennedy had different priorities: "I'm not that interested in space...Everything that we do ought to really be tied into getting onto the Moon ahead of the Russians." (Presidential meeting in the cabinet room of the White House, on Supplemental Appropriations for NASA, November 21, 1962.)

on the steps of the Michigan Union covering it. Two in the morning. It was late. The streets were full of young people, just like today for McGovern and in 1968 for McCarthy and going all the way back.[2] This is the first time I think, the phenomena of so-called "new politics" with a candidate reaching out to new constituencies had appeared. This whole street in front of the Michigan Union was full, and Kennedy gave an impromptu speech, which everyone was excited by, in which he endorsed the idea of a Peace Corps. I rode upstairs in an elevator with him later, asking him questions like an idiot, journalists' kind of questions. That was the only time I ever saw him, and it's strange, because the last time I saw Robert Kennedy was in an elevator by accident also, going up, one week before he was shot.

*It was a time when international events seemed to forecast change along with independent struggles over civil rights here. Did that affect you?*

Yes. First, there was a sit-in. I was sitting in my newspaper office in Ann Arbor, and Al Haber, who founded SDS, came over. He was the campus radical. He had a beard and a lot of books, and he just knew a lot, and he was much older than anyone else, and he came over to talk to me about this sit-in movement that was starting. He explained to me sit-ins had been used by the labor movement, how black students were using them, and it was important to come to their defense and see this cause was our cause. He was into organizing northern conferences and support demonstrations. Picket lines started in Ann Arbor that spring, I believe at Woolworth and Kresge stores, that students were trying to boycott in the South.

---

[2] U.S. Senator George McGovern (1922–2012) from South Dakota was the Democratic Party nominee for President in 1972. He was defeated by incumbent Republican President Richard Nixon by sixty-one percent to thirty-seven percent in the popular vote and 520 to 17 in the Electoral College. U.S. Senator Eugene McCarthy (1916–2005) from Minnesota was a candidate for President in 1968. He lost the Democratic nomination to Vice President Hubert Humphrey.

## Tom Hayden: The Rolling Stone *Interview* – Part I

Even then I felt uncomfortable, and I went on the picket line a couple of times, but I had to be talked into it, and I didn't have any contact with the South or with the black students until the fall of 1960. In October, I went down to Atlanta one weekend as a student editor, and I covered a South-wide conference of black students who were in SNCC, and it wasn't until then that I was moved by them, by the concept of direct action, by the concept of being able personally to make a difference.[3] Before that, it was in the air. The other thing in the air was that the students were on the move all around the world. Being a student editor, it made me hyper-conscious of the role of students. The news was always coming in from around the world about uprisings in Turkey, Japan, and Latin American countries. It suddenly became a visible world-wide phenomenon, and when black students in the South started demonstrating, that was the beginning of students becoming a social force around the world.

*In June, there was a demonstration in San Francisco against HUAC.*[4]

I didn't understand that well. The same person who told me about the farmworkers was carrying around *Operation Abolition* and I must have seen it about four times, and as soon as I got back from Berkeley, I arranged for it to be shown on the Michigan campus.[5] I don't know why this took place, but the room was packed. There were three hundred people, at that time an unprecedented

---

[3] The Student Nonviolent Coordinating Committee (SNCC) emerged from the 1960 sit-ins at segregated lunch counters in Greensboro, North Carolina, and across the South. Through interstate bus Freedom Rides and voter registration drives, SNCC became identified with moral and physical courage.

[4] The House Un-American Activities Committee (HUAC) was the U.S. House counterpart of the U.S. Senate committee chaired by Joseph McCarthy of Wisconsin, which investigated accused domestic subversives.

[5] *Operation Abolition* was a documentary film about HUAC's San Francisco hearings, produced and distributed by the Committee.

number, even though I don't think people understood the formal issues involved well, like contempt of a congressional committee. Redbaiting was a new word. Witch-hunting was a new word. Nobody was tied into the tradition of the thirties or the fifties that would make those words have an emotional meaning. It was clear, though, there were outdated and irrational people on this congressional committee behaving in, you know, insane ways. As allies, they were enlisting the San Francisco police, who were washing young people like ourselves down the stairs of City Hall in San Francisco. People were falling down stairs, pregnant women tripping on the water-filled stairs and heads were being broken. I never saw anything like it in my life. After all, the people on the stairs were like us.

*Dick Flacks: All right, this time we're talking about is the early sixties. What did you think American students could accomplish through direct action or other forms of action? Is it possible to think back to that?*

At this time, the Kennedy administration was giving some legitimacy to this worldwide student phenomenon, and to the Peace Corps and the National Student Association, which we now know was a CIA-run organization whose primary business was helping to infiltrate and shape the international student movement. Then they were supportive of the sit-ins, supportive of the idea of a world student movement, in other words, the very movement that turned out to be revolutionary in the form of the Panthers and SDS in the late sixties.[6] But it had two sides. It was easy and legitimate to support, and we didn't have any idea what the CIA was.

---

[6] Huey Newton (1942–1989) and Bobby Seale (1936–) founded the Black Panther Party for Self-Defense in Oakland in 1966. Students for a Democratic Society (SDS) was a national New Left student action organization founded in 1960 in Ann Arbor, Michigan, by Al Haber. It lasted until 1969.

## Tom Hayden: The Rolling Stone *Interview* – Part I

It was unimaginable that the National Student Association was a CIA front. That's important to take into account when you say Kennedy had something to do with legitimizing the student movement. In reality, the forces around him were trying to take advantage of the discontent of youth and channel it into certain directions that could be beneficial to the image of the United States. We didn't know that. We didn't know about the Peace Corps until bitter experiences within a couple of years proved that was so.

At the same time, Kennedy was sending Green Berets off to the jungles of Southeast Asia. They were supposed to be in the service of humanity—a counter-insurgency force that could, through building roads, hospitals, and schools, learning the language, living with the people, accomplish much the same ideals young people here were talking about in the Peace Corps. Meanwhile, he was involving the United States in a direct combat capacity in Vietnam.

The National Liberation Front of South Vietnam was formed in 1960. While we were going through the Beat Generation and the apathy of the late fifties, they were going through the massacres and roundups of the Diem administration. They also decided to organize, to do something about it at the same time the other movements arose around the world. That one in Vietnam was temporarily beyond our gaze. Kennedy did not legitimize that one. There was no talk of how wonderful it was that the Vietnamese were rising from their knees and starting to fight for their freedom. Nonviolence and reform were acceptable, violence and revolution were not.

There was talk about the morality of the black students in the South, the students in Turkey, the students around the world. That became campaign rhetoric by Kennedy, at least in the areas where student movements were progressive, in favor of civil rights and peace and so forth. They also were subject to control and manipulation. We didn't understand we were being controlled and manipulated, not only directly by people being in our ranks from the CIA, but also in our minds. The emergence of the National Liberation Front in Vietnam was immediately treated as the emergence of the "Viet Cong," the terrorists.[7] They were not to be included within the framework of legitimate uprisings, nationalist movements and student movements that were the atmosphere of the early sixties.

Now, when you look back, it's the National Liberation Front that has brought forward and exposed all the problems of American society. Other movements and organizations have been exposed as CIA fronts, have gone into the McCarthy or McGovern campaigns or have dissolved in idealistic futility. Many progressive-minded people of today were swept up in this kind of movement. I was approached to go to the "Communist-oriented" World Youth Festival in Helsinki in 1962 by an innocuous-enough group called International Student Travel, a branch of NSA which turned out later to be CIA-funded.

The civil rights and student movement energy of the early sixties was not then considered a menace or a scourge by the American establishment, although it was by HUAC and the ultra-conservatives. It was considered perhaps a positive thing that could embellish the image of the United States. The establishment was into funding us to go to Helsinki Youth Festivals and other places to show how, with all our problems of racism, there were Americans who were aggressively trying to abolish discrimination. We didn't know it was the CIA. We thought the people who were the "liberal establishment" were bad and probably couldn't be revived—as we see it still is today nearly

---

[7] The South Vietnamese fighting against the United States were National Liberation Front (NLF) soldiers. "Viet Cong" is a term of contempt invented by pro-U.S. newspapers in Saigon. Journalist Wilfred Burchett wrote that in the NLF's view, the term is for those "who accept the myth that if a label like 'Viet Cong' can be hung on Vietnamese, they automatically become foreigners in their own country, with no rights except to be annihilated." Wilfred Burchett, *The Furtive War*, New York: International Publishers, 1963.

in power through the McGovern campaign—but not the people who are the organizers of it. Not those people. We didn't know they were CIA then, but we sensed they were intransigent.

For example, in the fall of 1961, I was at the NSA Congress in Madison, Wisconsin as the outgoing editor of the *Michigan Daily*. It was still unclear whether I would work in SDS as a field secretary. I was out of school two months trying to decide whether to help form SDS or whether to go in and be the "left wing" of the NSA. As events turned out, I went south and was a field secretary for SDS, worked there one year, came back, and we formed SDS as a chapter-based organization in the spring of 1962 at Port Huron.

But in the fall of 1961, when two or three of us were going around trying to form an organization, and seeking moral and financial support from liberal and labor organizations, I was also a candidate for national affairs vice president of NSA. Other people there who later became the leadership of SDS were also either running for office or involved in the power politics of NSA. That's where you learned to be an American politician: delegations, bloc voting, hustling people, campaigning, becoming a monster. The people we were against we called the NSA "foreign policy elite" because they ran the international affairs section with a heavy hand, they were stationed all over Europe, and they seemed to fly in from European capitals and regulate what would happen at the Congress.

They were people in their thirties, older people, and it all became a little more chilling when one day we were in the office of NSA President Richard Rettig, from the University of Wisconsin, just before the Congress and found on his desk a chart written in his hand. Haber and other people, SDS people, were listed as being the Left on this chart, then there was a Right, and there was a Center, in terms of power blocs. And at the top, there was a group called the control group [*laughter*] called Control Group—capital C, capital G—and he was in it, and all the other people from abroad were in it and a couple of select people from the national office. Rettig and virtually every one of these people turned out to be CIA. We ran against them, attacking them as an older elite that wasn't from the campuses and was too much into the Cold War.

We narrowly lost. Their string-pulling stopped a couple of our candidates by a narrow margin, but one of us won. Paul Potter was elected national affairs vice president, not knowing what he was getting into.[8]

## The Old Left

The people we thought were intransigent were the people who were the heads of our parent organization, proclaimed socialists, like Michael Harrington, and labor leaders.[9] They were frightened at the prospect of a student movement, thinking it would inevitably disrupt the tradition of the liberal left community and take the side of revolutionary movements, which it has. They were perceptive at the time, but they also taught us. They were unbelievable. They locked us out of our office. They called us things we had never heard of before, "Leninists."

*At NSA?*

No, the parent body of SDS, the League for Industrial Democracy, old socialists and trade unionists. When we published the Port Huron Statement, they considered it too far left. Haber and I were in Senator Joseph Clark's office a couple of weeks after Port Huron collecting literature on disarmament.

---

[8] Paul Potter (1939–1984), SDS President in 1964–1965, was best known for his April 17, 1965 speech at the first national Vietnam peace demonstration in Washington, DC, at which he said, "We must name that system. We must name it, describe it, analyze it, understand it and change it."

[9] Michael Harrington (1928–1989), was the author of *The Other America: Poverty in the United States* (1962) and a founder of Democratic Socialists of America (DSA) in 1982.

We got a phone call from New York telling us to come back because we'd just been fired. We spent the summer after that fighting for the right to organize against people who said they were socialists and who were accusing us of being too radical. We didn't know what they were talking about.

The best of them were part of the CIO tradition—the sit-ins in Flint and the other factories.[10] For the most part, they supported the New Deal and then in World War II, they fought against fascism. But most of them by this time had been hoisted into government slots in the system.[11] The Wagner Act had legitimized the labor unions regarding their rights to collective bargaining. Others had gone into government positions, and they accepted the American system as being a viable system to work within and reform. It was therefore easy for them to purge the Communists, or so-called Communists, from the labor movement in 1948, and to take the side of the United States fairly unswervingly in 1950 on, to be silent during the Korean War, and to sell themselves to the CIA as cultural workers. They formed the Congress for Cultural Freedom. From that time until 1972 they represented the Humphrey-Meany wing of the Democratic Party.[12]

They did think working that way was the most progressive thing to do. By the late fifties and sixties, you can imagine what kind of people they were. They were utterly absorbed into the

---

[10] The Congress of Industrial Organizations (CIO) was a federation of unions organized industry-by-industry. The American Federation of Labor (AFL) organized unions by craft. The two federations merged into the AFL-CIO in 1955.

[11] Sometimes "system" is used to refer only to the government, especially the police. In other contexts, it refers to the entire apparatus of authority in a society—political, social, cultural, and economic.

[12] Hubert Humphrey (1911–1978) was a U.S. Senator from Minnesota and the U.S. Vice President under President Lyndon Johnson. George Meany (1894–1980) was President of the AFL-CIO union federation from 1955 to 1979. Both were liberal anti-communists who strongly backed the war.

system. They retained a liberal or radical rhetoric, but their real job was to be the Left gatekeeper of American radicalism, on what was legitimate.

I'm getting to how the early SDS people and others perceived them in the early days of the student movement. It wasn't so clear-cut at the time what the nature of this grouping was. Haber went to the League for Industrial Democracy to see whether a student organization could be developed out of it, right? There was an effort to get support from the labor unions, from the League for Industrial Democracy, because their rhetoric said they were for civil rights and they were for domestic reform. We felt the forces these liberal leadership people represented could be renewed—intellectuals, liberal professionals, parts of the labor movement and the church community. We thought that the Democratic Party could be reorganized. It was called "realignment." Now, a lot of these concepts were imported into SDS, as I look back, by people who were already ideological and joined SDS.

We accepted the theory for a while that moral students taking moral actions, especially black students from the South, could energize the sleeping liberal wing of the Democratic Party. Our first experience, from 1962 to 1965 was mainly one in which any hopes of that happening was stripped from us because it started with our being accused of being too radical. SDS almost wiped out at its inception. It went from there all the way to the 1964 Democratic Convention in Atlantic City when Hubert Humphrey and others who represented this tradition engineered a compromise which was no compromise that prevented Mississippi sharecroppers and the Freedom Democratic Party from being seated at Atlantic City. That group symbolized all the work and all the hopes of the whole civil rights movement. The rejection of them, when their cause was so clear-cut, was the final disillusionment with working with the liberal establishment. The left wing of established American politics at that time is what SDS was trying to relate to and thought it might be part of.

*ADA, like Hubert Humphrey, for example ...* [13]

We were against the co-opted leadership.

*Dick Flacks: The Democratic left community had many differences within it, but we thought it existed and SDS was part of it. Yet when we started to take certain positions, a lot of those people tried to destroy it right at the outset. The positions had to do with ending the Cold War, seeing something positive, go on with that. What was it in our view that Michael Harrington regarded as anathema at the time?*

A lot of it had to do with our refusal to respect the standing leadership of the labor movement or the old guard of all the liberal and socialist sect groups. They had an elite view of the so-called masses and this feeling that when people are inspired to do things, large numbers of people are liable to take to the streets unless they have proper control.

*Dick Flacks: Proper control! [Laughter]*

Proper control. "Those people can go anywhere. They can overthrow the government. They can cause total disorder, bring on repression"—and here we were, young and ready to go. We didn't understand how what we were doing was going to bring on repression or a Communist dictatorship. [*Laughter*] We wanted to do something about the arms race, Cold War, racism, and so on, and it was like two different frames of reference.

We were something new, which to them was called the "youth culture"—many names since the Beat Generation—but whatever we are, we didn't know what to call ourselves then, and they much less so.[14] We were a new phenomenon in the history of

---

[13] Americans for Democratic Action (ADA) was a liberal anti-communist organization founded in 1947, with Humphrey as its most prominent member.

[14] The Beat Generation was initially a small group of experimental authors in New York and San Francisco after World War II, notably poet Allen Ginsberg and novelist Jack Kerouac. Their influence spread throughout the culture.

the United States—the first massive movement, the first massive dropout phenomenon, and we didn't have any language for that. We couldn't explain that. We just were that. And they couldn't understand that any more than they could understand why we easily identified with people taking to the streets demanding their rights. They couldn't understand either.

It was natural for us at first to think the people who seemed to be the closest to us—liberal groups and so forth—would be the ones we would approach for support, because all of us were, like I described myself, divided. One part of me was an insane beatnik, who would go off on strange tangents and not know what to call that, but I knew other people were the same way. Another part of me was this rising, ambitious member of the establishment, at that time the establishment of college newspapers and so on. It was normal to try to get the support of the people in that second group, the liberal establishment, and to believe it could be done. In part, we were like them.

We didn't realize we were not like them until some experience had passed. We concluded by the mid-sixties the potential of a recharged liberal movement to win some reforms was a real possibility, but those reforms would never be enough to deal with our underlying alienation or the root causes of racism and poverty and people feeling like they have no power. We began to become radicals after the failure of the civil rights movement in the South and with the escalation of the Vietnam war. It was at that time.

Today, looking at McGovern, the same thing could be said, especially now that the issue of the war has ripened to a point where it can probably be solved if McGovern were elected. You can say reform energy can make some progress or implement certain reforms, but it will never be enough. It will never go far enough to satisfy the real needs of most of the people in the country.

It was something no one even imagined was possible. It was taken for granted that this was a stable society which dealt with its problems for better or worse through orderly parliamentary means. I was on my way to some meeting in Minnesota, and the plane landed, and the pilot announced Kennedy had been shot and killed. This guy with a Goldwater button jumped up and cheered behind me, and I was disoriented. I could only say for myself, but it may not have been so much the killing of Kennedy that was radicalizing as the way they covered up the assassination through the Warren Commission.

Two days later we watched Oswald, the "patsy," shot to death fifteen to twenty times on the TV set. The way he was treated made no sense and made me more suspicious of the system than the killing of Kennedy itself would have. The suppression of evidence, the hysterical insistence that it was only one man who could have done this, that he was a loner, made us invent the category of a "lurking class." In all bureaucratic societies, millions of people must be alienated and willing to be hired to carry out tasks like this. To call them individual assassins or loners is to miss the point that their social type is created by the kind of society we live in.

It started to become clear that the people investigating the assassination were the people who should have been investigated. That had the longer lasting effect. The reason I wasn't so shattered by the killing of Kennedy himself, except in the sense you're upset by anybody being killed like that, is from the experience from 1960 to 1963, a certain distance had set in between Kennedy and a lot of us. For one thing, he was enlarging our involvement in Vietnam, and by this time we knew, at least in a beginning sense, what that was about. That was about sending these tall, blue-eyed, blond Special Forces in to manipulate and sabotage a legitimate independence movement.

More direct than Vietnam was the Southern civil rights situation, which, for those of us who were there, was an embittering experience. It was obvious the Kennedys felt they were on the side of civil rights, but that meant for them the legalization or extension of certain legal rights. It didn't mean dealing with poverty. It didn't mean dealing with all the economic problems of blacks in the South. It meant channeling blacks through registration drives into the Democratic Party. It had some resulting success with people like Julian Bond, who was in SNCC then and is now a major figure in the Democratic Party.

But the government was never there when the tension was on. You'd find the Justice Department agents working out of the local FBI office because they didn't want to go around the FBI. You'd find they were slow to investigate anything. They didn't want to ruffle any feathers. They didn't want to offend any Southern officials unnecessarily. When Kennedy started appointing conservative judges to the Southern bench to rule in cases like this, and when you found the Justice Department officials of the North were cooperating with the FBI, you started to wonder what's going on. At first, you thought, the Southern system is a historical vestige that somehow has continued for the last one hundred years without our noticing it. Now that we're bringing the spotlight to it, it will fall away like a vestigial organ in any other healthy body. Instead, we found out that the structure of power in the South was tied into the structure of power in the whole United States. You'd find that Harvard was investing in Mississippi Power and Light, a company that economically dominated Mississippi. You'd find the Southern wing of the Democratic Party held all the seniority positions in Congress, ruling on all the fundamental questions that affected the whole society, not simply the South, and so on.

The first time I was in Mississippi was in fall, 1961. I was with Paul Potter, and the voter registration drive was just being put together by Bob Moses and Chuck McDew and some other people.[15] We went to Mississippi to investigate and get the word out through NSA about what was happening in the South. I also

---

[15] Bob Moses (1935–) became SNCC Field Secretary in 1960 at twenty-five years old. The next year he became Director of SNCC's Mississippi voter registration and education project. In 1964 he was the main organizer for Freedom Summer and co-founded the Mississippi Freedom Democratic Party. Chuck McDew (1938–2018) was SNCC Chairman from 1961 to 1964, after Marion Barry and before John Lewis.

went for SDS to write for the same purpose, and no sooner had we arrived than we started to realize what later became a radical point of view.

This was the day of nonviolent civil rights, supposedly. That's how history now records it. We had to separate ourselves from Bob at the airport. The whites go in separately, and we had to stay in a motel and arrange, by clandestine means, to meet a car in a darkened section of the black ghetto in a Mississippi town. We had to be let out of a rented car and lie on the back floor of a parked car in a parking lot. Somebody then picked it up and drove us—because it would have been too dangerous for whites and blacks to be in the same vehicle, even at night. They drove us to a house where all the shutters were down, the windows were reinforced, and we had a meeting in the cellar with Bob and some other people to talk about the voter registration campaign. In other words, we had to use, at that point, clandestine means to discuss the most conventional kind of tactic, namely the registration of voters, because what we were up against was a whole organized system that was out to kill us.

That was a devastating thing to discover. We couldn't even believe it as we experienced it. The next day Paul and I were dragged out of the car while we were observing a nonviolent civil rights demonstration. We were beaten in the street one at a time in a premeditated way by the people the sheriff had put on us. Then we were taken to the police station, where somebody from the Mississippi Sovereignty Commission arrived immediately, an influential guy who walked straight in.[16] He interrogated us much the way a congressional committee looking for Communists would, and he told us that we had a choice of going to jail or leaving town.

---

[16] The Mississippi Sovereignty Commission (1956–1977) was a state intelligence agency created to investigate and intimidate members of the civil rights movement.

We decided our job was done. We wanted to get this article out, so we decided we would leave town and go immediately to Washington to bring attention to what was going on here. As we were leaving, the photographer who had taken pictures of the whole incident came up to me and said, "They're planning to get you tonight if you stay at the motel." We decided it was probably a good idea that we leave town. They had destroyed his camera, and he had slipped the negatives into his pocket, and the papers carried the pictures the next day. It was carried all over the world that we'd been beaten up. I was wearing a suit and tie, short hair, and I didn't know what had hit me.

Paul and I, thinking we were respectable, flew to Washington, straight to the Justice Department. Paul, after all, was an NSA official and we met with John Doar, a Kennedy person in charge of civil rights at the Justice Department. He was kind to us, polite, but told us, first of all, that there was nothing that he could do about the case because of jurisdictional questions, questions of the law. Secondly, he advised us not to go back there anymore and do what we could to persuade Bob Moses and these other people, whom he liked, not to stay there. In other words, this Justice Department official, a top U.S. law enforcement officer was encouraging us not to register people to vote in one area of the United States that was supposedly under his control, because we would be getting into trouble of the kind he could do nothing about. From that time on, it was clear.

*There was also a Cold War awareness among the generation of the 1962 Cuban missile crisis that came along that must have had a good deal of effect in terms of introducing people to what Cold War politics were.*

That alienated us from the Kennedys also—the idea that we should all die, people all over the world should be killed over this kind of question. Dan Ellsberg was in the Cuban missile crisis discussions, and we started to realize we had nothing in common with the kind of person who could traffic in human life this way over a question of international image or prestige or something like that. We were in Washington and had a strange experience. We thought the crisis had peaked, and the United States was going to attack the Russian ship and the missiles would probably be fired at the United States from Cuba anyway, provoking a World War. I.F. Stone told us this in a church in Washington.[17] Everyone was in utterly stunned silence, and at that point, I felt my body detach itself from my mind as if I had already given up everything but the spirit. I was marked for death, and what I wanted was to be together with my closest friends who were there. We went out to a restaurant upon hearing the news that the Third World War had been provoked.

*Dick Flacks: I remember Stone said, "Six thousand years of human history is about to come to an end." [Laughter] Everyone believed it in that church.*

We went out and had dinner, and afterward, we turned on the radio and discovered a crisis hadn't happened.

*Dick Flacks: One of the ways the changing consciousness of this period was reflected was in the idea which grew in SDS that we should not just restrict ourselves to campus educational activity and normal political activity but move off the campus into community organizing. That began to develop by 1963. And I've always felt that represented in part a disillusionment with that coalition idea. What led you—can you remember?—to think the role of the student was not so much in campus politics and intellectual activity per se, but in a more direct kinship with poor people and so forth?*

I think it was a mistake. I think it was a misapplication of the lesson of the South, where black students dropped out of college and became the organizers of people in the communities through SNCC. They established a line or a mood, even in the North,

---

[17] I.F. Stone (1907–1989) was a journalist and author, best known for his immediate debunking of the Gulf of Tonkin incident. His *I.F. Stone's Weekly* newsletter, with a circulation of 70,000, shaped public opinion and inspired young radicals.

that students had no business being in school, that they should be the revolutionary inspiration and catalyst to community movements. I think that was the case. Of course, the mistake had to do with race and racism. A black middle-class student could relate to a black sharecropper because they shared the same racial oppression. It wasn't so clear why a white student could organize in Appalachia or white working-class industrial areas, much less organizing a black community, which is what I did for three years. Not that the work was irrelevant, the work produced some results. But it came more from trying to follow the SNCC motto—"Let the people decide"—than from disillusionment with campus activities.

Two camps came back together then. One was to leave the campus and organize in the community, around rats and roaches and high rents. Another approach was to take the experience of organizing the civil rights movement in the South and bring it back to the campus, which is what triggered the Free Speech Movement in Berkeley, and both happened simultaneously in the 1964 to 1965 period.

*I would like to talk a little about the summer of 1964 because that was probably the high point of feeling that white students could leave the campus and move out in the South and the North as catalytic forces, and of course Mississippi was the big moment of that. To pick up on something you said before, there was a sense in which that whole drive was endorsed by or approved by certain elements of the liberal establishment. What do you remember about that phase? You already alluded to the Democratic convention in the summer of 1964 as being a central experience. Did you go to Mississippi that summer?*

No. Mississippi came to me in a certain way. I was in the South from the fall of 1961 to the spring of 1962. I was intermittently there throughout 1963 to 1964. I did a lot of writing on Mississippi, and I was close to some of the organizers in Mississippi. Our idea in the summer of 1964, to go into communities like Newark, New Jersey, leave the campus and become organizers in these communities, was inspired by the SNCC decision to go into communities in the South. It was virtually a Northern counterpart of the summer project in Mississippi.

At the beginning of that summer, three people were killed—Schwerner, Chaney, and Goodman, although their bodies were not found until weeks later.[18] That created a ripple of tension throughout the entire movement. The tremendous tension growing between the black communities, us, and the police all that summer made people being shot in Mississippi not seem foreign or removed.

Then came an experience that was traumatic for that whole generation of activists, and that was Atlantic City, 1964.[19] We drove down from Newark for just a day and a night and watched the rest of it on TV. The Democratic Party, primarily under Hubert Humphrey's management, trying to manipulate the removal of the Mississippi black delegation from its legitimate claim to the seats, and seat in their place the regular Mississippi Democratic Party, which wasn't even going to support Johnson. It was more or less pledged to Goldwater, and it excluded blacks from participation in its structure. This black delegation was the result of several years of civil rights work in the South, the summer project, the loss of all these lives and here were these people utterly resistant to it. And nothing could have been more perfectly structured in terms of working within the system. The Democratic delegation of blacks supported the national ticket and met all the qualifications for seating and simply wasn't allowed to because of power.

The other thing tied into that was the bombing of North Vietnam began at the same time. It began August 4th of that year, the day of the funeral in Neshoba County, Mississippi, for

---

[18] James Chaney (1943–1964), Michael Schwerner (1939–1964), and Andrew Goodman (1943–1964), all Congress of Racial Equality (CORE) workers, were killed in Philadelphia, Mississippi by the Ku Klux Klan.

[19] The Democratic Party held its National Convention at Boardwalk Hall in Atlantic City, New Jersey, August 24–27, 1964.

Chaney, Schwerner, and Goodman, and it was immediately before the Democratic convention. Bob Moses tied the killings in Vietnam to the killings in Mississippi and to the universal use of brute force by American police and generals against people who were simply trying to have a share in making decisions and people who wanted to decide their fate. That was the beginning of the young radical or New Left movement into the antiwar movement.[20] That was the height of disillusionment with liberalism as such, because, the same Humphrey who kept the blacks out of their seats in Atlantic City, partly to demonstrate he was a reliable politician, became the Vice Presidential nominee at that convention, on a platform committed to rhetoric of peace in Southeast Asia and then escalated the war.

We now know from the Pentagon Papers that at the same time they were stamping on people's rights in Mississippi, they had already laid out plans for the escalation of the war. They were not going to integrate people of color in one place while bombing them in another and, besides, they needed Stennis and the other Mississippi regular politicians to support the war.[21]

## Newark

*Dick Flacks: At the period we're talking about, you were in Newark. Why don't you talk about that experience—what you learned from those years and how these external events like the escalation of the war and Berkeley affected you in Newark.*

---

[20] The New Left was an international political tendency, beginning in 1956, which combined a "rejection both of capitalism and of the bureaucratic communism exemplified by the Soviet Union, anti-imperialism, and an orientation to decentralized direct action, violent or nonviolent." Staughton Lynd, "The New Left," *Annals of the American Academy of Political and Social Science*, Vol. 382, March 1969, pp. 64–72.

[21] John Stennis (1901–1995), an ardent segregationist, was U.S. Senator from Mississippi from 1947 to 1989, and Chairman of the Senate Armed Services Committee.

# Tom Hayden: *The* Rolling Stone *Interview – Part I*

The escalation of the war and the growth of the student movement aimed at the administration and complicity with the war, rather than just off campus, impinged a lot on Newark. It made clear there was a new role opening up for people like ourselves, who thought there wasn't a foreign policy question around which to organize. We hadn't felt there was a mass base in 1963 for on-campus demonstrations or other actions. At the same time, the Newark experience was also impinged on by the rapid growth towards a situation where Black Power and self-determination as a program became politically correct. The feeling in the black community from 1964 to 1968 switched—that was just the period we were in—and that was always looming and making it necessary for us to leave or else it would have meant we didn't agree with those principles.

The whole Newark experience was immeasurably valuable for understanding how community work is done and how consciousness grows and how cooptation takes place, and above all, in just teaching me what the ordinary problems of day-to-day people are, and the problems of getting out and organizing people. We went in there, and our numbers would rise and fall. During the summers, there might have been thirty or forty of us, but always there were at least ten. We would live in one or two apartments in a Spartan way. We had not heard of collectives, but we lived that way. We lived on a few cents for each meal, we cooked collectively, everybody slept in the same houses, and personal relationships were always at the center of discussions among the organizers.

*Dick Flacks: Mostly white students.*

Mostly white, and there we were in the center of a black community. The overwhelming need was, of course, to prove that what we were doing was worth something by creating an organization we would gradually phase ourselves out of.

The important ego and political experience involved is that usually, you find, at least among middle-class people, there's a

23

vying for power and control, and you want to be at the center of things. The whole concept of organizing the community, however, especially when in a certain way you were separate and strange to it, was that you had to organize your way out of it and away from having a traditional kind of power. You would also have to become accustomed to making new friends all the time while organizing instead of surrounding yourself with the same old faces. Those two lessons were driven home.

It taught me a lot about the problems of how to create an organization in which people participated, not always depending on the original leaders. We had tried this in SDS, and now we were trying in a community, where it was even more necessary. Always reaching out and being among new people taught me a lot about sectarianism and how to avoid it. It also taught me a lot about not getting cloistered in small groups of people who reinforce each other.

The political lessons from that were that people who are seemingly lifeless on the surface, those people are just amazing. There can be no city in America that more derogatory things have been said about than Newark, especially in those days. It was seen as a dumping ground situated next to New York. Stewardesses on planes would joke about its smell when you would arrive there at the airport. Anybody with talent raised in New Jersey would always think of themselves as going to Harlem if they were black or the Village if they were white and never stay in Newark because supposedly nothing was happening in Newark. Also, the people there, most of whom are black and poor, are not supposed to be able to contribute to society except to give their body for manual labor. These people were considered to have no political potential at that time.

As you pointed out, we would go to the labor leaders, political leaders, and they would tell us that the people outside of the organized industrial working class could not be drawn into a social movement. They said that first about farmworkers in California because they were migratory. They said that about welfare people and permanently unemployed people and ghetto youth, because they had no solid tie to the means of production that grouped them, as in a factory, where they could be organized, and so on. We found that all those social claims, all those concepts by organizers, all those stereotypes about Newark were false, and if they were false in Newark, they would have to be false everywhere.

It was related to Vietnam, the concept of slow, patient organizing, and the cadre going out among the people, ideas we didn't know existed in Vietnam. It wasn't until shortly afterward we began to understand.[22]

We'd break down into groups of two and take a block, meaning both sides of a street, seven or eight or ten blocks long, hundreds of apartment houses on it, many with twenty or thirty families. We would equip ourselves with a list of property owners on the streets and the tenants and the outside landlords, and the absentee landlords. Then we would go door-to-door. Here we were, young, white students in a town people said no one could organize, where everybody is supposed to have an inferiority complex. We would invite ourselves into homes and tell people we wanted to help create an organization in the community. We told them we believed people could solve their problems by themselves. We said we see ourselves as a help in getting people together, but we want to organize a meeting on the block in which everyone would talk about their immediate problems, and some organized form would be created that would maybe allow for dealing with those problems.

Of course, many people regarded us as strange and many people we couldn't reach, but we were surprised there was not a great deal of hostility to it. In case after case, we found people

---

[22] A cadre organization within a political party consists only of well-trained disciplined loyalists. By contrast, mass organizations include people with less experience, training, and available time, and often are interested in one issue.

expressed a feeling that they had been waiting for years for something like this to happen, and they knew what their problems were, especially their immediate grievances. They usually had to do with rats and roaches and streetlights and police brutality they had witnessed.

We found there was always a sufficient number of people willing to come to at least a first meeting and somebody who was willing to have it in their home. In the meeting, we would try to get the people to select a person to chair the meeting and have a discussion of what were all the problems everybody has in common, and then start with simple steps, like the redress of grievances. Let's see the landlord collectively. Let's go to city hall and see the building inspector collectively. Let's go to the police station. When those channels of redress didn't work, which they often didn't, then it was time for a demonstration or publicity, and out of that grew a community organization of the leaders from the different block groups who operated the same way and a political program.

After a year, we had an office in the community. We had a group of thirty or forty people who were well-versed in all the problems of the community. They were also becoming familiar with the hang-ups of students or the lifestyles of students. They were becoming familiar with the antiwar movement. They saw themselves as part of a larger movement around the whole country. We had a poor people's national conference in Newark in 1964, and people from Mississippi came up, including Mrs. Hamer, the principal spokeswoman for the black Democratic delegation at Atlantic City in 1964.[23] She became a heroine for a lot of people, and she related how what we were doing in Newark was like what was happening in the South.

---

[23] Fannie Lou Hamer (1917–1977) was raised as a cotton sharecropper in Sunflower County, Mississippi. She became a field secretary for SNCC, founder of the Mississippi Freedom Democratic Party, founder of the Freedom Farms Cooperative, and co-founder of the National Women's Political Caucus.

## Tom Hayden: The Rolling Stone Interview – Part I

The whole organization, which gained notoriety and controversy and was identified by the police as the principal enemy in the city, grew. In the end, it became difficult, because we took over the poverty program. It was the only poverty program in the country that had community elections, and we were the only organized group of poor people, so it was easy to use the electoral process to take over the poverty program in a certain area. But then they changed the poverty program. They eliminated the democratic structure. Eventually people were faced with the problem of whether to stay outside the poverty program and go on in a situation where they did not have an economic base and were bound to lose their welfare checks, lose their jobs in factories or lose their unemployment checks. The alternative was to stay in the poverty program and work from within as a progressive force, which they decided to do more after we left in 1967 and 1968.

Some of us went to the white section of Newark, and those people are there now, eight years after the project began. There is now a freedom high school in the white working-class section of Newark, organized by people who came there in 1964 and 1965. The blacks who were organized in 1964 and 1965 are still in the poverty program, still fighting for social change, but broken down into individuals.

The rebellion in Newark that happened in 1967 was a situation in which all the problems we had been talking about came to a head. The police tried to blame the rebellion on, not only the blacks in our group, but on me. The rebellion released so much national consciousness and so much energy that it laid the foundation for the election of a black mayor and the creation of what we now have in Newark.

Anyway, the important thing I found out was how, if it was possible for them to keep body and soul alive, people at the bottom, ordinary people who have no qualifications as judged by society, can run their affairs. This is a big secret kept from most white Americans and most college students. As long as the secret is kept, you can always think of yourself as having to look out for others and do for them, playing a beneficent role in relation to them. You'll never be able to understand people's war, never being able to understand the revolutionary movements in this century where people have come to power. You have to get this experience.

*It was at the same time students were discovering their powerlessness—oppression if you like.*

Plus, seeing yourself. Berkeley students were saying, "Do not bend, fold, staple, or mutilate me," realizing they were part of a whole punch-card process. Then, we discovered it was Selective Service System policy to view us as elements in a manpower channeling system that sent some people into war and other people into vocations that were good for the national interest. And then, people who were drafted started discovering their lives meant nothing to their commanders, and that feeling gave rise to the GI movement.

The women's movement came out of the same recognition that the life of being a housewife or an appendage or a sex object meant you wasted all of your energy and creativity for fifty years. Different people were simultaneously discovering all of these things in different places.

*Did all this mean young people saw themselves as a generation oppressed?*

I'm not sure, because you can have several identities, some more fundamental than others. I don't think black youth or black young people are oppressed the same way white young people are. I don't think they think of themselves as young in the same way, and that's because they're black. They're more unemployed because they're black. They're more subject to police violence because they're black. But at the same time, young blacks have an easier time understanding rock and roll culture or student demonstrations or the GI movement than maybe the oldest generation of blacks because of the youth tie.

I don't think we felt too badly about the ideal of integration, either, for that matter. It was just that—it just became clear it was a myth.

What hurt—I didn't get it so much personally, but a lot of people did—was this feeling of being rejected by your black friends. When you discover it wasn't personal, but it was political, that it had to do with a different view of America and what America was and how it was going to be changed, people readily agreed.

Even though it's not altogether true, the myth of integration lives on. It lives in Miami Beach at the Democratic Party convention, although even their quotas were being used to ensure representation. It lived in Berkeley during the community control of police campaign. We found a lot of white liberals and many students who had a hard time agreeing with the principle that the black section of the community should have its own police, the young whites should have their own police, and the middle class on the hill should have their own police.

We said, "No, no, no. It'll be coordinated, it won't be separatism, it will just be that the people living in their neighborhood, which happen to be racial and generational and class neighborhoods, will have control of their affairs for the first time and select the people who will patrol them." That got a lot of resistance, even though the principle passed the white youth ghetto overwhelmingly, it wasn't as supportable as the candidates for office we put up, and the concept was trashed in the hills. They voted ninety percent against self-determination on that question. Many blacks, because of the way it was worded, and because they thought with a black-white coalition they could take power in an integrated Berkeley, chose the route of running candidates for office to take political power in a black and white coalition rather than the community control of police route.

Even today significant numbers of blacks and whites who have progressive views, who I identify with, feel there is a longevity to integration.

As we got experience through the civil rights struggle, we started to realize the full scale of our oppression and to find the language for it. Some people did it through, you know, the act of wearing their hair long and doing all sorts of cultural things, but not in the way of the beatniks, of personal withdrawal. This was mass disaffection. Everybody was visibly out front in their repudiation of the code of ethics and lifestyle of society. Other people did it in more political ways, especially around resistance to the draft and resistance to the war.

*Dick Flacks: Part of what was learned in the sixties was how intransigent, intractable, fundamentally difficult these problems were. I'm sure that in 1962 the people at Port Huron did not think the kind of struggle that lay ahead was going to happen, partly because we were too simple-minded, because we'd accepted a liberal ideal. Does that make sense?*

We became branded as radicals because we did not accept the concept that a progressive extension of the welfare state was good. When you were organizing tenants in these prisons called public housing, and you were organizing people on welfare and saw the abuse at the hands of administrators—people breaking into houses in the middle of the night and pushing people around—you realized this went far beyond extending these services. These services were new forms of servitude, and even though they kept people from starving, it didn't make the servitude any different. We started having a critique of what we called corporate liberalism, welfare liberalism. A critique that, in some ways, is shared by George Wallace, but he begins with the standpoint of racism.[24]

---

[24] George Wallace (1919–1998) was a white supremacist, three-time Governor of Alabama (1963–1967, 1971–1979, 1983–1987), and a four-time presidential candidate (1964–1976).

*Dick Flacks: I guess the other thing that was learned in Newark and by people in other ghetto communities was something about the nature of power in America, which you've already touched on, but maybe you want to expand on that.*

Only that what the revolutionary textbooks say about the cycle of redress and petitioning, leading to a confrontation, leading to repression, proved itself to be classically true by the time we were being blamed for causing the riot. The repression, the use of military force in this kind of society comes when efforts to pacify or channel or manipulate or materially satisfy people have failed, and one look at that, just the five days of looking at the streets of violence, was radicalizing. It was one thing for most Americans to read about ghetto rebellions in the papers. It's another thing to live in a black community and observe it take place—and observe the papers.

It was so like Vietnam. It was supposed to have been provoked by an incident that was fanned into a big social cause. The Newark police beat up a cab driver in front of a lot of other people who thought he had been killed because his whole body and face were streaming with blood. There were demonstrations called. The police suppressed the demonstrations, and the looting and burning broke out. It was not addressed to white neighborhoods, it was not addressed to downtown, and it was not addressed to police, at first.

God, the whole thing was nothing like the power structure said. They said "they" were going to attack the suburbs, they were going to attack downtown, that terrorists were standing on the rooftops shooting, even though months later the state commission considering it could not find the alleged terrorists. In the meantime, the police did a crackdown on the whole community. Before my eyes, they stopped innumerable people. Twenty-six black people were shot and killed. None of them, according to later investigations, were doing anything which would qualify them as a target in U.S. Army terms. They were unarmed people shot in the back in broad daylight.

Afterward, we went to the victims' homes, trudging through the rubble, asking their families what happened, getting eyewitness accounts, and working with lawyers on affidavits. It was just unbelievable. We used to go sit out on a rooftop at night and watch these guys. It was straight out of Vietnam. They'd come down the street with bayonets, with automatic guns, pushing people around and shooting. They couldn't subdue the people for five days.

That introduction of violence as the final form of power couldn't have been made clearer. That liberals would do it was clear now, in my mind, not only in Vietnam but in Newark.

In the middle of the fifth night, some of the governor's staff, who were progressive-minded people, turned out to be looking for me to bring a black person before the governor and his aides to make a presentation about what he should do. They wanted a critical presentation, just as I suppose was done at the White House, with hawks and doves vying to get various points of view brought before the President.

I was picked up in the middle of the night at the poverty program office in a state trooper's car. State troopers in New Jersey, like most states, are virtually all white, and they need to be he-men to qualify for their job. They're all about six feet two inches or six feet three inches, and they weigh one hundred eighty to two hundred pounds. Five of them in the car and me, and we drove eighty miles an hour around this cordoned-off city to the darkened side of the Federal Building. All the time, you know, it was just like we were in enemy territory. They had their guns at the windows as if, if anything flashed by their eyes, they would fire back. We got to a street where it was perfectly quiet. It's right by the Federal Building. Nothing there. They jumped out of the car at full attention, guns pointed at the rooftops, pointed at the trees and ushered me into the building as if at any moment guerrillas would come crashing down on the car.

In we went to a giant room converted to the command center. By this time, twenty-six people have been killed. It's four o'clock in the morning, and here is kind, Irish, liberal Richard Hughes, Governor of the State of New Jersey, raised in a prison-and-police-oriented family, coming over smiling to shake my hand and another guy's hand as if we were at a political convention or he was welcoming us to a roundtable discussion about the New Left. Flanked around him were his liberal advisers, including Paul Ylvisaker from the Ford Foundation who was the dove. The hawks ranged over on the other side of the table, including the National Guard, the state police, and so on.

Here's Hughes, a liberal Democrat, part of the populist left wing of the party, part of the progressive wing, the New Deal, the welfare-state man. He had just given orders which resulted in the death of twenty-six people in the last four days, the city is burning, several thousand troops are occupying it, and his only protection is the police. They're everywhere. There are state troopers at the doors, and here we are in a room with his hawk and dove advisers.

He asked for our opinions, and we gave them strongly, and it was exactly like Vietnam. We said, "You are the outside aggressor. There is no justice in your position. There is nothing for you to do but get out. This would not have happened if you had not taken the initial incident and escalated the violence, made the community resist that violence, which they had every reason to do, poured more violence onto them and now killed twenty-six people. It appears you have the stronger hand because you have the entire city occupied, but the violence against your officers you predict from the people hasn't begun, nor against anything except stores in their community.

"Instead of people submitting, obviously they're going to start getting violent against the troops, and then the troops are going to massacre more people, and you're going to go down in history as one of the biggest killers of all time. You'll still not be able to withdraw the troops if you demand that the community surrender first. Surrender means go in their homes, stop demonstrations, do nothing to resist oppression. Your repression will breed resistance, which you will then have to repress, which will create more resistance, and you will be destroyed in this process. You have to withdraw troops unconditionally."

He listened and turned to the state commander of police and asked him what he thought. The commander's advice was it was too dangerous. It would be a bloodbath if the troops were withdrawn. [*Laughter*] Because then, if the riot hadn't stopped, obviously if you withdrew the troops, that would be an incentive for people to kill all the store owners, all the white people, all the bosses, wherever they could find them, right? The dove advisers were saying some intermediate position should be found, short of total withdrawal. The Governor said, "What about withdrawing from certain areas where it can be assured there will be no violence when we withdraw." [*Laughter*]

I said, "I don't know who you could get assurance from. You just killed twenty-six people. But my personal opinion is if you withdraw all the troops tomorrow morning the violence will subside because blacks haven't killed any whites. But the killing of whites will start if the white troops stay. If you want to protect the ghetto stores, forget it. They've all been destroyed. If you want to protect the downtown businesses, then you can withdraw troops to the downtown area and occupy it for the shoppers. If you want to protect the suburbs, you could withdraw the troops to the suburbs and occupy the suburbs. All roads lead into the suburbs. Just get out of the ghetto." And this went on for it seemed like hours.

At the end of this time, he made no commitments, thanked us much like a good Irish politician, and took a card with his name on it out of his wallet. It said, "Richard Hughes, Governor of the State of New Jersey." He wrote "Good Luck, Tom" on it. [*Laughter*]

He said he hoped to see me again sometime, and we left.

The next morning the troops were withdrawn. I have no idea what happened. But to see a person concerned about his image in the press—you've got to be tough and being tough meant he could not risk a withdrawal if there was going to be further property destruction. Being tough meant punishing them with their lives for what they did to white property and getting immediately into the cycle of Vietnam. It was so parallel it, that kind of thing fixes patterns in your mind about the way decision-makers behave. I'm sure that's the way John Kennedy and Lyndon Johnson found themselves deliberately, consciously backing into Vietnam by thinking it was out of control when, in fact, they were consciously doing it.

### Vietnam

*Dick Flacks: You got invited to go to North Vietnam.*

The North Vietnamese representatives were at a European meeting where they encountered an American Communist historian, Herbert Aptheker. They asked him if he would see if he could find some people in the American antiwar movement who would like to visit Vietnam, which by then had been bombed for seven or eight months. He said he would. He returned and asked Staughton Lynd, who had been one of the main speakers at our SDS April 1965 demonstration, the first national demonstration against the war in Washington.[25] Twenty-five thousand people were there, and Staughton had probably been the most effective and was by then the most well-known figure organizing resistance for the war among intellectuals, students and so on. Staughton said he would consider going if he could pick the third person.

Staughton asked me if I wanted to go. This was probably because, first, we had known each other when he was in Atlanta,

---

[25] Staughton Lynd (1929–) has been a history professor, author, attorney, director of the SNCC Freedom Schools in Mississippi, and radical pacifist antiwar leader.

and he, like myself, was involved first in the Southern civil rights movement. Secondly, he thought there was a connection between the Vietnam War, the antiwar movement, and the young SDS radicals working in areas of poverty, and these were worldwide issues.

*Dick Flacks: To set the stage, do you remember much about your attitude toward the war before you went to Vietnam? You were not particularly involved in the antiwar movement up to that time. You were primarily based in Newark.*

I was aware of Vietnam as early as 1962 or 1963. We used to discuss how neither the Soviet Union nor the United States posed any solutions, although they might contribute some aid or something. They never posed any solutions to the Third World countries then emerging as the new force—China, Cuba, and there was this country of Vietnam. I remember reading Burchett's book on the guerrilla war in South Vietnam.[26]

In 1964 there was the connection made by Bob Moses that everyone shared. In the winter, there was an SDS National Council meeting, where people came in with the proposal for the first national action on the war, a march on Washington. I was active in that national meeting, although I was mainly working in Newark, and I took part in the decision and the planning. Then I went back to Newark and was only marginally involved in the organizing for it. We came to the demonstration with a delegation of community people from Newark. I remember being excited about the developments.

*Dick Flacks: SDS, when it formed, had some good relations with the established peace organizations, pacifist groups, and liberal peace*

---

[26] Wilfred Burchett (1911–1983) was the most important source for information and viewpoints from "the other side" of the U.S. wars against North Korea and Vietnam.

*organizations. There was a group called Turn Toward Peace and so forth, and all of those were reluctant to deal with the Vietnam War.*

They were ban-the-bomb groups and reluctant to be involved with the war, partly because they couldn't see the direct connection with nuclear war and because it implied support for revolution and communist-led movements. SDS decided to go ahead with a national march on the war before the full escalation by Johnson. SDS planned and organized this march without the co-sponsorship of the establishment organizations. For the first time since the thirties, a national peace demonstration was being organized which permitted Marxist groups to participate in their own name. We did not see how you could exclude any groups from an antiwar demonstration and we did not share the elder group's paranoia about being used by tight-knit cadre organizations. And this combination of things led to a new attack on SDS by a lot of leaders of the established peace organizations. We were red-baited.

We had Senator Ernest Gruening speak, and I.F. Stone—they tried to intervene with that—but at that time the bombing of North Vietnam began full scale, so we marched with a new significance.[27] By the time of the march, there were twenty-five thousand people, which made it the largest antiwar demonstration that had ever occurred in the United States—far beyond what anybody had expected.

*Dick Flacks: Wouldn't you say there was a tension between working on the war issue and the local community organizing as a prime direction for people's energy?*

---

[27] Ernest Gruening (1887–1974), a Democrat, was Governor of the Alaska Territory and then a U.S. Senator from the new state from 1959 to 1969. He was one of two Senators to vote against the Gulf of Tonkin Resolution in 1964, which approved unlimited escalation of the war in Vietnam.

Yes, it just became something you did double-time on. It was the same problem for Rennie Davis later.[28] He was doing community organizing work in Chicago. He saw involvement with Vietnam as posing a deep personal crisis for him. I wanted him to share the crisis I was in. I tried several times to get him to see the Vietnamese and finally, he agreed in the fall of 1967. He left Chicago and went to Bratislava with us, and then he went to North Vietnam with five other people and me.[29] From that time on he and I were full-time activists in the antiwar movement.

This was a month after the Newark rebellion, and it was clear that now was a good time for me to leave Newark, and it was a good time for him to leave Chicago. I had stayed in Newark from 1965 through the summer of 1967. I had written a book on the war in the spring of 1966 with Staughton, and I did a lot of speaking at a lot of teach-ins as that developed, but I stayed in Newark. This was partly because I thought people had to be rooted in the community and partly because I thought it was important the different wings of SDS, the community organizing and the antiwar, should be bridged, and partly because I was personally unresolved about what to do. I had made a long-term

---

[28] Rennie Davis was national director of the SDS community organizing programs, called the Economic Research and Action Project (ERAP), based in Ann Arbor. Later, he was indicted as one of the Chicago Eight protest leaders at the 1968 Democratic Convention. Davis led the Mayday 1971 civil disobedience in Washington DC, resulting in the largest mass arrest in U.S. history—12,614 people.

[29] The September 6–12, 1967 Bratislava Conference in former Czechoslovakia, now Slovakia, brought together thirty-eight Americans from SDS, SNCC, Southern Christian Leadership Council, and the Quakers to meet with Vietnamese students, teachers, editors, social workers, and officials. Fifty years later, former Deputy Prime Minister Nguyen Khanh, a Bratislava participant, said, "The U.S. people whom we met in Bratislava absolutely took us by surprise at the first sight, as their dressing style was very simple. They were very friendly and open-minded. It did not take us, the strangers, much time to turn into friends." *Vietnam Times*, September 23, 2017.

commitment to Newark. I didn't want to leave, but by the time of the 1967 rebellion, the conditions were such that it was good for me to leave.

*Dick Flacks: Supposing in 1965 when you went to Vietnam, someone had prophetically said to you, this war is going to go on for seven more years at least, the majority of American people will come to oppose it, the key media in the United States will feel the immorality and injustice of the war, the majority of the U.S. Congress will be opposed to it, and yet the war will go on for seven years. Think you would have believed such a prediction at that time?*

I thought it was fundamental, but that didn't mean I had any projection of where it was going or what would be revealed by it or anything of that sort. The antiwar movement was in such a state of infancy that long-term questions were not as easy to answer. We had no foundation, no experience, no ideological grasp of what this kind of war could lead to in terms of the structure of our society. The last one like this happened when we were five or ten years old, the Korean War. There was no antiwar movement against Korea. I was so fundamentally affected that the immediate thing to do was to come back and explain to people how changed I was by it, and that involved teach-ins and organizing draft resistance, but the tactics—you couldn't see far ahead.

*Dick Flacks: What changes did you mostly feel?*

I was an American boy from the Midwest, and my furthest travel and contact with other peoples had been a year in the South and the Newark ghetto, and, I didn't accept any Cold War rhetoric. I had no idea of what was going on. In the space of one month, I was in China for five days, and I was in Vietnam for two weeks, and it was the other side of the world. They were socialist societies. I'd never been in a socialist society, where people are producing for themselves, building for themselves, educating themselves. These were nonwhite societies—the only time as a white person I had ever been in a country that was entirely of another nationality, and this would take us into a long discussion of the Vietnamese people.

We wrote later about our feelings. Staughton at that time was a pacifist. As for myself, we wrote: "Tom feels, perhaps, a more direct identification with the National Liberation Front, especially the young organizers, who build while they fight, without whom he fears the revolution would be crushed and Vietnam made into an American colony."

*Dick Flacks: Was there anything you experienced in Vietnam that you found hard to explain even to antiwar people back home?*

Yes, that the United States was being defeated, the Vietnamese people could preserve their freedom and independence, and the Vietnamese people had special qualities, which I'm still trying to understand, that made them the most extraordinary people now living in the world, setting a standard of morality and sacrifice for the whole world.

I'm still convinced that's true, but to explain it you need to go through a lot of complicated arguments you don't even realize are within yourself. First, all the anti-communist conditioning like in *The God That Failed*, that communists commit terror, that communist states and communist parties and organizations are dictatorial, authoritarian, heavy-handed, call it what you want, repressive, that culturally they're bleak.[30] All of that I'm prepared to believe has been true in some places at some times, for instance in Eastern Europe. But here I was confronted with people who sang us songs, who knew a great deal more about our history and culture than we knew about theirs, who were and still are the gentlest people you would ever hope to meet. Even though they were fighting against other Americans, they were gentle towards us and gentle among themselves.

---

[30] *The God That Failed: A Confession*, is a collection of essays of disillusionment with communism, by Louis Fischer, Andre Gide, Arthur Koestler, Ignazio Silone, Stephen Spender, and Richard Wright (New York: Columbia University Press, 1949).

It's hard not to feel you're naive, that you're romantic. You're told by the media when you come back you're naive. Other people tell you it's simply your petty bourgeois romanticism that makes you say this and your lack of sophisticated understanding of communism and so forth. Those arguments have a telling effect on you to a point where you wonder whether you're in your right mind or whether you did see and experience what you know you saw and experienced. There may be a tendency on the part of some people to close off their experience with the Vietnamese for exactly that reason because it's unexplainable.

Now, however, I feel more confident about it because the understandings are there. I didn't realize them at the time. After all, Vietnam is unique of all the countries in the world in having the longest continuous struggle against the foreign aggression of any country that has retained its national identity. Therefore, it's understandable they would be amazingly able to withstand suffering, that they would have rich solidarity among themselves. They have gathered an infinitely complex set of experiences about how to fight wars and how to organize a resistance, far beyond what other peoples of the world have. Being a small country, they would not think of themselves as potential conquerors of anyone or conquerors of other races or countries. Rather they would think of themselves in the way you do in any contest between the small and the large, whether it's the martial arts or whatever.

You would try to isolate the problem rather than attack the whole set of problems behind it. You would try to fight against those who are invading you, but you wouldn't fight against those who stayed home in the other countries. You would evolve a distinction between the aggressor attacking you and people in the country the aggressor comes from. They are not susceptible to racial appeals for unity, because Asians as well as Westerners have invaded them. The Chinese and the Japanese have invaded them in the name of racial solidarity. There are many concrete reasons why you come to the conclusions considered to be romantic about the Vietnamese and, yet, at the time, that was the hardest thing to explain, and for most people today it's still the hardest thing to explain.

*Dick Flacks: On one of your trips, didn't you go directly from Vietnam to meet Averell Harriman? Was there anything in that contrast you would know of and could talk about?*

The second time I saw Harriman, in 1968, I was with Dave Dellinger, and we were trying to discuss his attitude towards a prisoner release. We wanted the Pentagon to keep their hands off any prisoners the Vietnamese might release.

It was Harriman's seventy-third birthday, and he was receiving messages from all of his friends about what a wonderful life he had led, this architect of the Cold War, and his young assistant, who had been one of the people from NSA who went into the State Department, was scurrying around, bringing him coffee and bits of cake, and out the window you could see Washington was on fire. We had a hard time getting into the building because the blacks were burning down the center of the city. Rev. Martin Luther King, Jr., had just been assassinated, and the city was burning. Here in the State Department you could observe the birthday party of Averell Harriman, talk calmly with him about the state of affairs regarding American prisoners, and not detect the slightest hysteria in him about the U.S. capital behind him being on fire. Luminous red flames were coming up from the business district. The only people who seemed hysterical were the secretaries, who were wondering whether the children would be all right, how they were going to get home—you know, ordinary people who had to go out there and get in cars and buses and face reality.

My experience with American officials has always been like that. The most frightening thing is they do not easily learn any of these lessons. The previous time was during the Tet offensive. We met Harriman's assistant because, at his request, he wanted to ask us questions about prisoners. Dan Berrigan was there, and

Howard Zinn, Dave Dellinger and me.[31] The NLF had just attacked the U.S. Embassy in Saigon in the second week of an offensive that hit one hundred fifty district capitals.

We asked the official something—some question about his cabling Saigon and telling them in the U.S. Embassy to leave American prisoners alone. Again, the same question—do not interfere with the release of American prisoners and do not make any propaganda about it. And he said, "I won't be able to cable the embassy, because our communications system has been destroyed." "You mean the American government doesn't have any contact with the American officials in Vietnam? It's come to that? Is the embassy surrounded? What's happening?" He said, "I don't, the State Department doesn't, we don't have any way to get through."

In other words, not only are they constantly unaware of who the Vietnamese are, but they are unaware their defeat is near. I don't know how you deal with people who are unable to be defeated because they're able to ignore it. The Pentagon Papers show every time the United States escalated in Vietnam, it was because they'd been defeated. The Saigon government had collapsed. The National Liberation Front guerrillas were everywhere. The economy was in chaos. The Buddhists were in the streets. Everything was falling apart. The CIA reports come in and explain everything is a catastrophe. In the face of the

---

[31] Daniel Berrigan (1921–2016) was a Jesuit priest, antiwar leader, and one of the Catonsville Nine, who used incendiary napalm weapons to destroy military draft files in Catonsville, Maryland, May 17, 1968. Howard Zinn (1922–2010) was an author, historian, professor and relentless civil rights and peace activist. Later famed for his "bottom-up history" book, *A People's History of the United States* (New York: Harper Collins, 1980). David Dellinger (1915–2004), a lifelong radical pacifist organizer, was imprisoned during World War II as a conscientious objector. He was a founder of *Liberation* magazine in 1956 and was tried for conspiracy to incite a riot at the 1968 Democratic Convention as one of the Chicago Eight. All eight went free.

catastrophe, they say, "Let's continue. Let's call someone and escalate the involvement."

*Dick Flacks: These are people who think they have the ultimate weapon and the ultimate shelter.*

That's right.

*Dick Flacks: In total contrast to the Vietnamese leadership, whose families are dispersed in the countryside, whose very lives are always in danger.*

Speaking of dispersal, that day in 1968 we also met with Sargent Shriver, who was about to become the ambassador to France, and it was again about the Paris peace talks, which were about to open. This was in the War on Poverty office while Washington's ghetto was burning to the ground. The only way Shriver could talk with us was during his dispersal, which took place in a limousine, which dispersed him from the basement of the poverty program out through a tunnel into suburban Virginia, where we were driven all the way to his mansion, twenty-five to thirty miles from the ghetto, a gigantic house hidden among the pines. As we rode in the limousine, he was in the back seat, and I was in a jump seat I could use to talk directly to him.

Behind his head I could watch Washington burning. We drove off to his home, and he never expressed an opinion about it. He wasn't embarrassed. I would be embarrassed to be in front of my enemies, my critics, with them observing the whole city I'm supposed to be pacifying being burned to the ground. Nothing. Nothing. It was talk about dinner, about what Paris weather was going to be like, and the matters we wanted to discuss with him about his attitude toward the prisoners and talks. He got out of the car at his house and ordered the chauffeur to drive us to the airport or wherever we were going, and that was it.

These people have negative freedom of some kind. There's nothing positive or good about it. They are free of any results of their policies. As Ellsberg pointed out, he read all the way through eight thousand pages of Pentagon Papers and never found a reference to casualties, morality, or destruction. Nothing. Just bureaucratic options—this option, that option.

Probably the most painful thing that ever happened to any of them was Johnson having to retire. Other than that, I can think of nothing. McNamara, having participated in plotting the death of tens of thousands of people, was moved to the World Bank where he can participate in the plotting on a larger scale. I know of not a single official who failed in office and was removed or publicly condemned. I believe a great number of these people who started the Vietnam War and then became doves because it wasn't working would be in the State Department of President McGovern if he's elected, unscratched by their experience, their souls, if they have any, never touched by what they did to the Vietnamese people. In their view it's all a mistake, an unwise allocation of resources, and they'll be back in the government on some new frontier.

1967–1968

*As you said, some significant realization came about in 1967 to 1968.*

Internationally, not only was there guerrilla warfare in Vietnam, but there was a cultural revolution in China people misapplied to America, thinking new men and women could be created here without state power, just as they were being created in China with state power. Regis Debray, a young intellectual much like ourselves, we suppose, was writing new books about guerrilla warfare. [32] They implied you could start the revolution with a gun, rather than finish it with a gun, and you could create popular support by militant action rather than militant action being seen as the last stage after popular support has become massive. Che Guevara was calling for the creation of "two, three, many

---

[32] Regis Debray (1940–) is the author of *Revolution in the Revolution?* (New York: Monthly Review Press, 1967).

Vietname."[33] Young people like ourselves were going into the hills in Latin America. The Black Panther Party formed inside the United States around the question of the gun. Universities were being closed, disrupted. Speakers were being prevented from speaking. Buildings were being occupied. In other words, things were happening. It was not a fantasy.

Then it climaxed in 1968: one, Columbia, two, the student-worker uprising in France, three, Chicago.[34] This whole period happened.

*Czechoslovakia.*

Czechoslovakia.[35] It's hard for people to believe it happened. And people now think, "You were living a fantasy." But it was not a fantasy at the time. The only fantasy part of it, which could only be proven afterward, was that it wasn't permanent. It was an international upsurge. People concluded it was the final decisive upsurge.

*Chicago?*

---

[33] Ernesto "Che" Guevara (1928–1967) was an Argentine-born physician and leader of the Cuban Revolution. On April 16, 1967, Guevara gave his "Message to the Tricontinental" (Organization of the Solidarity of the Peoples of Africa, Asia and Latin America), saying, "How close we could look into a bright future should two, three, or many Vietnams flourish throughout the world with their share of deaths and their immense tragedies, their everyday heroism and their repeated blows against imperialism, impelled to disperse its forces under the sudden attack and the increasing hatred of all peoples of the world."

[34] "Columbia" refers to April 1968 antiwar and civil rights protests at Columbia University in New York City, during which students took over many university buildings and carried out a general strike. "Chicago" refers to protests at the Democratic Convention in Chicago in August 1968, discussed later.

[35] "Czechoslovakia" refers to the Prague Spring period of democratic reforms in that country, beginning in January 1968. The experiment was crushed by Soviet armed forces in August 1968.

No, that whole period. Chicago was simply part of a decisive upsurge which, we thought, was going to bring down the American government faster than any of us could predict.

*Why?*

That period, 1967 to 1968, all those events happening at once.

*Why did they happen at once?*

It happened largely because of Vietnam. Vietnam was the revolutionary model the Chinese leadership used as the example, in Lin Piao's phrase, of the war in the countryside that would encircle the cities.[36] Vietnam created the upsurge in Europe, which led to an anti-Vietnam War movement there, which swiftly led to a student movement and uprisings against conditions in Europe. Vietnam was the immediate cause of the radicalizing of the U.S. student movement from 1965 on. Vietnam was the inspiration to Che. I wish I could say it — I think it's true, but I'm not sure of it — Vietnam at least contributed to the consciousness of the black militants as they participated in the urban insurrections and then when they formed the Black Panther Party. I think they were acutely aware of guerrilla warfare and revolution, primarily through reading Fanon.[37]

Their uprisings came mainly from the experience of the civil rights movement, the police repression and then the Party—but you'll have to ask Huey [Newton]. I don't know, but I think even there Vietnam had a lot to do with shaping black consciousness. Stokely went to the 1967 Latin American Organization of

---

[36] Lin Piao (1907–1971), now "Lin Biao," was the Chinese Vice President and Minister of National Defense.

[37] Frantz Fanon (1925–1961) was born in Martinique in the eastern Caribbean Sea, and lived in France, Algeria and Tunisia. He analyzed the psychology of colonialism and racism, notably in *Black Skin, White Masks* (New York: Grove Press, 1952) and *The Wretched of the Earth* (New York: Grove Press, 1961).

Solidarity (OLAS) conference and was greeted as a hero there.[38] The OLAS conference was inspired not simply by Che's message, but by the presence of Vietnamese, by the "two, three, many Vietnams" concept, and then Stokely brought that concept back into the United States. I don't want to make everything seem to come from Vietnam, but it did. Vietnam triggered all that.

*People went to Chicago that summer with what seems to be an assortment of reasons.*

But our reasons were much shaped by Vietnam.

*But the people going to Chicago at least turned into a phenomenon out of this wild assortment of purposes.*

I don't know. There was a national focusing of the contradiction between two kinds of energy, the energy of dinosaur imperialism and the energy of resistance and opposition of all kinds that had been going on and brewing in the United States for eight years, that had intensified from one year to the next and finally came to a showdown there. That's why it became epic, because it was a showdown of all the forces that had been facing off with each other, skirmishing, testing each other, and exploring each other. It had finally come to a deadlock. There wasn't any going forward with this Democratic Party and these New Deal liberals, who had tied themselves to the military-industrial complex, and they, in their way, were making the same judgment about us. We might be middle-class but we were not going to be integrated into their world. We were not going to be acceptable. We were not just temporarily radicals who could be brought back into the American dream. Therefore we had to be punished and made an example of.

---

[38] Born in Trinidad, Stokely Carmichael (1941–1998) was a SNCC Freedom Rider, a voting rights field organizer in Mississippi, and then SNCC Chair from 1966 to 1967. He later joined the Black Panther Party and the All-African People's Revolutionary Party in the Republic of Guinea. He changed his name to Kwame Ture in 1978.

*Both sides intended it as a conclusion and came away from it as a disastrous beginning.*

There was some premeditation, but more it was like a ritual confrontation that brought everyone's recognition to the highest emotional focus they had ever experienced. Like a ceremonial confrontation, an encounter in which people finally have stripped away all pretense and show themselves to each other for what they are—and fight. [*Laughter*]

*Dick Flacks: Several phases were leading up to Chicago, what people thought Chicago would mean before it happened, right? First the idea that Johnson had no legitimacy. Then there became the possibility it wouldn't be Johnson. There was slim hope that the alternative to Johnson was Bobby Kennedy or Eugene McCarthy or something would emerge, which I guess might have been a period where people thought there would be just millions of people coming to Chicago to reinforce that possibility.*

And again SDS, as usual, would have nothing to do with it. It was another case of the original early SDS leadership coming back to carry out something our experience told us was the right thing to do, while the SDS national office fought against the action all the way, in any form it was put forward. If Johnson was nominated, there would be repression. We couldn't survive repression. If Kennedy was nominated, then Rennie and I were running dogs for Kennedy, preparing to lead all the people SDS had radicalized into a demonstration that would result in everyone cheering Kennedy. It was just the early versus the older SDS, the different styles again emerging.

*Were you close to Robert Kennedy?*

No. I met Kennedy twice.

*Before he was a candidate?*

Yeah, it was spring of 1967, but it was not long after Staughton and I returned from Vietnam, and a journalist friend of mine, who was writing a book on Kennedy, suggested to Kennedy it would be good for him to hear our views on Vietnam. So Staughton and I and Staughton's son met with Kennedy in New York one day to talk for a couple of hours. It was after Kennedy made that trip to Paris and while Kennedy was deciding to take an antiwar position. I was impressed by his willingness to have these arguments and willingness to consider opposing the war, which after all he had had a lot to do with starting. By now it's normal to have among your friends many people who started the war, but then it was unusual to meet somebody who started the war and who was preparing to oppose it.

He seemed isolated by his wealth and power and not sure of what was going on and still thinking in terms of Cold War categories about the Communists taking over the coalition, and Communists didn't believe in free elections. He told us somebody in France had told him Communists don't believe in free elections. "This is the great problem," he said, "how can we resolve this conflict in Vietnam when we don't agree on the means of solving it since we believe in free elections?" He was telling me this when he would have called Lyndon Johnson an election rigger from way back. He said we were for free elections, that was our proposed solution, and they're not for free elections. He wasn't entirely up to date on what was going on in Vietnam. That was the only conversation I had with him.

I had one other accidental meeting with him the week before he was killed because I was doing some articles on the McCarthy and Kennedy campaigns. I was talking to some journalists in the hotel where he and McCarthy were staying the week of their debate in the California primary. I was going up to the floor where Kennedy's staff had all their apartments because I wanted to see some people, and by accident, he came in exhausted from a day of campaigning looking gray and the skin on his cheeks and hands all worn out from that and said hello. He was with Fred Dutton and

John Glenn, and we got on the elevator and went upstairs.[39] I was going several floors above where he got off, and in the elevator, he asked me if I was campaigning for him with a hopeful look because he was so exhausted, and the election was so close.

And I said no, I was working on peace demonstrations and organizing for Chicago. He just looked tired but polite, and he got off the elevator, and I never saw him again. SDS attacked me for being a running dog for Kennedy, based on that set of facts.

*Dick Flacks: You were written up as having been at the funeral at Saint Patrick's.*

Yeah.

*Dick Flacks: Did that embarrass you?*

No. Why? What do you mean by that?

*Dick Flacks: I don't know. People attacked you.*

I didn't feel that much respect for Kennedy or McCarthy, but I certainly would have wanted them to be in office now instead of Richard Nixon, for the sake of Vietnam. I did have respect for and feel a closeness to the people who supported Kennedy and McCarthy. Especially Kennedy, because so many Irish and working-class people in general, black, particularly, and young people . . . It goes back again to whether you relate to experience and what is taking place or whether you relate exclusively to an ideological framework for judging abstractly what a person's politics are. He, just like Martin Luther King, was politically part of the establishment on one level, but the feelings and hopes they

---

[39] Fred Dutton (1923–2005) was campaign manager for Robert Kennedy's 1968 presidential campaign. Previously, he had served as Chief of Staff for California Governor Pat Brown, and Assistant Secretary of State for the Kennedy Administration. John Glenn (1921–2016) was a Marine fighter pilot in the Korean War, the first American astronaut to orbit the Earth, and a U.S. Senator from Ohio from 1974 to 1999.

aroused among young people were ones you would have to share and identify with if you were a human being.

*Dick Flacks: Why have the Kennedys developed this mystique that still survives? Teddy Kennedy takes it over.*

Because of hope. Their family has represented hope for ten years, and secondly because that hope has been denied in the most traumatizing way imaginable by having their heads blown off in a spectacular form of political violence everyone saw. So their family represents an abortion of hope.

As long as the Kennedy program is not allowed to be implemented and fulfilled, for better or worse, millions of people will never know whether the sixties didn't have to happen or whether they were inevitable anyway. Nor will they know whether America was supposedly benign and would have pulled out of Vietnam and gradually worked against racism and poverty—not without struggle, but with a relatively nonviolent struggle, or whether their killing was no accident. Nor whether it was part of the character of the way power is wielded in America or whether any reformer is doomed to run up against the same kind of thing.

It's not a mystique based on charisma or sex appeal or something like that. It goes to the deepest question in the soul of the American people about our country, and to some extent that's an open question. We never had a test in the sixties of that question. McGovern again raises that question. I'm hardly one who believes peaceful reform towards the kind of changes I'm talking about is going to happen. People ought to draw the lesson that our country is run by murderers. All the assassinations of the sixties were political conspiracies, not isolated acts. If some of our officials use violence everywhere else in the world, there's no doubt they would use it here. But this point is frightening, perhaps, to everyone, even those who are most verbally committed to revolution—frightening to draw that conclusion in absolute terms, that there is no residue of hope within regular channels, only violence awaiting you.

*Especially when it's never been real.*

The reason I went there the night before the funeral is because I shared with a lot of other people these feelings of loss and despair and grim, grim days ahead. I was thinking of Chicago and Vietnam. Other people may have been thinking of their civil rights or all the bloodshed in the South. Whatever it was, people were upset. I was with some friends who knew or were covering the Kennedy campaign that night the coffin was flown in, and I decided to go with them to St. Patrick's. We got there in the middle of the night. It was two a.m., and a lot of ordinary people were already gathering outside for what was to become the funeral the next day. I think Fred Dutton or Adam Walinsky recognized us and let us into the sanctuary.[40]

I had with me a green military hat from Cuba and I didn't recognize for the longest time the coffin was there. I don't know if you've ever been in St. Patrick's when it's empty. It's one of the larger Catholic churches. I noticed the Irish cops and the Irish workmen putting together this scaffolding from which the next day the television cameras would record the scene. The faces of the Kennedy staff, which were absolutely gray and wasted, showed how the only reality for them was in this person, that their lives were attached to this person. They were shaken but didn't have the benefit of dying. They were simply zombies.

Then in the middle of all this, I noticed Robert Kennedy's coffin. This person, who was so inflated larger than life and who could pick up the telephone and wield power and write a check for any sum of money and affect millions and millions of people with the statement of and wield power and write a check for any

---

[40] Adam Walinsky (1937–) served as a Justice Department attorney in the Kennedy Administration, and as a speechwriter for Robert Kennedy from 1964 to 1968.

sum of money and affeca few words, was now nothing, an unnoticed body in a coffin in the corner of a vast room which was to be the last spectacular scene of his life. Just the incredible vanity that was involved, the vanity of his life for one thing, but also the incredible way everything in his life, including his death, would have the packaged nature of the continuing spectacle now going on even without him. Even without him, they were getting the television cameras ready, whether he liked it or not.

For all I know, if he had been shot and lived, he might have taken a different view of power and ambition and so forth, but now his will was being carried out without him, and the people would have no friend as they saw it. It would be reinforced for them in a way that would cause infinite sorrow the next day by televising this funeral. You could tell he was nothing now, but he was going to be elevated to the level of sainthood and focus all the grief of people who were hoping for reform. That moves me to tears, which are not hard for me to shed.

The coffin was being neglected in the assembling spectacle, so they decided some people should stand by it amidst all the hammering and clutter. Since there were only about fifteen of us in the church, they asked me and others whether we would take a turn doing that for fifteen minutes. I did that with my Cuban hat in my hand, and I was so upset I don't remember who else was there. I don't regret that. Anyone who would feel that was politically incorrect would be exactly the kind of person I wouldn't want to work with too closely because I think they have no touch with the American people.

*Dick Flacks: Or even with their feelings.*

Or even with their feelings, because of this fear of suddenly discovering they were American or something. I drew a distinction. I had an invitation to the funeral that came by telegram, to ride on the train to the gravesite. On the whole, the people on the train had not proven any interest, as far as I could see, in the grassroots people that cared about Kennedy. I didn't want to say no. I didn't reply to the telegram. That's been escalated into my having attended the funeral services with Robert McNamara or something like that [*laughter*]. I don't think I've ever seen Robert McNamara, and I didn't go to the funeral.

# Chapter 2

# Tom Hayden:
# The *Rolling Stone* Interview
# Part II

### Chicago

*Rolling Stone: What happened in Chicago was epic in terms of what had come out since Port Huron, civil rights, the new youth culture, Yippies and so on, and Kennedy was the focus of it. Yet it wasn't a coalition. What was it?*

It was a coalition by the end. There were ego rivalries that kept people apart. There were simplified categories like, "those people are apolitical, those people are too political," between the Yippies and the antiwar forces, but in the end, since we were all treated the same way [*laughter*] it became rather absurd to magnify the difference.

Everyone expected something different. I don't know what people expected. Do you mean "people people"? Or do you mean planners? People expected just what happened, the drama they inevitably want to be part of as a further step in discovering their identity and American identity. That was the ultimate reason people came.

On the planning level, all of us planned events which we thought there was some chance could work. They were rational. One was a Festival of Life that would have all these rock groups, and which would, by its example, expose and cause a cave-in of the Democratic Party's authority to the extent it had any. The antiwar people wanted to have a march that would be representative of the American people that would go to the convention and fulfill the same results.

Woodstock and the Moratorium, which happened one year later, were close to what the original image of Chicago was going to be. On the other hand, just speaking for myself and Rennie Davis, there was always the feeling we were getting into something that was not rational, that was not going to happen as planned, that we were up against forces we still did not understand, and that did not want us to have a legal organized protest. And we were aware of that, not simply from negotiations with the City and the vibes in Chicago from the Chicago police—and those vibes had turned out to be correct, but we didn't know why.

As it turned out later, that was the period in which the armed services first started putting their intelligence apparatus onto domestic protest. Army, Navy, probably CIA, and local police surrounded us. We didn't know the American military, as the Pentagon Papers now reveal, was coming home, just as we had speculated in our rhetoric. They were starting to deploy forces. We didn't know that was happening during January to August 1968, but we did have that scary sense from the city and the government officials we talked to something was happening beyond what we could grasp, and it was frightening. There was a chemical mix in the air that was dangerous.

The other part we sensed was from Vietnam. Rennie and I had been in Vietnam with several other people in October and November, just before the idea of Chicago seized us and we started talking about it. Then I was in Cuba for three or four weeks in January with Dave Dellinger, and there we had already decided upon a plan for Chicago. Being in Cuba made it clear the demonstrations should have an international effect. They should not simply be aimed at domestic things but should have the effect of making the U.S. government stand exposed as starting to lose domestic support in the eyes of the people of the world. That would cause an upsurge of world support for our antiwar movement in the United States. It would lift expectations that American policy in Vietnam could be stopped if the world's governments would only get together. It would show America was not Nazi Germany with a unified or suppressed people and a government out of control, but that America was a divided country in which progressive people and real human beings were starting to emerge and fight their own government's policy. The world could choose between the two Americas.

Then back from Cuba, saying my goodbyes to Newark after experiencing the rebellion there four months before. I had gone from the Newark rebellion to North Vietnam to Cuba back to America. I was in America two and a half months before Columbia happened. I was at Columbia for a week, living in a building with people who felt such international solidarity with people around the world and such solidarity with students across the United States and such revolutionary pride in their ability to live together communally for a week under such danger. In that building, there were the ingredients of Chicago and the ingredients of the Weatherpeople, Mark Rudd and others.[41]

From there came the spectacle of France. The students were shaking the government to its foundations. They seemed to have almost overthrown it, and then Germany, and then Rudi Dutschke being shot in the head, then Martin Luther King being shot and killed, Bobby Kennedy being shot and killed.[42] Lyndon

---

[41] "Weatherpeople" refers to an SDS split-off group detailed later. It was originally called "Weatherman," but later changed to "Weather Underground." The name comes from a Bob Dylan lyric: "You don't need a weatherman to know which way the wind blows." ("Subterranean Homesick Blues," 1965). Mark Rudd was a leader of Columbia SDS and later joined the Weather Underground.

[42] Rudi Dutschke (1940–1979) was a prominent voice for student radicals in Germany in the sixties and the anti-nuclear Green movement in the

Johnson dropped out of the presidential race. The sense something epic was happening was hard to miss. All you had to do was get to Chicago, and it would happen.

It didn't seem any more planning was necessary. There was no way to avoid everything coming to a showdown. I don't mean a real showdown in which the government would be overthrown or the Left would be destroyed, or any existing forces would be permanently put out of action. It was another kind of showdown, a liturgical showdown that everyone would participate in and be affected in the whole country and the whole world. Out of that came a lot of things that still aren't understood.

First, the present reform of the Democratic Party was made necessary. We proved there was no alternative but their disappearance from American history. Second, the American government required a restructuring of some kind, preferably by extrication from Vietnam.

Instead, what we got was the Nixon Doctrine, which was aimed more at the American people than anyone else, the troop withdrawals, the lowering of draft calls, the cutting back of pressure on the American people. Nixon cynically believed what we care about is whether our taxes are too high or whether our sons are going to be killed, or whether we're going to be drafted.

*Dick Flacks: And the eighteen-year-old vote.*

Eighteen-year-old vote, yeah. That all stemmed from Chicago. But the other thing we got was the end of SDS because the strain was just incredible. Those of us who could have gone from Chicago to continue organizing SDS, that is the original leaders of SDS like Rennie and myself, were too much at odds with the SDS national office, which still thought of us, even during Chicago, as being dangerous reformists.

---

seventies. In 1968 he survived three shots from an assassin. His assailant committed suicide in 1970. Eleven years later, Dutschke died from brain damage he suffered in the 1968 attack.

We were also blocked from taking leadership in the antiwar movement by too many disagreements with Mobilization people, who were from sectarian or liberal organizations with a stake in keeping "dangerous, violent" people like ourselves out of leadership. Rennie came to that later than I did. He stayed with it.

I felt, given the situation with SDS and the antiwar movement and given my continuing doubts about a national role, it seemed the thing to do was again to leave the "center of power" and go to a community, in this case, Berkeley, and remake myself into a normal human being who could relate to other human beings. I think of this now as short-sighted and irresponsible. In retrospect, it might have been necessary, because nothing about SDS was reformed. Anyway, what happened to me isn't the point here.

The conditions for the demise of SDS were at hand. Number one, early leaders like Rennie and I were too much at a distance from them to go back in. Number two, they could not have related to Chicago. Still, at the time, Chicago was happening, they had the elite view of themselves that their role should be to supposedly radicalize McCarthy workers, as if the chief danger, while the blood was flowing in the streets, was people would be coopted [*laughter*] by liberal Democrats. Third, SDS was tied up internally by the Progressive Labor Party, which was still arguing students were not where it was at, and you had to go to the ranks of the industrial proletariat.[43]

## Weather Underground

Finally, the overall total effect of everything from Columbia to Chicago was to create the Weatherpeople. I believe they were not artificial, not an old left graft, not people who were living in abstract fantasies in the way they have been considered, but the final natural generation of SDS, the true inheritors of everything

---

[43] Progressive Labor was founded in 1962 as a split-off from the Communist Party USA. In the mid-sixties it appeared inside SDS as a faction.

that had happened from 1960 on. They let what was left of SDS as an organization collapse because of their disillusionment. All the disillusionment, all the failure of the civil rights reform effort, the anti-Vietnam War reform effort, the liberal Democratic reform effort, the community organizing efforts in the ghettos—each one of these had ended in someone's blood, whether it was the blood in Birmingham, the blood of blacks in the Northern cities, the blood of Martin Luther King, the blood of the Vietnamese, the blood of Robert Kennedy, and finally our own blood in the streets of Chicago. It had all crystallized.

Their views came out of their experience more than has been realized. They made judgments from their experience that have proven to be wrong, but at least those judgments came from experience. First, time was running out. Second, a revolutionary force had emerged in the world that was engaged in a life and death struggle with the United States, and it was in Vietnam and the Third World. Third, the U.S. response was not going to be cooptation, but violent repression. Fourth, it would inevitably bring down thunder on the heads of dissenters in the United States. Repression would begin here. And fifth, the student movement, because it was so white and privileged and reform-oriented, would never see this danger in time. Therefore, those who could see it in time would have to, at least for the present, give up on the majority of whites, even students, being able to form a resistance.

Instead, look for whatever whites from SDS and possibly some poor whites—street gangs, since at least they were potentially violent [*laughter*]—but basically link with blacks and link with Third World people in the United States and around the world. Get ready for a resistance movement that would in the long run possibly provoke political consciousness. Don't stand out there carrying the placard and expect those people to respond to your demands anymore. Get out there and form an underground that will allow you to do things.

## Tom Hayden: The Rolling Stone Interview – Part II

One objective was to show them that in the face of repression they will not stop the protest. The protest will continue even in the form of guerilla bee stings and sabotage. Another objective was to debunk the overwhelming myth they rely on domestically, which is their technology and firepower is too much for anyone to bear up under. Show them action could be taken against them and be gotten away with. By staying underground, encourage a feeling of resistance among other Americans, particularly Third World people and young whites. Finally, they wanted to issue a warning to people around the world that there are some Americans who will resist in the way some French resisted the Nazis in France, the Danish people resisted the Nazis in Denmark, and so on.

I try to describe the Weather position in the best possible way because I respect where it came from. It came from experience, from a true glimpse of horror and a desire to react genuinely. Nearly every Weatherperson was a person I knew from the early or middle period of SDS, and I know they experienced these things. They were not simply university intellectuals who read a book on Mao Tse-tung thought and took off for the hills. They tried. They knocked on doors in Cleveland. That's where Terry Robbins, who now is dead, and Kathy Boudin, who now is missing, came from.[44] They went through all the steps. They went through all the disillusionment, and they were true children of the sixties.

---

[44] Terry Robbins (1947–1970) died with two others—Diana Oughton (1942–1970) and Ted Gold (1947–1970)—when a bomb their Weather Underground collective was assembling accidentally exploded in a Greenwich Village townhouse. Kathy Boudin (1943–) survived the explosion and later went underground following a 1981 Brink's truck robbery that left three people dead. Boudin served twenty-two years in prison and is now a professor at the Columbia University School of Social Work.

Tom Hayden on Social Movements

Dick Flacks: One of the important things about them is they either had been committed pacifists or had certainly been raised in an environment of extreme nonviolence.

True. Terry's friend who was killed, Diana Oughton, was as kind and peaceful a person as you could ever meet. The men had a lot of macho and aggressiveness. Diana is portrayed as a terrorist now, but she was a flower child.

Dick Flacks: That may be part of what was the problem. To become what their experience said they had to become, the transformation of identity had to be so extreme they couldn't speak about that transformation in the language you were just speaking about. It had to be a total rejection of civilized language. Having been pacifists and intellectuals, they had to totally transform themselves to consider employing violence. As a result, they could show no signs of softness to people not in their immediate group.

I relate to what you say because I've done it myself innumerable times, whenever I want to go on a campaign or something like that. The arguments in SDS over whether I was opposed to the realignment of the Democratic Party became personality confrontations between me and others when I wanted to go work in community organizations. I got into a frame of mind where I virtually thought people who didn't want to go to work in the ghettos were irrelevant or worse. The Weatherpeople, therefore, were repeating a familiar cycle, except when they were doing it, I was on the other side.

We had such painful arguments in which they would say I was not seizing the time. I was not willing to risk everything. The woman I was living with should split. I was opportunistic.

Then I would say, "Look, I agree with so much you're saying, but I know you're becoming extreme in a way that's going to result in making major mistakes. You're either going to get caught, or you're going to get killed, or you're going to burn yourself out because your hope is going to run into reality. Reality isn't going to change as much as you think, and you're destroying your relationships with other people who you're going to want to be your friends then. This is not simply a question of personalities and conflicts and styles of political work at stake. It's a political and moral judgment about America because your writing off friends can only lead you to conclude you also must write off the American people."

They were right regarding the need to become more determined. They were also right in recognizing the New Left of the sixties could go the way of the European Left of the last one hundred years and the American left of the thirties and forties. The New Left could become a bunch of settled, complacent people who talk socialism and raise their children in the most oppressive ways and give rise to new radicals who hate their parents in every generation. They were right about that. But they're wrong in the sense they think violence will give you moral authority. I argued with Terry Robbins not too long before his death. He said the act of violence would anoint the doer of violence with moral authority. It didn't.

The good thing about them was they learned, because they are in touch with their own experience. They are not counterfeit radicals. They learned from the hardest thing possible. They learned from their killing themselves in the townhouse they had become too militaristic, too hateful towards everyone, that they had forgotten the gradual step-by-step process which had brought them to their consciousness. They had not been made into violent revolutionaries in a day. They had grown up in America as Americans, gone through high school, college, the fifties, the sixties, and only after a long process had they come to view the government as the enemy. They could not short-circuit that process with a few bombs.

Then they switched maybe too far in the other direction and glorified the youth culture for a period. I don't have any way of verifying this except their actions and writings, but slowly they've come to a more balanced, long-term recognition of themselves as an illegal part of the American revolutionary process. They are capable of doing some things, releasing some prisoners here and there, hiding fugitives who are running from unjust courtrooms, striking violently against institutions that are the symbols of genocide, and waiting to see what develops.

They've done a lot too—not military damage, but they've done damage to the reputation of the FBI and the CIA and all the secret agents who are supposed to be so sophisticated. We found out from the FBI papers stolen in Media, Pennsylvania, that this is a calculated program on the part of the intelligence service to make everybody think there's an FBI man behind every mailbox. Those were the exact words. The Weatherpeople, like no other group, have shown no matter what sophisticated techniques the FBI, CIA, and others have, they are not able to catch well-organized fugitives. That's been a thorn in their side. It led to the demystifying of Hoover and a lot of other things.[45]

What this accomplishment reveals is not only the weakness of the emperor. It tears down another myth about the emperor's strength. This is important because a lot of people are paranoid they're being watched, that they can't get away with taking an hour off from work to go to a demonstration without getting fired.

It also probably reveals the Weatherpeople are healthy and in touch with their experience, because I don't think they stay hidden so well and get around so well by technique or by outdoing the FBI. How could they? I don't know how much money they have, but it's not millions of dollars. They have a thousand agents looking for them at all times. They don't have the technology. They have a few bombs and maybe some machines, cars to drive around in and maybe some false ID. That's their technology, so it must be they have rooted themselves in American life. [*Laughter*] Popular support would be too strong

---

[45] J. Edgar Hoover (1895–1972), the first FBI Director, dedicated his agency's resources to destroying the civil rights and peace movements with false charges, wrongful imprisonment, provocateurs, and assassination.

a word, but there is a sufficient climate of understanding to make it hard for the FBI to penetrate wherever they are.

This wasn't true ten years ago, but it is now. If you talk to the average person in America about police and not call them pigs and not call them the strong-arm men of the ruling class or something like that, but say anything about the police harassing you, you'll be believed. The average person will believe you if you walk into a restaurant and say, "God, I was just grabbed by some police and thrown up against the wall in an alley and searched, and then they said they were looking for somebody else, but first they hit me in the stomach with a club." Anyone in America will now, with few exceptions, believe that would have happened.

That climate of distrust of the government and police is there. If you understand that, you understand the Weatherpeople were wrong in believing the American people were impossibly conservative. You also probably can see the reason why the Weatherpeople haven't been caught, that they've gotten wise to this factor. They've started to understand a person who today may be conservative, tomorrow can change.

I've gone on too long on that, but I think the Weatherpeople were wrong in the beginning in their judgment of the American people. But they've been trivialized or thought of like a cartoon character, mad bombers, or crazy and they're not. America made them what they are, and they are as American as can be, and I think they'll reappear from time to time in our history. I don't think the sects will reappear and make any contribution to American life.

## Restructuring the Movement

*Dick Flacks: I was interested that you said Chicago meant the demise of SDS, but it certainly wasn't the demise of the student movement. Two years after that was the highest point of student revolt.*

That was a total misjudgment and one we'd do well to digest. Just at the point of maximum confrontation of 1968, where it looked like the establishment was hopeless and we were outnumbered militants, was exactly the point where we could have relied most on an upsurge of popular resistance. What was planted by Chicago—while we're on the verge of total disillusionment—was a widespread popular understanding that the establishment was out of its mind, that the people in Chicago, the antiwar movement, and the counterculture were in the right. One year later you had Woodstock and the Moratoriums. Eighteen months after, you had a massive upsurge around the time of that conspiracy trial and the Cambodian invasion.

And where was SDS? Gone. Where was the organized Left? Gone. Just at the point where everything we had worked for—a nationwide student movement, antiwar movement, youth culture where people could express themselves as human beings without it being a crime -- was finally taking shape in the form of millions of people doing it and believing it, where were we?

*What happened?*

A shambles. What came next was a long, experimental, sometimes painful, sometimes immensely creative search for new forms. It was no longer just the simple expression of identity like a be-in or something from 1966 to 1968.[46] It was more serious. People were more convinced something new was happening, not simply a radical restructuring of society, but a restructuring of the movement itself. This wasn't an entirely new concept. SDS from the beginning thought participatory democracy had to apply to the organization, not simply to some blueprint for society. It was an acceleration of this because none of the forms after 1968 — simply organizing large-scale antiwar demonstrations or festivals of life or SDS chapters — seemed to make any sense.

In the wake of what happened in Chicago, people started to look for alternatives. They were found in the growth of youth

---

[46] The first "Human Be-In" took place in San Francisco's Golden Gate Park on January 14, 1967. Its name came from Richard Alpert, now Ram Dass, who said about an earlier event, "It's a hell of a gathering. It's just being. Humans being. Being together."

communities like Berkeley and in new movements like the women's movement which seemed to embody a much deeper understanding of the need for people to relate to each other differently, not simply to relate to the establishment differently. Collectives emerged as the form in which the new culture and new movements would express themselves. The women were reacting to the shambles of the male-dominated SDS and the sectarianism and the factionalism, and so were freaks in a different way.

*Didn't that channel create the basis for what you were talking about regarding the participatory democracy, whatever degree of it was exhibited at the Democratic convention? Because what did happen after it, it seems to me, after 1968, was people began forming collectives. They did begin identifying in a collective sense with something less politically defined, but a much more culturally defined identity of their own. But it was formless in the shambles of the movement.*

And the feeling people had been ripped off on a widespread basis by the absorption of rock music into the commercial culture, by the absorption of Yippie-type theatrics into the media, by the sense the kind of things that were supposed to be naturally ours becoming if not part of the system, at least out of our control. It was no longer like SDS, which had some semblance of democracy, even if it was structured in such a way certain groups couldn't make much impact. It was much more like people were becoming consumers of something that didn't even represent them and they couldn't control.

*Dick Flacks: By the time of the Chicago trial, you and other people had become national figures whether you wanted to or not. What are the personal consequences of being placed in that kind of situation?*

One political consequence was that you become a caricature of yourself as portrayed by the media. When people would invite me to speak, they would think I was a freak, and I would do handstands onto the stage, turn over the podium, hand out matches because that's what they thought the Chicago trial was about. It was radicalizing because it would make people distrust the media to see me the way I was, a barely articulate, dull, slow kind of analytic person.

The media and the establishment have a major hand in selecting who should be the people's leaders. Not that there shouldn't be leadership and not that it won't come from people who have been around a long time, but there's always something deliberate about the escalation of a leader into a personality, into a myth. It's part of the media. They may find it convenient to run campaigns against Jerry or Abbie.[47] I don't know. People get put in the position of being led by figures partially selected by the media.

Another political thing that happens is there's no way for people to be like a mythical figure, so you're not setting an example anyone can follow. People feel oppressed by their leaders whose faces they see in the papers, who are not like them. They can't be like that. The worst result is the groupie-ism that affects rock and roll stars. People feel more powerless because they can't even control what they thought was their movement.

What happens to the person involved is a cycle. Not inevitably, but likely, you become addicted to the media environment, to the crowd environment. Your identity gradually becomes so involved in that you don't know who you are except in relation to media, and crowds who wire you up and who begin to determine what you do more than the other way around. This is especially true of cooptation in America because of the advanced technology and the role of communications in organizing society,

---

[47] Jerry Rubin (1938–1994) was an organizer of the Vietnam Day Committee in Berkeley, California, and the October 1967 March on the Pentagon. He founded the Youth International Party (Yippies) on New Year's Eve, 1967, with Anita Hoffman, Nancy Kurshan, Abbie Hoffman, and Paul Krassner. Abbie Hoffman (1936–1989) and Rubin were indicted as part of the Chicago Eight for conspiracy to riot at the Chicago Democratic Convention of 1968.

what people consume and what people can see. It would be less true in other kinds of societies in the Third World.

Once you pass a certain point, it's not clear anymore that you will ever be able to re-grasp your identity, and you have two choices.

One choice is opportunism and becoming entirely a media-oriented personality, negotiating for more power and starting more or less to live entirely in the world of the media. [*Laughter*] That may have some educational advantages. You may be able to educate some people, but gradually your self dissolves.

The other choice has been an attraction-revulsion thing a lot of people in SDS have had towards power: ambition, followed by having power and status, followed by thinking better of it, followed by succumbing to the pressures involved and your self being threatened by a crack-up. Then comes total withdrawal into a much simpler lifestyle where you're no longer effective in the original sense, but you are more human and perhaps in some other sense more effective.

Unless those two choices are overcome, and they're not the only two, it's hard for me to see where movements would get leadership.

What happened after Chicago intensified this. It happened to almost all of us. I'm not talking about Bobby Seale for a second. Dave Dellinger's period of being a vital organizer behind coalitions started to dissolve somewhat in his relationship with masses of young people who come to those demonstrations. The gap became greater and he, in response, started changing. There were struggles around collective leadership in *Liberation* magazine. Rennie went on organizing a bureaucracy to carry out a project, which climaxed at May Day, a gigantic confrontation. During that, he, too, was lashed back and forth about elitism and his role. The result was an important struggle to try to get him to change in some way, but it wasn't clear how people wanted him to change. Jerry and Abbie were attacked for elitism and by people whose egos had been hyped up by the Yippie environment.

I thought there were exceptions to this rule (mainly myself!) and I would somehow peacefully resolve this contradiction by becoming involved in a collective in Berkeley. Not that a lot of work didn't get done around the war and community control of the police, but we were never able to resolve the internal conflicts about how a "movement heavy" relates as an equal in a small group. In such a group, if you continue to use the contacts and influence built up over the years, you can only make the other people in the collective become extensions of you or live in your shadow, which is now unbearable for people to do, especially women. On the other hand, you could arbitrarily decide all your power is an illegitimate privilege and cut off that influence, cut off those contacts, become someone else, become absolutely a "no-one" like everyone else and deny you're Tom Hayden or that anything you were before still exists.

Neither is possible. The pain involved in both is too great and the choice seems too sharp. What happened wasn't so much like a factional split, but just a separation of people after about a year of trying to make it work. People still worked together, all of us, all over California, but trying to live together and struggle together in the same block in the same house never succeeded.

I still haven't been able to put together what the proper resolution of the problem is. I don't know who can. It was necessary to confront the personalities and the power and the resources we had built up due to the publicity and coverage of the conspiracy trial. The movement can't be built around that kind of star trip.

*People in the movement today have had varying ranges of experience. There are a few who have had ten years of experience, while others have had, say, five years. Each is historically connected, and I wonder whether people are aware of or have a sense of their history.*

People certainly don't. A view of your history isn't encouraged by the way the media records history because it's inevitably recorded around the biographies of personalities. The people who have been around a long time must keep active, keep organizing, and in that sense, provide leadership, but it has to be directed at teaching, including the teaching of our own history. It must be directed at just what Dick said, helping people understand the energy has come from them and not from the organizers. Often in any period where there's a new burst of energy, organizers are a restraint on it rather than real guidance. That's true in all these cases, the black movement in the South, the draft resistance movement, the bursting of SDS on the national scene. Nearly every creative turning point has been accomplished by some group no one has heard of and in nearly every case threatening established leaders.

That's not to glorify spontaneity. That's to point out new directions can come from below and not from above. That's why it would be a mistake to say we don't need leaders. That would ignore that every new act is preceded by preparing public opinion, prior examples of martyrdom and sacrifice, and the writing of books somebody reads and passes on the ideas to somebody else.

The continuity is only possible with leadership, with people persisting year in and year out to influence and educate and talk to and learn from everybody around them. That's what in Vietnam they would call the function of a cadre. The organizing is not for the sake of building a bureaucracy with an elite at the top. The function of organizing is to create continuity from one generation to the next, one person to the next, to summarize experience so when somebody does discover something new, which they do every day, it gets passed on to other people. That can only happen by organizers, writers, people talking.

*Dick Flacks: Berkeley, where you spent some time, has the highest concentration of post-student movement young adults with some degree of community among themselves in the country. Do you think there's anything emerging in Berkeley that provides directions to people there and elsewhere about how you can create a place and you can continue a lifelong relationship to revolutionary change?*

If you lower your ambition in terms of a standard of living, which many people have done, and which is an important decision, you can get by for little in this society even with a family. That means you can work outside of the career structure of advancement and higher and higher salary at a variety of jobs that don't take all that much time. Sometimes you can work at several jobs over the years. That's an answer for people who don't see anything in the job structure but need an income. The other thing is creating a community of support. By living collectively and being in communities like that, people can economically support each other and make life cheaper and free themselves for more time to do political things or to do experimental things with their lives.

The other things that come out of the community like that are alternative institutions. They still have to struggle with the established institutions for legitimacy and can't be like a separate society in themselves, but they do result in some services for people, result in people getting skills and experience and taking care of their affairs by themselves cooperatively, and showing the way like beacons or alternatives. Like the variety of counter-institutions that support a lot of people, small businesses, trades, and hippie crafts. Still, most people aren't living in Berkeley, and there is the question of how to live like that while at the same time struggling over the direction of the institution where you work. That applies whether you teach in a college or high school or work in a factory, and how to conduct that kind of struggle is just as fraught with problems of becoming conservative as is living in Berkeley, which is a much more comfortable environment.

The early SDS people divide into both. A lot of SDS people have created counter-institutions and, in a sense, employed themselves in their activity, and others are following journalism or teaching or some other form of work and are like a center of radicalism within whatever institution they're in. In either case, it's a false issue to say there's such a thing as working inside or outside. Who do you reach? Who are you teaching? Are you incorporating into your life and style of work values that make you different from the establishment in such a way that you and your work become an alternative for other people?

## Organization

*Dick Flacks: By 1976 there are going to be sixty million American adults born since 1940, that is, people between eighteen and thirty-five years old. The evidence so far is their consciousness, in a high proportion, has been deeply affected in one way or another on central issues. If you had your way, would you like to see a new party created?*

Eventually, there has to be a party that comes out of the collective experience of all the protests and works out a program that reflects the wishes of the majority of people and that can be carried day to day through alternative institutions, as well as posed in legislative struggles and so forth. Because of the fundamental nature of racism, I have always felt such a party can't exist without the initiative coming from the Third World people inside the United States, in the way the organization of SNCC in the first part of the sixties led to the organization of a student and an antiwar movement. We were not simply an arm to SNCC but were charged and inspired. And in the same fashion, the Panthers inspired and set an example for and encouraged organization during the late sixties. In other words, I don't think beyond organizing a student movement or an antiwar movement or a women's movement you can put together anything that would resemble a party until the most oppressed people in the country called for it and organized for it.

In the meantime, a more provisional goal should be put forward. A student movement would have to be built now by this present generation of students on the campuses, not by the early founders of SDS. It will be more difficult because SDS came out of the vacuum of the fifties, a time of innocence, a time when you could stand up with great hope, great enthusiasm, and feel you were something new on the face of the earth. To form a new organization out of the carnage and sectarianism of the last several years is more difficult. People are more cynical. People want to know whether what you're proposing works, and lurking in the wings are all kinds of groups that will probably try to interfere with the development of the new organization. It has to be done, and it has to be done by students.

It is not too late for the antiwar movement to take shape in a way that makes it visible and clear to the American people. I don't mean building a single organization.

I think the war is going to come to a climax this year or next year or the year after that. Every effort should go toward deepening and developing an antiwar movement on a clear basis that has programs and politics and structure people can relate to. As the war comes to its climactic stage, people need to know it's a struggle between Nixon and Kissinger on the one hand and the majority of American people on the other, represented by an antiwar movement, not represented by a dove or two from the Senate. The latter case would look like something out of the Middle Ages. Here comes the dove on the white horse jousting with the hawk on the black horse and they fight it out, and we, the serfs who have been the cannon fodder and spectators all along will have nothing particularly to do with this contest.

If people can feel their organizing and efforts and resistance in all the forms it's taken over the years against the Vietnam War is what resulted in the war ending, then I think there'll be an upsurge by people to want to organize for more changes. There'll be a renewed belief in organization as a way to make change.

It's unfashionable today, but there was a point when certain people did believe you could make a revolution by your personal growth—everyone touch each other with their growth. That became a persistently argued point of view in meetings, in projects like Newark, in national SDS meetings, in debates between SDS and the first generation of freaks. And then it became popularized in the establishment by the *Greening of*

*America* by Charles Reich.[48] When people read that they started to realize, "Oh, no, that's not what we meant." [*Laughter*] But everyone from freaks to Democrats has now put forward this idea, the "Greening of the Democratic Party," the immediate description of the Democratic Convention. Herbert Marcuse gave at least the impression there was an ideological case that could be made for this, and there you have it.[49]

*Dick Flacks: It seems hard to create an organization that allows such a theory to evolve within and yet nevertheless maintains an organizational framework people can relate to. The surviving organizations are highly dogmatized, doctrinally. Most people who don't want to have that imposed on them won't join those organizations, but it's difficult to create an organization without a dogma, one of whose purposes is to evolve a theory. It's hard for people to grasp. It wasn't so hard in the early sixties for some reason, but it is much more difficult now. Does that make sense?*

Yeah, except first, I think it's too precious. It should be a question of your attitude towards that. You may have the attitude that things are just growing forward like weeds that will tend to solidify into an approach to life that never yields to theory, never yields an organization. It can itself become an ideology. It's a self-serving viewpoint. Or, you could grant no such theory exists now that can be accepted by everyone and such a theory and an organization will only make sense after there's been more development of the American scene and our experience. Then you could have the attitude — which I think is better — that you must focus your mind at all times on thinking through these questions, examining experience, sharing and arguing about it with other people, forming organizations for learning to work collectively,

---

[48] Charles Reich, *The Greening of America* (New York: Random House, 1970).

[49] Herbert Marcuse (1898–1979), German-American philosopher and writer.

77

creating pockets of people that can do the things it takes organizations to do. The future theory and the future party will come out of that experience, not out of the experience of greening.

Second, to show what a bad result this greening attitude can have, you only need to look at Vietnam again. Here is a problem that overwhelmingly begs for organization, for continuity. I know that because I have been actively organizing around the Vietnam War for seven years, and I know many antiwar organizations filled spontaneous needs. The need for an emergency reaction to the 1965 escalation created the teach-in, for example. But there was no attempt on the part of those live, vital movements to form an organization that would continually educate more Americans to the realities of the war. Because of that vacuum, leadership in the antiwar struggle passed to bureaucratic and old left organizations who never had gone through the sixties' questioning of organization, people whose second nature, or should I say their first nature, is to be overly organized and bureaucratic.

In 1962 SDS fought for the right to exist as an organization. It was threatening to many bureaucratic people because it was spontaneous. People were shaken up by that. Having fought for that right, we fought for a second right in 1964 and 1965, which was to put students and young people in the vanguard of the coming battle against the Vietnam War, and we were threatening to traditional organizations once again. We won that battle. We organized the first mass demonstration, and the spirit was incredible. It was a great moving event, and immediately after that SDS got into this debate about whether they should participate in what we should maybe call a mass movement, or whether they should be "radical." It was a debate which was not objectively necessary, as things have turned out. The debate measured the distance we had come from real experience and study of the real world because it started with what I think, just my personal feeling, the greatest misunderstanding of the decade, which was the underestimation of the importance of the Vietnam War.

Maybe you understand better why I think Vietnam is everything in this. People have treated Vietnam as just a symptom, and single-issue radicals could maybe start a campaign against the war, but liberals would finish it. They have regarded Vietnam as not a sufficiently radical cause, merely a symptom to organize people around.

Imagine being Vietnamese and hearing you were a symptom or a tool. Imagine being told your country was an organizing tool in the long-range plans of American socialists. Not only would you be offended, but it would be ideologically absurd because Vietnam has fought the two greatest colonial powers of modern times. It's the only country in the world that has fought on the battlefield and defeated the French and are on their way to defeating the United States. It is the focal point of all the Third World peoples, all the suffering peoples of the world, a great example to them, a country which has—more than any other country in the world—shattered a whole set of assumptions about America for the rest of the world and the American people. It has given radicalism a chance to be relevant in the United States for the first time in thirty years and has given Americans the first chance in a long time to see ourselves as we are.

America has a genocidal birth pain to rediscover. The rulers of America have always tried to divide and conquer and keep secret primal genocide by writing various Pentagon Papers over the years. The way rulers maintain their rule is not simply by committing genocide and massacring a given population, whether it's the people in San Salvador Christopher Columbus killed or whether it's My Lai or anything in between. The way they maintain their rule is to erase from human memory any consciousness or image of resistance to make the people who are ruled feel happy and free. This is especially true in a system of rule that uses democratic structures and talks about free speech, civil liberties, freedom of the press, religion, assembly and so forth. You must make people participate in their enslavement by giving them a lobotomy, not with a physical instrument, but through manipulating their consciousness to a point where it no longer contains any capability for recognizing the facts. So many people are beginning to recognize the facts today that this represents a failure of the whole system of rule upon which control of America rested right from the beginning.

*Dick Flacks: Go back to 1959 and compare it with today. You might say one of the great achievements of the movement in the sixties was to de-lobotomize a significant proportion of the people of America.*

Right. Marcuse calls it a one-dimensional society. That's what I'm talking about. That would be the complete lobotomy—to make everyone feel this is the best of all possible societies, that freedom consists of spending eighty billion dollars for missiles and invading or entering forty, fifty, sixty countries. But that has failed, and society has become two-dimensional. That is a measure of progress and a testimony that our minds have not been completely ruined, our personalities have not been completely warped. Warped, yes—completely, no. The passing on of the truth from one generation to the next is important in forestalling and resisting genocide.

The example that affected me the most was this May, in Los Angeles. In the Unitarian Church, there was a cultural presentation by the Vietnamese students on AID scholarships supposedly to make them into what *Fortune* magazine calls good industrial managers for the future of South Vietnam as a part of the Western economy. In other words, they're brought here to receive the best of American capitalism and values and then go back to introduce those values to their society. Instead of being dressed in suits and ties, they were dressed in black pajamas, standing on the stage presenting through stories and poetry and song a real expression of their national identity as Vietnamese on Ho Chi Minh's birthday.

On the stage with them was Tony Russo who, seven years before, was interrogating NLF prisoners for RAND Corporation as part of a study of how to manipulate and undermine the NLF better.[50] The study, by the way, became President Johnson's chief paper rationale for the air war over Vietnam from 1965 to 1968. Tony had been a prisoner for two months in Terminal Island and was just out and now is facing thirty-five years in jail for helping release the Pentagon Papers.[51] Also on the stage was Jane Fonda who, four years ago, was participating in exporting a cultural image of a certain sexual standard to the entire world. *Barbarella* was shown throughout the entire Third World so peasants and others being driven into cities could appreciate what was good and attractive about America. Now she has traveled to North Vietnam and over the last two years has probably been the most active, well-known personality against the Vietnam War. The highest authorities of our country have accused her of treason.

At the same time, she, too, like the Vietnamese, like Tony working for RAND—Tony had come from Princeton—had received the best American society had to offer, the Academy Award, riches, all this. Then doing security in front of the stage for the cultural presentation were Vietnam veterans dressed in the same uniforms they used when they were committing war crimes in Vietnam, some only a year ago. One of them had been shot by the NLF at the Dong Ha River, where the Vietnamese crossed in the first days of their offensive to capture Quang Tri Province. Paralyzed from the shoulders down, he was in a wheelchair right in front of the stage, probably appreciating the program more than anyone else. He had just been arrested twice and thrown into the streets by Los Angeles police for leading antiwar demonstrations protesting the mining of Haiphong.

---

[50] For more on the RAND study, see Barbara Myers, "The Other Conspirator: The Secret Origins of the CIA's Torture Program and the Forgotten Man Who Tried to Expose It," *The Nation*, June 1, 2015.

[51] "Terminal Island" refers to the Federal Correctional Institution built on an artificial island near Long Beach, California.

Who were they protecting the Vietnamese against now, these Vietnam veterans? They were protecting them against remaining Vietnamese who were still in favor of the dictatorship that sent them to this country and, apparently, in favor of the massacre of the rest of the Vietnamese. Other Vietnamese were demonstrating outside in favor of Thieu and calling their brothers and sisters inside communists.[52] And the Vietnam veterans who once fought to save them from Communism were now protecting them from planned disruption of the meeting.

It's just not an accident the leading resisters of the Vietnam War are Vietnam veterans and Vietnamese students because they've had the greatest chance of any Americans to see the truth and the most urgent stakes in changing that policy. What's reflected in this story is that people change. People exposed sufficiently to reality and the truth will accept it. That's what is so frightening to the government. Once the movement was created again in 1960, once it reappeared in American life, it was only a matter of time from then on. Once the conflict was joined between the movement and the system, even if people weren't conscious yet of their roles, time from that point on was on our side. The system only survives because of the lack of consciousness of the people. When people become conscious and form a movement, it is because they're beginning to recognize the authorities don't serve them and don't tell the truth. They start creating alternative ways to serve their needs and find out what the truth is.

From then on, the government must begin losing popular support. It's inevitable. The movement can only receive popular support. That's what I mean by saying time is on our side. As long as that process remains continuous, it's predictable, not

---

[52] Nguyen Van Thieu (1923–2001) was the U.S.-backed President of South Vietnam from September 1967 to April 1975. He fled South Vietnam four days before the Vietnam War ended. He left South Vietnam for Taiwan, and then London, England, before settling in Foxborough, Massachusetts.

accidental, that we would discover everything. We will discover the entire history of America just as we've discovered in gruesome detail the entire history of My Lai. We will discover the entirety of America, the good and the bad, the truth and the lies. People who took part in the bad and the lies and are trying to perpetuate it will find fewer people accepting their authority. Those who stand for the better part and truth will have more authority. That's why continuity of movement, continuity of organization is so important.

## George McGovern

*Dick Flacks: Among the people who feel the most energy now is probably those working for McGovern, many of whom are doing that because they feel convinced that's the most practical thing to do to stop the war. What would you hope the McGovern volunteer of that kind would be doing and trying to think about in terms of not just the specific campaign, but the future? How can they use this experience?*

Don't make the mistake we made of thinking the Peace Corps or the New Frontier was the simple answer, that you could find a place for yourself in there and use new, more modern imagination to solve the problems of the poor people of the world. That would be a misreading of the possibilities of working within the system. The system itself sets the priorities we have, distorts the facts, and twists our brains. The system itself would have to be changed to change priorities and make it possible for us to see what's happening. That's the danger.

What disturbs me may seem like a small thing. It has not been noticed or mentioned by anybody about McGovern. After his nomination, he went to Custer, South Dakota, to his cabin in the Black Hills, which were taken from Sitting Bull and the Sioux Indians only one hundred years ago at the time of his great-grandfather. McGovern showed the press around to the resort areas. What was once the land of the native people of this country has now become rich people's vacation areas. He was promoting

South Dakota as a resort, and if that wasn't bad enough, he then showed himself campaigning around South Dakota wearing a cowboy hat and cowboy jacket. I don't know if he had boots on.

This perpetuates the worst image and tradition of America. More than anything else, it shows on the deepest level of personality and character he is not an alternative to the frontiersmen, to the adventurer who has taken us to Southeast Asia and other parts of the world. The cowboy. If a person doesn't see there's something obscene about today appearing to be a cowboy and doesn't see there's something obscene about encouraging tourism in the Black Hills, then they haven't got out of the civics book imagery of America. That imagery is the cause of our aggressiveness and arrogance and misunderstanding of the real nature of history in the world.

The grassroots McGovern workers could seize the opportunity to focus peace sentiment and heighten the desire for peace to come to Vietnam by finally ending American involvement. They could stress, not McGovern's personality, but the issues which transcend McGovern in importance and should not die if he loses the election—the redistribution of wealth, the cutting back of the defense budget, that sort of thing. If so, there could be a widening of the base of social understanding of things that need work in this country.

People who work for McGovern, even if he loses, have shown themselves capable of putting together a real organization, real machinery capable of building opposition to Nixon, resistance to the war, in an effective way. If they do it with confidence in themselves, rather than illusions about McGovern, then they'll be a progressive and powerful force in American life in the seventies without having to go through the illusions and traumas and frustrations the people of my generation did from 1960 to 1964. They're going through it with their eyes open.

The Port Huron Statement predicted there would be a broad-based progressive coalition, and radicals would be independent catalysts within it and set the stage for a debate about a fresh set of

## Tom Hayden: The Rolling Stone Interview – Part II

issues going beyond the Cold War. The myths about anti-communism would break down, and the question of quality of life in America would emerge. We would go right through that period into more radical ones as soon as we overthrew the baggage of the Cold War because it would increase people's feelings of power and they would be able to talk about what was on their minds. Here we are ten years later, still facing Nixon, who has run the country from elected office one way or another for most of our last twenty years.

*Dick Flacks: Maybe we are at the beginning?*

It was not a diversion when the civil rights movement failed, the Kennedys were killed, King was killed, and the Vietnam War was escalated to genocidal proportions. What did happen from 1963 to 1968 is conservatives reasserted their power, just as they are going to try to do in a unified way against McGovern today. They reasserted power back then, but they got overextended. They could not fight the war in Vietnam. They could not govern the whole world. They could not quell protests in America, and they were defeated. That is why they're being faced again today with the possibility of a liberal reform movement replacing them in power because they failed to accomplish their goal.

*Dick Flacks: This is self-serving, but it seems to me one of the more remarkable things about the New Left was this: A small group of young people who, along with a few other intellectuals, pacifists, and so on, ten years ago saw the empire was over-extended and beginning to crack. It's taken ten years for that even to be instituted into part of the Democratic Party. And it's not at all clear McGovern represents a stable force within the establishment at this point.*

Since I've been aware of the world, all the national elections have been times for focusing feelings. Kennedy in 1960 helped awaken students and young people to politics. Johnson in 1964 confirmed a growing sense of betrayal. Nixon and Humphrey in 1968 shaped a universe without alternatives.

And now, after all this history, comes George McGovern, with the rhetoric, in part, of the Port Huron Convention of ten years ago. Is it a measure of the New Left's success or are we being absorbed into the status quo? Both are true. Neither is true. Whatever happens this November, radicalism will find its way forward through a lot of dead ends. But I'll say this: If we don't do everything we can to defeat Nixon, voting as well as other things, we will be blind to the suffering of those people who most have opened our eyes, the people in Indochina. And if we can't see their needs, what will we ever be able to see?

Whoever wins the election, the war will be a big issue in the campaign, and the antiwar movement should be present to cut through all the rhetoric and deceit. Public opinion may not count for much in America, but in election years it counts for more than usual because all the politicians are looking to capture or pacify it. For three years, we have heard this war has been "winding down," but as Tony Russo says, for Nixon down is up. Here it is once again, the biggest issue in a Presidential election.

Nixon is killing more people than ever before, has dropped four million tons of bombs on those people, is spending twenty million dollars per day on the war, still has one hundred eighty thousand troops over there, and is using most of our B-52s, fighter-bombers, aircraft carriers, and destroyers. Nixon is changing Vietnam, heaven and earth, body and soul. The heavens by seeding the clouds. The earth by poisoning, burning and bulldozing the land and forests. The bodies by chemical war, napalm, tiny crippling fragmentation bombs, and by face and body operations to "beautify" the upper-class women in the Playboy image. The souls by pouring a flood of consumer goods into Saigon to create a Honda culture, a brothel culture, a Hollywood of Indochina. All that is corrupt in us is being concentrated in pure form for delivery there. If the better part of us does not end this war, we will have lost a big struggle within ourselves as a people.

# Tom Hayden: The Rolling Stone *Interview* – Part II

One hundred years after killing the Indians, we read bestsellers celebrating Sitting Bull and condemning our ancestors' atrocities. Why wait one hundred more years to recognize this war in Indochina is the same? Twenty years after the German people blinded themselves to genocide we still are righteously asking, how could they? Now is the time to prove we will act righteously. Now is the time to prove we've progressed beyond the state of numb denial. If not, what will our answer be to the same question for the next twenty years?

Maybe Nixon can't be beaten. Maybe too many people have been confused by his troop withdrawals. Maybe McGovern is too threatening to the majority even though the majority wants the war over. Maybe, maybe, maybe. All I know is our responsibility is to let people know what is being done in their name and make them aware that supporting Nixon is supporting murder in Indochina. There are other reasons to oppose Nixon—the conservative Supreme Court judges he will appoint, the racist neglect, the wage-price freeze, but above all, the war.

Nixon could end it if he feels threatened enough by McGovern. Or it could be ended if McGovern is elected and his peace plank implemented. I know from being fooled many times that having any illusions about politicians and elections is bad, but blindness on this question is worse. McGovern is virtually the creation of the antiwar movement if you trace the roots of his career. The difference between him and Nixon has been created primarily by events the people have shaped. The failure of the United States in Vietnam has made most people sick of it, sick of the policy within which Nixon is trapped. And McGovern has been nominated not because he's a shrewd politician, but because of the frustration and rage that comes from Vietnam.

Having given birth to the McGovern phenomenon doesn't mean the peace movement should die and turn Democrat. The people have done it before and can do it again. The time for a renewal of feeling about the war is right now. If we all slumber through the election and Nixon wins, it will be far more difficult to build up antiwar protest again. That's when it will be most needed, but it can only be started today while the war's an issue in politics once again. So, with a lot of other people, I'm campaigning for peace.

*Dick Flacks: Are you saying the antiwar movement should devote its entire energy to electing McGovern? That is the way to end the war?*

No, not at all. I am saying McGovern could be the Pierre Mendes-France of 1972.[53] Mendes-France was a part of the French political establishment in 1954, no different than other politicians. The French people, however, were sick of the war and France was suffering from a lot of economic and domestic problems. The Vietnamese were giving the French a beating on the battlefield, which climaxed at Dien Bien Phu. At a critical point of negotiations the incumbent French government was stalling, the same way Nixon is—trying to prolong a war everybody thought was immoral or a bad investment or something like that. The French parliament had a mechanism for removing the Prime Minister, so they replaced him with Mendes-France, who was elected on a pledge to end the war through negotiations in thirty days. He set a specific date, just as McGovern has set the date of ninety days. He went to the negotiations in Geneva, and by the thirtieth day, he was almost done. The French stopped the clocks to give him a few more hours. They stopped the clocks. He was done on the thirty-first day, ending the French phase of the Indochina war.

That wasn't because the French people rose up on the side of Mendes-France. That was because French public opinion demanded peace. French workers sabotaged some arms shipments, French students and French women lay on railroad tracks. French organizations held mass demonstrations, French intellectuals called for resistance and spoke of the duty of the

---

[53] Pierre Mendes-France (1907–1982) was the Prime Minister of France from June 18, 1954 to February 23, 1955.

## Tom Hayden: The Rolling Stone Interview – Part II

intellectuals to oppose the war. A French antiwar movement grew that politicians could not afford to dismiss. This was combined with the primary factor, events in Indochina itself, which created a situation in 1954 which ended the war.

That is what is so exciting about what is shaping up this year. No one in France today recalls Mendes-France as a leftist or radical. He might as well have been from South Dakota. Few have ever heard of him in the United States, so it's clear he did not represent a sharp "turn to the Left" in French history or anything like that. He simply served a vital function at a critical point in the history of France and its relations with Indochina, and he broke the connection. He broke up one hundred years of French colonialism. France still took part in new colonial wars.

France today is a repressive society, and all these are parallels with McGovern. McGovern is not now and never has been a radical. If you look at his positions on almost any social question, they merely reflect many of the official recommendations of the President's commissions. Even on the question of the Vietnam War, he has not been the honest man of integrity he has portrayed himself to be for the last several years. He had an opportunity, for example, to release the Pentagon Papers. He agreed to do it but wanted a week to think about how. Then, he decided on the basis of expediency not to do it at all. It was too risky.

During our trial in Chicago, which involved indictments of antiwar organizers who had challenged the Democratic Party warmakers in 1968, McGovern, as I recall, criticized equally the behavior of Judge Hoffman and the defendants alike. During all the long years of peace demonstrations, he has always argued for activity oriented primarily to getting elected officials into office. He has always condemned demonstrations that were more confrontational, though those confrontations, as we look back, had a big effect in waking people up. He considers himself an alternative to radicalism, not just an alternative to Nixon. He thinks change can take place within the Democratic Party under his benign guidance.

The point he misses is he would not be the nominee today if it weren't for the bloodshed in the streets in 1968. That confrontation forced the question of reforming the party, which created the conditions for McGovern to set up the commission to reform the party and bring in at least those elements of the street demonstrations in 1968 who wanted to be brought in. There they were on the convention floor in August, as if this had happened merely through his clever and sophisticated political manipulation of the Democratic Party! It had not. The Democratic Party was faced in 1968 with becoming irrelevant or opening itself up to these new forces, and that was caused by the people who stood in the streets outside the system and confronted the police sent by Mayor Richard Daley and Vice President Hubert Humphrey.

The face of the system will be changed in a drastic way compared to the way it was in the fifties and most of the sixties when there was no Left-Right within the supposed arena of debate, the political party system. The two-party system is supposed to, according to the Port Huron Statement, clarify issues, polarize alternatives, create for people real choices between alternative programs. Instead, according to the Statement, it stifles debate, stalemates the people's will, diverts attention from real issues.

That period now may well be over. Within the political framework of city councils and local governments all the way up to the political framework of the Democratic Party, there will be progressive, even revolutionary ideas aired, though not carried out. When you heard those people at the Democratic Convention saying from the microphones, "We from Wisconsin who oppose the bombing of the dikes of North Vietnam," or you heard other people saying, "We gay people want this platform plank adopted," you see something that will not go away. It has become so widespread it has to have representation in the forms representation is supposed to occur in, namely the electoral forms.

This is going to be a very complicated period, because no fundamental change will occur through these forms, just as none has occurred on the level of more people participating, a new climate of the opinion growing in the community and some token changes here and there that don't amount to anything for large numbers of people. It will not be a period of which we can say we are entirely closed out of society, as 1968 was. If we fail to see the danger in Nixon, for example and thus stay out of this election, we will be sentencing the Indochinese and ourselves to hard times. But while what we do in this election is an urgent matter, it still is not decisive. There will also be the great danger of simply going into the electoral arena and the most fundamental need of all—for a vital, active, independent movement—will be threatened, because it will be more tempting on the part of more people to go into electoral institutions.

To illustrate the price, the illusion, of going into electoral institutions, remember the Berkeley City Council would not have opened up if it were not for ten years of revolutionary cultural growth there. This included confrontations, street battles that during People's Park stretched out seventeen days against the National Guard, resulting in one death, one blinding, and one hundred fifty people shot or injured. That's what created the base from which it was possible to intervene in the electoral system and stop certain politicians from going on and on repressing people from one generation to another. Similarly, the skulls cracked and repression in Chicago, merely the peak of eight years of growing protest and bloodshed, caused the reforms of the Democratic Party and the "opening" of the Democratic Party to the McGovern reformers. If we remember that, we remember where power comes from.

A lot of people are going to forget, and they're going to have to be reminded of it by discovering how helpless and powerless they are once they are elected to office. A lot of other people are going to see things none of us have ever seen before, namely democracy, dry up right before our eyes as we seize it. We're going to see supposedly democratic institutions cut back as the poverty program was cut back in Newark when we seized control of it. We're going to see a showdown between the public sphere as we become a majority there, and the private sphere, the corporations and the Pentagon, which is used to manipulate the public sphere comfortably.

### A Force in the Center of Society

That's going to mean a radicalism that once was supposedly isolated and alien to American society is going to be a force in the center of society, insisting on its democratic liberties, insisting on the enforcement of the Constitution, insisting on its right for radicals who are duly elected to hold office, insisting on the right of the people to decide on the distribution of wealth, control of polluters, control of corporate investment, and control of foreign policy.

Against us will be the private power centers seeing the emergence of people and people's demands, and those with private power will be deciding whether to make major concessions, which can only help us, I think, no matter how much they temporarily coopt us. One would be absolute withdrawal from Indochina. Another would be the beginning of a review of withdrawal from other regions of the world, even if it's only a review, which it will only be. The third would be the cutback of billions of dollars from the defense budget, which will still leave the military-industrial establishment secure but will directly threaten their interest concretely for the first time. So, those are concessions I wouldn't mind because those concessions can only make people feel more of their power and strength.

On the other hand, what is more likely, except perhaps on the question of Indochina, is a policy of no concessions. Indochina, they must concede eventually, because the Indochinese people are resisting, and the American people know too much about it and are sick of it. Guatemala, for example, they don't have to concede yet. They probably think they don't have to concede the defense budget.

Instead of major concessions to the public there will be an increasing tendency towards more secrecy at the corporate and political level, more creation of foreign policy by private means, more attempts at repression, more disinclination on the part of the wealthy class to spend their tax money on government institutions that don't support them, more of a tendency to withdraw from the United Nations, and a polarization around democratic rights and the need of the people for peace. Most people will side with the movement on those issues. I see hundreds and perhaps thousands of city councils affected by that, thousands of labor locals, thousands upon thousands of schools feeling this polarization.

*Dick Flacks: All professional institutions.*

Yes. Anything but the military and corporations. That's a struggle in which time is only on our side. We have to seize it, of course.

# Chapter 3

# The History of the Antiwar Movement

## August 28, 1974

*This talk was given to an Indochina Peace Campaign Organizers School at Lake Arrowhead in the San Bernardino Mountains eighty miles east of Los Angeles. It took place sixteen days after President Richard Nixon had resigned and amid hints from both North and South Vietnam that a final offensive was in preparation. The prospects for peace had never been better.*

☙

We are part of an insurgent thrust over the last generation that has forced our rulers into such a state of crisis, many of them were tempted to abandon democratic forms of rule and destroy what they had built up over two hundred years. We should not underestimate the importance or the stakes at all.

We ought to view the sixties and early seventies as positive history, of which we can be as proud of as any people can be proud of their history. This is not to say you can't be upset, disappointed, or critical of aspects or even main tendencies of this history. It's a question of whether we identify with the upsurges of our past, or whether we turn away and think it's a negative, useless history or a failure. I think the proper way to view it is in this dialectical process of every upsurge having its positives as well as negatives. Those who succeed find a way to build upon the positive and strip away the negative.

# Tom Hayden on Social Movements

## 1960 to 1964

In the early period, 1960 to 1964, people in the New Left had little awareness of Vietnam. We knew about the Third World, however, and there was an identification with the Cuban Revolution. There was some knowledge of the "Viet Cong." The National Liberation Front in Vietnam was founded in 1960, the same year as Students for a Democratic Society and the Student Nonviolent Coordinating Committee. We heard about them sooner than they heard about us. If you look at the early SDS documents, there are references to Vietnam as one of the examples of "unrest" or the "revolution of rising expectations" in the Third World.

Our minds were not primarily there because the focus of problems for our country was shifting from the international to the domestic level. The civil rights crisis was then the focal point. There was a feeling in the air the Cold War was tapering off, and the possibility of war with the Soviet Union was less. The threat of Third World revolution was obscure to the American people, although not to the CIA. What obsessed American society from top to bottom was the focal point around race.

A significant movement built up. Its pivot was race, and it also had a peace orientation because there had been a disarmament "ban-the-bomb" movement in the late 1950s. The movement's origins were more in the abhorrence of violence, especially thermonuclear, class, or racial violence. It was accelerated by the talk of peace from the New Frontier, the Peace Corps, and the thaw in the Cold War. The civil rights pressure by black people, starting with students, gave impetus to the whole idea of domestic reform. Of course, you would have to turn away from the arms race and the Cold War to redistribute funds for social progress at home. The early programmatic idea of SDS and most activists in the early sixties was that domestic priorities take precedence over the Cold War and the arms race. The civil rights movement provoked this consciousness of domestic priorities.

## The History of the Antiwar Movement

It was not a simplistic reform consciousness either, because the civil rights movement had revolutionary aspects, especially in its active form. You were thrown into the streets and then into jail. By 1963, over four thousand people had been arrested in Southern demonstrations. There was a lot of currency in the word "revolution," especially among the young black students who formed SNCC. There was a lot of talk about ending the Cold War and having a revolution for democracy inside the United States.

The implications for the economy were clear: this would mean moving in the direction of public control of the economy. People even frequently used the word "socialism," although that was frequently rebuffed for two reasons.

First, black people, especially black students, had a healthy bias in some ways against white people coming down from the North who suggested socialism was the answer to their problems while they were in a Mississippi prison and couldn't get five dollars for bail.

Second, being part of the New Left meant believing the old left had foundered. Most people knew what that meant from firsthand experience because they were in organizations where they had to get into a "generation gap" conflict with the elders. People who stood for socialism in name were always putting down or lecturing the New Left, discrediting what they stood for in the process.

There was also an understandable "born yesterday" complex since the old left had been killed. There was the idea that if you were New Left, you had to be entirely, thoroughly new, and what you said had to come out of your direct experience. It was almost existential. Things were not valid unless you could put them in natural terms. You spoke from your experience, instead of doing one thing with your body and speaking as if you were a talking book.

All these things were healthy in some way. They delayed, however, the introduction of Marxist ideas or at least Marxist talk while in fact, the people involved had little doubt they were moving in a revolutionary direction. There was a lot of study of

## Tom Hayden on Social Movements

many authors, some discussion, and not much self-definition as "socialist" or "anti-imperialist." This led some leftists in the seventies to dismiss the early sixties simply as, "Well, that was a period of empty reform or liberal reform" or "That's when everybody was following John Kennedy." Instead of seeing it as a stage on which to build, they see it as an early illusory period that had to be overthrown. I think that would be a mistake.

The movement was so threatening by 1963, it became a crisis when demonstrations rocked the city of Birmingham, Alabama, leaving blood everywhere for people to see on television. I think part of the reason for the Vietnam escalation was the insurgency inside the United States.

While we didn't use the word "focal point," we did use the idea. The South was the focal point, and Mississippi was the focal point within the South. The South was the weak link in the American power structure, and Mississippi was the weakest of the weak links. Over half the Mississippi population was black, and it had the most reactionary white power structure in the country.

The idea was you could build, using today's words, a united front—a broad campaign of everybody outside the South, all the northern liberals—to put maximum pressure on the South to either break with segregation or lose its role in the Democratic Party. There was a tremendous success in store for us if the balance of forces had remained constant, that is if there had not been a war. That's because many people in the North, conservative and liberal people, were shocked at seeing black people killed in the South, seeing Jim Crow, seeing white students going down there, having their children involved.

It was an enormous international problem for the United States. Dean Rusk said civil rights was America's number one foreign policy issue, a frank admission of where the focal point for imperialism was.[54] Things were moving.

---

[54] Dean Rusk (1909–1994) was the U.S. Secretary of State under Presidents Kennedy and Johnson.

Then, when this more conservative coalition seized power and escalated the war, the result was a reversal of almost everything. Now, the southern segregationist senators who we were trying to isolate during the civil rights period couldn't be isolated anymore. They were key to the northern liberals who were starting the war. They occupied the military committees and the key votes in the Senate. To fight the war in Vietnam, you needed the support of the conservative racists, whom you might dump if the only question was race.

It was the Democratic Party, at least in name, which started the war. It was Johnson who started the war.[55] It was a constellation of people who declared themselves moderate, if not liberal. These people suddenly changed coalitions. A coalition of the civil rights movement was building under Kennedy, an objective coalition of forces (and I don't mean working together). There was a sudden reversal, and civil rights people, activists, and SDS'ers were isolated against a new coalition of forces, which included the Democratic and Republican parties, north and south, who were starting this war.

## 1965

The antiwar movement formed in the summer and fall of 1965. At the same time, SDS was forming on the east coast and the

---

[55] This much-debated assertion originated in 1967 as Robert Kennedy was preparing his 1968 presidential campaign. Kennedy wanted to distance his older brother and himself from the war. Peter Dale Scott followed with articles and books beginning in 1971. Oliver Stone popularized it in his film, *JFK* (1991). The story evolved from "Kennedy wanted to withdraw from Vietnam," to "Kennedy gave the order to withdraw," to "Hawks killed Kennedy to reverse his withdrawal order," to "LBJ started the war, not Kennedy." In 1993, Noam Chomsky critiqued this argument in *Rethinking Camelot: JFK, the Vietnam War, and U.S. Political Culture* (Boston, Massachusetts: South End Press, 1993), substantiated by Frederik Logevall in *Choosing War: The Lost Chance for Peace and the Escalation of War in Vietnam* (Berkeley, California: University of California Press, 1999).

Vietnam Day Committee (VDC) was coalescing on the west coast. VDC came out of the civil rights movement, organized big teach-ins, fantastic demonstrations, and almost got into a confrontation with the police as early as spring 1965. Standing face-to-face with the police, the VDC decided not to go through the police line, turned people around and marched back. People would argue for years over whether that was a sell-out or the correct thing to do at the time. The VDC was more local than SDS, but it was probably bigger and more militant than the east coast wing of the antiwar movement.

SDS suddenly had leadership. It surprised itself by organizing a march of twenty-five thousand people in April 1965, the biggest in years. Traditional groups went along, although they were uncomfortable with our politics. SDS then blew its leadership with its hang-ups about power, organization, and leadership. A vacuum was created for new coalitions.

So, who moved into the vacuum at the national level? The groups that had waited throughout the forties, fifties, and sixties. They saw the space, moved in and secured the leadership, some better than others, all of them different from the New Left.

The best people were the radical pacifists who came out of the 1940s and 1950s.

The first reason they were appealing to young people is they were action-oriented. They were in favor of getting arrested, putting your body on the line, jamming the streets, and civil disobedience.

The second reason they were liked was they were non-exclusionary. In this great debate among the old left, they decided to break ranks and say everybody could participate.

The third likable thing about them was they were the least obnoxious coalition-builders. Being non-violent and pacifist, they had a nice, less bureaucratic way. For example, I'm talking about Dave Dellinger and Staughton Lynd. A.J. Muste, who passed away in 1967, was their leader. He took over the problem of building a coalition. He was in his seventies at the time and lived an active, simple life. He spent about fifteen hours a day talking with people.

The second element moving in were the groups from the traditional left. The Communist Party and the Trotskyist organizations would continue in different coalitions.[56]

The Communist Party USA was pretty much serving as an extension of the Soviet Union. It took the position the United States was wrong, and North Vietnam and the NLF were right. They also felt negotiations were the answer, and they wanted a quick end to the war. In the fall of 1965, their recommendation to the North Vietnamese was to start negotiating soon, at a time when the Vietnamese did not want to negotiate at all.

For instance, I went to Hanoi in the company of a representative of the Communist Party in December 1965. We stopped in Moscow, and he had meetings with the people in the Soviet Party and then went on to Hanoi. He told us what he was bringing as advice from the Communist Party USA and the Soviet Party is "they should not underestimate what they could gain by going to the negotiating tables." They didn't want this to escalate into a larger war, perhaps causing a confrontation between Russia and the United States.

That wasn't exactly our position. The Communist Party was not happy with the New Left. It didn't participate in building the New Left. Over ten years, it didn't form a single organization contributing directly to the New Left. Instead, it tried to channel young people into alternatives.

---

[56] Leon Trotsky (1879–1940) was one of the leaders of the Russian Revolution of 1917, and subsequently led the Red Army in the Russian Civil War (1918 to 1922). Trotsky split from Joseph Stalin in the 1920s, was exiled in 1929, and assassinated on Stalin's order in Mexico City in 1940. Organizations that follow Trotsky's views are called "Trotskyist."

For example, its 1964 alternative to SDS was called the W.E.B. Du Bois Clubs.[57] But the Communist Party didn't like the Du Bois Clubs because their offices were in San Francisco. The Clubs started to relate to the growing youth culture, and the New Left and SDS on a generational basis, not feeling this gap. Gus Hall, the head of the Communist Party, had a secret meeting with people from the Central Committee, and they decided to yank the Du Bois Clubs out of the Bay Area because they were too infected by New Left thinking. They reinstalled them in Chicago, which was considered a safer, working-class town, where there weren't any of these upper-middle-class students running around making a big fuss.

That was the Communist Party. The positive side was it did support the Vietnamese and oppose the United States, and it brought a lot of older people into demonstrations who we couldn't have gotten without their approval, and it added a great deal of organizational support and advice when nobody else would.

Then there was the Socialist Workers Party—the Trotskyists. They also converged into the space where a new coalition would be formed, and big fights would occur.

I remember Staughton Lynd and Dave Dellinger would go to these meetings where there were discussions about forming the first coalition. There would be about eighteen hours of screaming and yelling, and they would come back and lie on the floor sleeping for an hour before the next meeting. They were part New Left and part radical pacifist, and they could not stand the sectarianism of these two groups. However, since there was no New Left group there, and the only organizations fighting over the coalition were the Trotskyists and the Communists, they tried to go in full of aspirin and try to deal with it. Of course, we

---

[57] William Edward Burghardt Du Bois (1868–1963) was an essayist and author. His works include *The Suppression of the African Slave Trade to the United States of America: 1638–1870* (1896), *Souls of Black Folk* (1903), *John Brown: A Biography* (1909), *Darkwater: Voices from within the Veil* (1920), and *Black Reconstruction in America* (1935).

wouldn't deal with it. Our attitude was just, "Can't stand it. It's all crazy." We had no long-term vision. Dave and Staughton would go in and try to deal with it.

The Trotskyist position was the Communist Party had killed Leon Trotsky, and the paranoia, hatred, and rancor flowing from it were unbelievable. Their view was every Communist Party in the world was Stalinist, including the North Vietnamese Party. They were against supporting Vietnam, they were against North Vietnam in principle, almost as much as they were against the United States. Some of them were equally against Stalinism and capitalism.

One important thing to understand about Trotskyism is its opportunism. It goes hand in hand in this society. Which means you hide your basic ideas if they'll be unpopular, and you put forward ones that will be popular. They wouldn't bring up that North Vietnam was evil and Stalinist. They'd put that in their magazines and cadre manuals. In the organizational meetings, though, they would always put forward the position that we should only talk about the United States, only advocate for getting "Out Now."

That flowed from two things. First, they didn't want to talk about the Vietnamese Revolution. Second, they didn't want to talk about anything like negotiations which is what the Soviet Union or, later, North Vietnam wanted. They could only stick to one position, which sounded more "revolutionary" than any other position. Their position was, "We want the United States out now—lock, stock, and barrel—unconditionally, not a single troop left. The United States doesn't have a right to be there one more minute. The United States doesn't have the right to go to negotiations. The Vietnamese don't have to talk to them. They should throw them out of their country. Anybody who thinks otherwise is a liberal fronting for imperialism."

Which brings us to the third group, the liberals fronting for imperialism.

It was a group of liberal Democrats who in 1964 were kind of for the war. By 1965, they were alienated. They were swinging away from the war. They, too, had an orientation which was reflected through the years and then became the Moratorium. Their position was "Negotiations Now." Their position was you couldn't get the United States to leave. That would be too anti-American. You could, though, get rid of the foremost problem, friction between the United States and the Soviet Union. They also wanted a return to domestic priorities. It was a naïve, uninformed position. They didn't know much about Vietnam, and they brought an administrative, liberal mentality to their position: if you could get the fighting over, if you could shift it from fighting to the negotiating table, then we could go back to the early sixties and start the Great Society. They were anti-Communist and frightened of the New Left. They would have nothing to do with the Communists or Trotskyists, and they would only have a little bit to do with the New Left because they knew we were indispensable for getting people to come to the demonstrations.

Fall, 1965, saw two incredible demonstrations.

One was a nationwide call by a group of mostly Communists and Trotskyists who worked out an agreement because of A.J. Muste's clever negotiating. It was called the National Coordinating Committee. The headlines were unbelievable, and at the time, one hundred thousand people demonstrated in one hundred cities everywhere in the United States. Those numbers were staggering to the Administration and us.

The liberal group had a march on Washington at which forty thousand people came to the Washington monument. Most of the speeches were about "Negotiations now" and "All war is wrong." It was mostly young people there, bored, waiting for something to happen.

Carl Oglesby, who was then the SDS spokesman, gave the speech which went beyond Paul Potter's speech in the spring of

1965 and became the manifesto of that period.[58] This was late in the day, and it got everyone standing on their feet, screaming, and a standing ovation at the end. It was reprinted in many forms for years afterward. He said, "The original commitment in Vietnam was made by President Truman, a mainstream liberal. It was seconded by President Eisenhower, a moderate liberal. It was intensified by the late President Kennedy, a flaming liberal. Think of the men who now engineer that war, the men who study the maps, give commands, push the buttons, and tally the dead. Bundy, McNamara, Rusk, Lodge, Goldberg, the President himself. They are not moral monsters. They are all honorable men. They are all liberals. But so, I am sure, are many of us who are here today in protest. To understand the war, it seems necessary to take a closer look at this American liberalism. Maybe we are in for some surprises."

Then he goes into the whole history of imperialism, country by country, and he says, "This is all the action of corporate liberalism, which performs for the corporate state a function similar to what the church once performed for the feudal state. Let me speak then directly to you humanist liberals. If my facts are wrong, then I soon will be corrected. But if I am right, we all face a crisis of conscience. Corporate liberalism or humanism? Which? For it has come to that. Will you let your dreams be used? Will you be a grudging apologist for the corporate state or try to change it? Not in the name of this or that blueprint or "-ism," but in the simple name of human decency and democracy and the

---

[58] Carl Oglesby (1935–2011) was elected SDS President in 1965. Previously he had worked for Bendix Corporation, a major military contractor. Fellow SDS'er Mike Davis said of Oglesby, "I'm not capable of accurately describing the kindness, intensity, and melancholy that were alloyed in Carl's character, or the profound role he played in deepening our commitment to the antiwar movement. He literally moved the hearts of thousands of people."

vision that the wise and brave men saw in the time of our revolution."

During the course of this long and amazing statement, he said, "What would Tom Paine think of McGeorge Bundy?"[59] This was devastating. It wiped out liberals for about ten years—this one speech. It was brilliant.

On the other hand, it did reinforce the notion that the war had been started by liberalism, which confused honest liberalism with corporate liberalism and made the interests who had escalated the war into liberals. Thus, all our enemies were liberals, and hypocrisy was the main problem. The notion of uniting with liberals to isolate the enemy to defeat the enemy was out of the question and seen as selling out. There was some truth to this notion that these liberals started the war, but it also put SDS in the odd position of not attacking conservatives much. It took them for granted as a dead reality, identifying the real problem as manipulative liberalism.

Those were the several groups, and they all continued in their various threads and ways over the next eight or nine years.

## 1966–1967

In 1966, the draft resistance started to catch on as the next form of New Left moral direct action, and so did the idea of electoral politics. Bob Scheer and Stanley Sheinbaum ran for Congress in California as Democrats on an antiwar platform in the spring of 1966.[60] The New Left, the VDC radicals, accused them of selling

---

[59] McGeorge Bundy (1919–1996) was the National Security Advisor to Presidents Kennedy and Johnson.

[60] Bob Scheer (1936–) wrote an eighty-page pamphlet, "How the United States Got Involved in Vietnam" (1965), a key document for the Vietnam teach-ins in the mid-sixties. He was editor of *Ramparts* magazine, a reporter for the *Los Angeles Times*, and is now editor of *Truthdig*. Stanley Sheinbaum (1920–2016) resigned as Administrator of the Michigan State University Vietnam Advisory Group in 1959 when he discovered it was a

out because you can't be part of the Democratic Party, you can't be part of the electoral process, and you're taking people off the streets and into the electoral arena. That idea paralyzed people.

In 1966, there were big national demonstrations including the pacifists, Communists, Trotskyists, and liberals.

In 1966 and 1967, everything intensified. For instance, in the fall of 1967, electoral-minded people who were coming from the liberal and New Left areas tried to form a *de facto* new party called the National Committee for New Politics (NCNP) and had a huge convention in Chicago. They were hoping to get Martin Luther King to run for President, but they were paralyzed internally by the New Left people who said community organizing, not electoral politics, was where it was at. They couldn't get an organization together.

SNCC had come out against the war in 1965. SNCC leader Julian Bond was elected to the Georgia assembly, thrown out for his antiwar views, and was admitted back in by a nine to zero decision of the U.S. Supreme Court. SNCC was the only black organization at the time against the war, and it pushed SDS to take a strong position. With his Riverside Church speech in 1967, Martin Luther King pushed liberals to be much more opposed to the war than before. They were hoping there could be a coalition of liberals and the New Left going into the elections.

That failed, leading to the Dump Johnson movement. "Forget the New Left. Just go for the students on the campuses who aren't so radical and put them together with the liberals." And that, in turn, led to the Eugene McCarthy campaign.

Another element leading up to the National Conference for New Politics was Vietnam Summer, the first attempt at community organizing against the war by thousands all over the country.

---

CIA front. He became an active critic of the war. He ran for Congress from Santa Barbara as an antiwar candidate in 1966 and 1968. Sheinbaum organized the Pentagon Papers Trial Defense team for Daniel Ellsberg and Anthony Russo, raising one million dollars from 25,000 contributors.

These were considered in those times the right wing of the New Left. They were already more into the day-to-day work of community organizing and less into revolution and confrontation. One wing did Vietnam Summer and the community organizing project. Then it did the NCNP. When it broke up, they didn't have a place to go.

Another wing of the New Left went toward draft resistance. It also had splits. For instance, when it looked like the Administration was going to arrest everybody for draft opposition, Carl Oglesby and Paul Booth rushed to Washington and made a declaration in 1966 called, "Build, Not Burn." [61] Their idea was, "Don't draft us for war, draft us to do community organizing in slums. We are a generation that does not want to burn villages. We are a generation that wants to help people develop their villages." It was not pro-Peace Corps, it was more like, "Pay us for doing what we've been doing in the civil rights movement."

The left of SDS immediately attacked it as being "the greatest formula for liberal sellout and collusion ever devised." That's what a telegram written by the next SDS National Secretary, Greg Calvert, said.[62] SDS in the Bay Area sent a similar telegram. They bolted the organization until the declaration was withdrawn.

Even in draft resistance, there was one wing that was into it as "put your body on the line," pro-revolution, anti-state. Another wing was more political, wanting to fight for the legitimacy of draft resistance and also trying to preserve organizations.

---

[61] Paul Booth (1943–2018) was a participant in the 1962 Port Huron SDS conference and in 1965 became SDS National Secretary. He spent forty-three years working for the American Federation of State, County, and Municipal Employees (AFSCME) union, first in Illinois and then in Washington DC, as organizing director and then chief of staff to the union president.

[62] Greg Calvert (1937–2005) was the National Secretary of SDS from 1966 to 1967.

You must understand the scale of the draft resistance. There were 2,500 people between 1966 and 1967 who signed cards saying, "We Won't Go." They felt by signing the card they would be taken from their homes and put in prison for five or ten years. It was a big thing for them.

The confrontational people who were not into draft resistance also had a great achievement in 1966 and 1967 with anti-recruitment demonstrations which climaxed in east and west coast demonstrations. The one at the Pentagon drew fifty thousand people, all night, face-to-face with bayonets.

The more militant one was on the west coast, called, "Stop the Draft Week." I think that was Carol Kurtz and Shari Whitehead's first demonstration and may have been Andy Truskier's.[63] This one was called, "Take over the streets of Oakland." It was like, "Last time, we refused to pass through the police lines. This time we're going." "Going" meant "going to occupy the area of Oakland near the Induction Center." It was amazing. Cars were pushed out into the streets and turned over. Thousands of people did this for a week.

These two things together at opposite ends of the country had an inflammatory effect on students and young people everywhere. It had a freaky effect on the establishment and the middle sectors of opinion because this was coming out of nowhere.

Of course, it wasn't coming out of nowhere because they had already seen three years of African-Americans doing this. The impetus again was blacks, I believe, because I was personally involved in the Newark rebellion at this time. This antiwar stuff was important to me but was parallel. In Newark, twenty-six people were killed in five days. One hundred buildings were

---

[63] Carol Kurtz later joined the national staff of the Indochina Peace Campaign in Santa Monica. Shari Whitehead was a leader of San Diego IPC. Andy Truskier (1943–1976) was a leader of the Berkeley peace movement and a founder of the International Liberation School.

burned to the ground, ten thousand troops occupied the city for a week with automatic weapons, and it looked just like Vietnam. You had a feeling it was one world, one struggle.

Detroit followed, with forty-two deaths. For the first time, troops were brought back from Vietnam to the United States. Daniel Ellsberg was flying back from Vietnam and saw Detroit, his hometown, occupied by the same troops that had been in Vietnam. That, plus draft resistance, changed him.

These things happened in August 1967, just before the fall demonstrations. At the same time, the first meeting between the New Left and the Vietnamese was in the first week of September. Fifty people went to Bratislava, Czechoslovakia, from all over the country, from all kinds of organizations, and spent a week with a delegation, headed by Mr. Vy, who later became a negotiator in Paris and Nguyen Thi Binh, who later became the PRG Foreign Minister.[64]

Rennie Davis and I went from Bratislava to Hanoi. He had been just a normal community organizer, getting more militant up to then. Between riots, Bratislava, and going to Hanoi, though, he completely freaked out. He was on the plane coming back to the United States carrying anti-personnel weapons. He arrived just in time for the Pentagon demonstration, where he spoke and was screaming for people to act.

The phenomenon of this linkage was just unbelievable. I'll give you more examples.

Stokely Carmichael left for Cuba and went to the OLAS conference, which is the conference of guerrillas from all over Latin America, and he was the hero of this conference. Fidel

---

[64] Nguyen Minh Vy replaced Ha Van Lau as Deputy Head of the Democratic Republic of Vietnam (North Vietnam) delegation at the Paris Peace Talks in 1969. Nguyen Thi Binh (1927–), known as "Madame Binh," was Foreign Minister, Provisional Revolutionary Government (1969–1976), and Head of the NLF/PRG Delegation to the Paris Peace Talks (1969 to 1972), and Vice President of Vietnam (1992–2002).

*The History of the Antiwar Movement*

Castro gave a speech, saying, "We're sending Stokely around the world. When Stokely gets back to the United States, if he's touched or any harm comes to him, Cuba will respond." Stokely is sent over to Africa, Syria, and he winds up sitting across the table from Ho Chi Minh, who is telling him how to form revolutionary united fronts.[65] He comes back into the United States. You can imagine what the left was doing, what the American people were doing, and what the government was doing. This seeming maniac who was held responsible for organizing five hundred insurrections in the United States, leaves for Cuba and Castro says, "Right on," and he goes to see Ho Chi Minh, and then he flies back to the United States.

At the same time, the Black Panther Party is formed in Oakland, and their first action is to patrol the streets with shotguns.

The Chinese Cultural Revolution can be thrown in, and Che Guevara's "Two, three, many Vietnams" proclamation.

Things were shaking. The Pentagon demonstration and the Stop The Draft Week demonstrations reflected this. It was not simply the New Left militants. There was a demonstration at the United Nations with 125,000 people, just unheard-of numbers. Martin Luther King and Stokely Carmichael spoke from the same platform.

Six New Left Problems

The New Left labored with six problems throughout all of this.

First, we didn't expect a long war, and we didn't gear for it.

Second, we thought Vietnam was a single issue, and we wanted to change the whole system. We couldn't see the role Vietnam would play in changing the whole system.

Third, we underestimated the process of opinion change in America, thinking only a few people would go into the streets and the rest were racist or apathetic. Partly it came from bitter conflict

---

[65] Ho Chi Minh (1890–1969) announced the Declaration of Independence of Vietnam at the end of World War II in 1945. He was President of the Democratic Republic of Vietnam (North Vietnam) from 1945 to 1969.

with liberals, feeling like, if they were the left wing of society next to us—how could the rest of society come around?

Fourth, we were still anti-organizational, and people went with great reluctance to any of these things. SDS opposed going to the Pentagon demonstration until the last minute, saying, "You should not demonstrate in front of the powerful. Single-issue is no good. Community organizing and resistance were all there was to prepare for. No organization."

Fifth, there was a separation between SDS and draft resistance as SDS got a more ideological mentality. SDS did not lead the draft resistance. It was tied up in paralyzing debates about what was the correct form of draft resistance. The draft resisters started to form a community and an anti-SDS "We Won't Go" organization. They felt betrayed by SDS for not having given support. SDS began to be seen as a lot of hot air. All talk about revolution, but no life on the line, no existential community of which to be a part.

And sixth, the prospect of revolution was real. It was not like SDS people had gone out of their minds thinking we were in a revolutionary situation because the media portrayed it that way. There were these events, the Chinese Cultural Revolution, the continental Latin American revolution led by Che, the OLAS conference, Stokely Carmichael, Rap Brown, the Black Panthers, five hundred ghetto rebellions in four years and, above all, our friends in Vietnam who were the center of revolutionary guerrilla warfare, and around us on the campuses.[66] Extraordinary things happening beyond our control fed into the ideas that action was where it was at, the revolution was action, everything else was talk, and the vanguard was always spontaneously emerging from below.

There were 3,500 campus protests in 1967. Out of seven million students, 350,000 students in a poll explicitly said they considered themselves to be revolutionaries. It didn't include people

---

[66] Rap Brown (1943–) now named Jamil Abdullah al-Amin, became Chairman of SNCC in 1967, following Stokely Carmichael.

who said, "I favor social change," or "I consider myself progressive." It was only people who said, "I consider myself a revolutionary." By 1970, the figure had tripled to 1.1 million students.

## 1968

In 1968 syndicated newspaper columnist Drew Pearson announced, "After extensive research, this column is able to report that there is an international student conspiracy." [67]

From the winter of 1967 until the spring of 1968, the following happened:

There were four thousand more campus arrests.

The police and National Guard were called onto campus 127 times in that college year, 1967 to 1968.

One thousand students were expelled or suspended from school in spring 1968.

There were 174 major bombings on campuses that spring, averaging one a day, not counting small arson attempts or unexploded bombs.

By the summer of 1968, there were 9,400 campus protests, including 731 arrests.

In this climate, repression began for real. As far as we know, this was the beginning of Pentagon intelligence and the CIA moving into the domestic arena. Military intelligence was moving in to supplement the FBI. All forms of intelligence escalated, coordinated out of a Pentagon war room. There was a shift in the priorities of the FBI almost exclusively to African-Americans, antiwar people, and students. I think there were seven thousand FBI agents at the time, with six thousand assigned to the New Left in one form or another.

---

[67] Drew Pearson, *Washington Post*, June 14, 1968.

It was also a time of indictments. Out of Stop the Draft Week, the Oakland Seven were indicted. Conspiracy charges, for the first time, were brought against a range of people including Dr. Benjamin Spock to show the establishment would not treat liberals any more lightly than radicals and older people any less seriously than young people.[68]

Liberalism was realigning. It was a distinct break from the sort of liberalism that had been in collusion with the state and with Johnson. A new liberalism, calling itself "new politics," with a mass base formed, symbolized by the Eugene McCarthy campaign in 1967 to 1968. It merged its left wing with the New Left and its right wing with the old liberals. There were always a lot of tensions within it. It was always vast enough for politicians, such as Eugene McCarthy and Robert Kennedy—who need to be opportunistic to some extent—to think they could run on it.

This had been after a period when the New Left had the initiative. Now, we're talking about the end of clear New Left initiative, and the rivalry between the New Left and liberalism, and the beginning of the liberal-left takeover of the political line of the peace movement. There was real growth in this period of the antiwar reform movement, with the war as its main issue. Of course, what they were really seeking was dumping Johnson and putting a new political reform government into office.

Revolutionary politics reached incredible levels in 1968, and problems began to appear at the same time.

For instance, SDS called for "Ten Days to Shake the Empire" in spring 1968. The national office was against doing it. By this time the SDS National Office seldom did any of the actions called for at meetings. It had become a floating reserve of revolutionary people, none of them students any longer. For the first time, the New Left had created its own world, and you didn't have to relate

---

[68] Dr. Benjamin Spock (1903–1998) was the author of *Baby and Child Care* (1946), which sold fifty million copies. In 1969, a federal court set aside his conviction for conspiracy to counsel and abet military draft resistance.

to the real world. You could live in a world of organizational politics, completely divorced from campus or community life, so large, so exciting, so many relationships spanning the country. That's where the national office was at.

## Columbia and Chicago

What was amazing was the level of identification with SDS. There were student strikes at fifty places in March-April 1968 and again confirmed the theory that despite what we do, the revolution will march forward.

It came true at Columbia University in April 1968 where the place was taken over and completely immobilized. Since it was in New York and a ruling class institution, it was on the front page of the *New York Times*, top of the news every night for ten days, twenty days. Mark Rudd overnight was what Mario Savio had been three years before.[69] He was compared a month later with Rudi Dutschke, the red menace of West Germany. Suddenly, you know, you had these new Lenins, vaulted into significance by the media, and seen as holy terrors capable of grinding the most important institutions in American society to a halt. *Fortune* magazine and *Barron's Weekly* came out with front pages screaming about the threat of these New Left people to the future of American business. It was incredible.

Then there was the 1968 Democratic National Convention in Chicago. It was unbelievable for all the reasons you know. Both Columbia and Chicago were instances of the New Left revolutionaries acting in a way that brought a mass base with them. They kept the initiative and leadership in a complex movement. It was about the last time it happened. The leaders acted to polarize the situation, and everyone else had to respond. I'm not sure what the reasons were. In both cases, there was an effective polarization where you had enough political support

---

[69] Mario Savio (1942–1996) was a leader of the 1964–1965 Free Speech Movement at the University of California Berkeley.

coming your way to escape complete repression and you also had enough political support to prevent cooptation. You were able to be in the pivot and throw the balance.

In Chicago, the revolutionaries threw the balance. They pushed the McCarthy movement and the Democratic Party delegates toward the left and even toward the streets in the following polarization. We even won some sympathy from the media. The Democratic Party did what we wanted it to do, choose between maintaining a Johnson continuity and a Vietnam continuity on the one hand and losing the election or changing its Vietnam policy and winning the election. We can see that's what happened.

They chose continuity, and therefore had to repress us, and therefore lost the election. If you look at November 1968, you'll see Humphrey on an upward curve in the polls, rapidly catching up with Nixon—but not willing to break with Johnson or the Chicago police. He was also not willing to criticize the Vietnam policy and so lost support from many voters who decided not to vote, lost many people who would have worked in the campaign, and ended up with a compromised image.

We knew what was happening to Humphrey, and so did Clark Clifford, his adviser. They couldn't decide what to do, so they decided to do the worst thing possible, in a sense, which was to give a phony peace speech in Salt Lake City. Even so, his poll numbers increased. Then Johnson started the Paris talks on November 1 in hopes of putting Humphrey over the top. Humphrey went right to the wire being loyal to Johnson and the Cold War coalition. He lost the election by about one percent, so it was clear we had the balance of power. If he had been willing to change the Vietnam policy, he would have won by between one and five percent.

This was the last time we were in a determining position for a long time.

I'd like to mention what some of the problems were in Columbia and Chicago because I think you've run into them.

## The History of the Antiwar Movement

In Columbia, there became a split between the two wings of the strike leadership. One wing wanted to up the ante, with more building takeovers and higher demands to stop the system. Another wing wanted to hold the buildings and negotiate for university reforms to end their connection with war research, bring black students onto campus, and so forth. The more radical wing thought it was "mere student power," just trying to get a role inside the system. They were against it. They seized more buildings and escalated their demands, and the rift got wider.

Finally, by summer, the group considering itself more revolutionary was now isolated. It had started the strike through its courage and its vision, the courage of taking a building and its vision of how to expose the university. During the course of the strike, though, they kept raising their demands and tactics higher, until it was easy for more reformist leadership to move in and take over the strike, do the negotiations, and win some university reforms. They didn't end the system, and they won some questionable reforms, but there was no doubt the revolutionaries had taken over and then lost control.

This is not a small footnote to history. These people not only went on to take over SDS, they then went on to become the Weathermen. It was Mark Rudd and a whole group from Columbia. Their position was, "We are the Action Faction." It was based on a twisted reading of Che Guevara and Regis Debray. Or maybe not so twisted. The idea was action is all that counts, and things are rotten, and people are apathetic because nobody is doing anything to create a confrontation. There was a lot of truth to this.

They started the strike and overthrew the old SDS chapter which they considered the Praxis Axis. There were a lot of heavy thinkers trying to figure out what reforms are correct, what books to read, everything. Then, Mark Rudd and two others walked out of the meeting, split the chapter and started the strike. From there they took over SDS and threw out anybody who was in the Praxis

Axis. This got blown into greater and greater proportions until it became Weatherman.

In Chicago, Rennie Davis and I were in the middle. We were the left wing of the mobilization calling people there, and seen as the right wing of SDS, which was opposed to the demonstrations happening at all for leftist reasons.

The right wing didn't trust us because we were confrontational and talked about stopping the city, as best as we could talk about it without getting into legal trouble.

The leftists, the SDS people, were against us for a whole mélange of reasons.

One, they were against national demonstrations, because they're "not real."

Two, we had to avoid repression. Bringing people into town would bring the Chicago police down on them and kill them.

Three—the biggest one—it was leading people into the illusion of electoral politics because inevitably we would get all the people there, McCarthy would be nominated, and it would turn into a McCarthy rally, with us standing in the background scratching our heads, after having delivered all these people to the Democratic Party. They were against what we were for, which was going there and aligning with the McCarthy students, believing their movement was just but would fail, and on the other hand we would have to have that unity to face the Chicago police. SDS disagreed. They thought you would get sucked into McCarthy on the one hand if you weren't beaten up. On the other hand, if you were beaten up, you would be destroyed, so you shouldn't do it.

We didn't have any help from them until—again, this always happened—when the action started. Then SDS came in heavy. Their main tactic during the week was to distribute a leaflet brilliantly written by Carl Oglesby advising the McCarthy kids, whom he called "the McCarthy kids," against putting too much hope in McCarthy. Instead, they should join SDS. In other words, as they arrive in the city, full of hope, the SDS was standing there arguing their politics were wrong. This began a strange form of action, which I associate with sectarian groups, of leafleting other people's actions. It was not the whole role SDS played. However, it was just the beginning of this sort of thing. Their hope was, as SDS leaders put it, the McCarthy kids would drop like ripe apples off the tree into the SDS basket.

For instance, at the end of the convention, there was vast unity. Everyone was against the Chicago police, in the broadest coalition brought together so far around something heavy. McCarthy said he wanted to come out to the park and get up on the garbage can and talk to the people.

It was a dilemma, so we decided to end our action officially the day before. If people wanted to stay in the park and have McCarthy speak, it would be fine. We didn't want to sponsor it. We would fall back and let it happen, let the McCarthy forces come into play.

We were sitting around the park and McCarthy comes out, thanking his followers, and they're applauding. Suddenly from the back of the crowd, you hear this voice screaming obscenities. There's this guy on the shoulders of somebody else being carried forward, towards McCarthy screaming and pointing his finger, and screaming. It was SDS National Secretary Michael Klonsky, who went on to be the architect of the October League.[70] His position was amply demonstrated in this act because he was almost beaten into the ground by the McCarthy followers.

By this time Klonsky had taken to calling Rennie and me "New Left oriented," as a put-down. You didn't have to say anything more, you say, "Oh, they're New Left." The good idea five years ago now was a bad counterrevolutionary category.

---

[70] Mike Klonsky (1943–), was briefly SDS National Secretary when the organization was collapsing. He was a leader of the October League, which became October League (Marxist-Leninist) in 1971. He chaired the next incarnation, Communist Party (Marxist-Leninist), from 1977 to 1982, when it went out of business.

Starting a few months or a year before, antiwar people began to dislike SDS, maybe not as much as Johnson. SDS people were closer, though, so it might be more emotional. It didn't seem to matter since there were millions of people who said they were revolutionaries.

SDS drew from this a theory which later led to the Weatherman theories, expressed in a slogan, "Vote with your feet." They called for "Two hundred, three hundred, many Chicago's" to occur around Election Day, November 5, 1968. About three people appeared, and it was a disaster. From there, it was only six months until the national convention split, destroying SDS and creating several factions.

### 1969

These trends continued in 1969, including the liberal-antiwar trend, with some pacifist-radical participation, and a lot of radical grassroots support. There were a million people at the Moratorium. Slightly to the left of the Moratorium was a group called the New Mobilization, a combination of the pacifist, the Communist, some New Left people, and some liberals. It also had a huge base for single action demonstrations. By now, the Trotskyists had formed an organization called the National Peace Action Coalition (NPAC), with a student arm called the Student Mobilization Committee.

All these groups grew, partly because of the vacuum of New Left organization. There was a lot of local action you couldn't credit to any national organization or tendency. There were hundreds of antiwar and resistance actions, against Dow Chemical, against Marine recruiters, and so on.[71] It got to a point

---

[71] The nationwide Dow Chemical campaign, beginning in February 1967, was aimed at ending Dow's production of napalm, an incendiary chemical weapon used by the United States in Vietnam. The campaign ended in June 1969, when Dow stopped making napalm.

*The History of the Antiwar Movement*

where corporate recruiters had to leave campuses in the fall of 1969. It was too dangerous to go.

Administration spokespeople stopped going to campuses to give speeches. SDS called this "institutional resistance," making the campus impossible for the warmakers to visit and thought it would weaken their capacity to make war. It was happening to an extraordinary extent.

On the national level, SDS had a convention in 1969, and split into two or three groups, depending on how you look at it.

One was Progressive Labor, an old left group. It started as Maoists supporting Third World revolution and then deciding in 1966 it was too adventurist.[72] It switched all the other way around and now wanted to identify itself with the white working class. Anything else was considered adventurist and dangerous.

The second group was SDS itself, which split into two factions. Revolutionary Youth Movement I (RYM I) fully identified with Third World people and black struggles in the United States and with the need to move toward violence in the hope you could bring white working-class people with you. The other faction, Revolutionary Youth Movement II (RYM II), was more oriented to a black and white interracial working-class movement with youth in its vanguard. It wasn't opposed to violence in principle but was much more into building mass organization.

RYM I became the Weather Underground in six months. Bob Avakian and Mike Klonsky were in RYM II, which split again, and again, forming several organizations, among them the October League and Revolutionary Union (RU).[73]

---

[72] Mao Tse-tung (1893–1976) was the leader of the Chinese Revolution, and the Chairman of the Communist Party and the government of China until his death. Organizations which follow his ideas are called "Maoist."

[73] Bob Avakian (1943–) was an SDS organizer at Bay Area campuses. He became National Secretary of RYM II. The Revolutionary Union became

Still, the struggle went on at this incredible spontaneous rate. The Chicago Trial began in the fall, and it was unbelievable. Our witnesses ranged from Ramsey Clark on the right all the way over to people who were into violent confrontation on the left.[74] At the end of the trial, there were three hundred demonstrations, called TDA's for "The Day After," involving tens of thousands of people. Most of them were violent and relatively spontaneous. We just put out a call for TDAs, and local radicals put out a leaflet saying gather here.

In Berkeley, a thousand people gathered in a park, and the police were caught off-guard. They thought it was one of these demonstrations where first you hear speakers, and then the crowd tries to move out, and the police block the street, and then you negotiate. Instead, this one guy gets up and says, "We know what we're here for," and in about forty-five minutes, one million dollars of property damage was done, and everybody went home. People started to get the idea that all you need to do is heat up an issue and people would gather around it like moths to a flame and explode. That's when the Santa Barbara Bank of America was burned to the ground.

## 1970

The Weather Underground formed then. I have no doubt a thousand bombings occurred between Fall 1969 and Spring 1970. I do not include the duds. Sometimes coordinated strings of bombings would occur from Santa Barbara to New York, and not only by the Weather Underground. The Catholic resistance movement was now into it, bombing the headquarters of big corporations. There were more bombings in 1969 to 1970 than

---

the Revolutionary Communist Party in 1975, and Avakian still chairs its Central Committee.

[74] Ramsey Clark (1927–) served as a Justice Department attorney through the Kennedy and Johnson Administrations. He was U.S. Attorney General, 1967 to 1969. Clark supervised the drafting of the Voting Rights Act of 1965 and the Fair Housing Act of 1968.

had ever occurred in American history in any concentrated period of struggle. In a country priding itself on having an established form of government to resolve conflicts, we can't exaggerate the effect this must have had on the establishment at all levels. That's what I mean about our movement dividing the establishment into factions.

This continued when Nixon invaded Cambodia. There was no organization. We organized a demonstration in New Haven in support of Bobby Seale, Ericka Huggins and nine other Black Panthers who were going on trial.[75] We worked hard. It was mostly the energy from the recently-ended Chicago Eight conspiracy trial. We get to New Haven, and the town is in hysteria, they've closed it down. On April 23, Yale President Kingman Brewster had said, "I am skeptical of the ability of black revolutionaries to achieve a fair trial anywhere in the United States." Vice President Spiro Agnew called for Brewster's immediate resignation. It was the President of Yale versus the Vice President of the United States.

We get into town. You go to the movement office, and it's all dark. You have to knock on the door, and someone opens it, they have a shotgun in their hand, and this is a twenty-year-old student who's been active for about four months. People come to your door at night and say, "Listen, we need you to help us with something, to carry this somewhere," and they hand you this basket. The basket weighs hundreds of pounds and has about one hundred fifty handguns in it. The National Guard is moving in on the town.

In the middle of this, fifteen thousand people arrive, Nixon invades Cambodia and castigates students as "these bums, you know, blowing up the campuses." We thought, "Oh, this is it."

---

[75] Ericka Huggins (1948–) was a founder of the New Haven, Connecticut, chapter of the Black Panther Party. Bobby Seale and Huggins were charged with conspiracy and murder. The jury deadlocked, and the judge dismissed the case.

## Tom Hayden on Social Movements

We're not leaving this thing." Yale University itself was teargassed and covered with smoke, and the faculty members and all those upper-class people are gagging and staggering around.

At the height of this, we have a rally. I'm supposed to speak and make some announcements, and John Froines hands me a piece of paper saying, "Read this announcement. A thousand people have just had a meeting and called a strike."[76] I read the announcement, and I didn't know what it said until I got to the end. "We declare a student strike, and we're going back to our campuses." Everybody in the audience starts screaming, "Strike! Strike!" and it goes on for about eight minutes.

Within one week four hundred campuses were closed for the first time in American history. I'm not sure what the organization was. Strike Centrals were set up by unknown people, who'd call you up and say, "Hello, I'm Harry Katzenjammer. I'm from Strike Central. We're going to send you fifty thousand posters." No one knew where the money was coming from, who was making the posters, or what was happening. There must have been five hundred bombings that week. This made real the idea that, no matter what mistakes you made organizationally, there would still be mass eruptions.

There were a hundred demonstrations a day for the first week of May. Sixty percent of American students were on strike, 4.5 million, according to establishment surveys. There were seventy-three violent confrontations in the first five days after the invasion of Cambodia. There were two thousand arrests in the first week. There were twenty-four instances of National Guard mobilization in at least sixteen states. There were 169 bombing and arson attacks, not including attempts, recorded in the first week. George Winne, Jr., a graduate student at the University of

---

[76] John Froines (1939–), an SDS member and chemist. Froines was one of the Chicago Eight—in his case, charged with making incendiary devices, specifically stink bombs, for protesters at the 1968 Democratic Convention. The jury acquitted him.

California San Diego burned himself to death in protest. Four students were killed at Kent State, two at Jackson State. On May 9, one hundred thousand people gathered spontaneously in Washington, D.C.

That's also when Vietnam Veterans Against the War (VVAW) grew into an organization to add to the spectrum of other organizations.[77]

The left, again, had a difficult role. There were seventeen thousand people gathered in Berkeley for one rally, and the left was allocated one speaker. He gave this presentation which typified the problems of the time. All these people ready to go, and his speech consisted of arguing, first, they should leave, Vietnam was no accident, it was a logical outflowing of imperialism, they were wrong to think it was a mistake and they shouldn't associate with people who thought that. Secondly, they shouldn't participate in electoral politics. Third, they shouldn't believe in nonviolence. By the middle of his speech, the booing started. I remember thinking to myself for the first time in my life, that I agreed with the people booing my friend who was in a related radical organization. He was booed right off the stage. That was the role of many local radical organizations by the spring of 1970.

They did not start it, they didn't think it was right, and they had no advice, tactical or strategic, to give it. They found themselves attacking spontaneous action of the people, and winding up booed and isolated, and in some cases hated. It was hostile. There were still enough people, though, who considered

---

[77] VVAW was founded in 1967 after the four-hundred-thousand-person April 15 Spring Mobilization to End the War in New York City. It began with six veterans who marched and grew to tens of thousands of Vietnam veterans around the country. In 1971, VVAW organized the Winter Soldier investigation of U.S. war crimes in Vietnam, and then Dewey Canyon III, in which Vietnam veterans returned their medals, ribbons, and discharge papers to the U.S. Capitol steps.

themselves revolutionary for this problem not to manifest itself as a great problem in too many people's minds.

## 1971

For instance, one year later at Mayday, another extraordinary thing happened with minimal organization, just a lot of speaking and propaganda. Fifty thousand people came to Washington, all "revolutionary" in the sense they were anti-government and pro-confrontation, not that they had high political consciousness or agreed on everything. They caused the largest number of arrests in American history in a single spot to take place, 12,614 people. It was the first time that kind of executive martial law had been invoked. They brought helicopters with troops from Vietnam into the nation's capital.

They were attempting rhetorically to stop the government. They didn't do a bad job of it, for something objectively impossible. It's not possible to stop the government in an action. All the people who work in Washington live in a few suburbs and travel on a few key highways. You could, then, imagine if just a few more people were there, and just a few more tactical decisions had been made one way or another, all the streets might have been closed to commuter traffic at a certain time. Perhaps they could have stopped the government for some days.

This provided people with the feeling, partially correct, and partially an illusion that the New Left was still growing, and organization was not as important as revolutionary action.

## Revolutions within the New Left

A problem was setting in. The New Left was starting to have revolutions within itself, becoming more convulsive, with women asserting their prerogatives against men, day-to-day movement workers their prerogatives against powerful leaders, people in collectives asserting their prerogatives against people who were mass demonstration-oriented, and locals their prerogatives against national.

This came out of frustration at not achieving our external goals and, having arrived at a large enough revolutionary movement, one had to be critical about what it did to your life if you considered giving your life to it.

It became more pronounced as each form of discrimination was transformed into a demand for liberation until it wasn't clear whether the chief priorities of the movement were external or internal anymore. Many people did argue, with a lot of legitimacy, that the chief problems were now internal and there had to be a revolution within the movement for it to be able to survive and succeed.

On the one hand, it had a positive effect in putting forward the ideas of collectivity, changing power relationships between men and women, eliminating some degree of elitism, and sweeping out a lot of garbage.

On the other hand, it also meant all the external issues were far removed. The isolation of the antiwar radicals from the mainstream peace movement just got greater until it was two different worlds. For instance, Mayday collapsed just three months after this most militant action in American history, not on any question about Indochina, but on the question of women's liberation and gay liberation and elitism within the organization. It occurred at a conference seen by many people as the heaviest, worst, most antagonistic conference in the history of the movement. I wasn't there, but I was at a preliminary meeting.

There was still an evolution toward keeping an antiwar force alive at the same time a multi-headed liberation movement was internally reconstructing itself. It took form in 1971 preparations for the 1972 Republican National Convention in San Diego. Of course, nothing happened because in the end the GOP didn't hold the convention in San Diego. They moved it to Miami. Nevertheless, the process was instructive.

On the one side, the preparation for San Diego was seen by the government as a continuation of Chicago, Columbia, Cambodia, and Mayday. It was going to be a mass force. This is where G. Gordon Liddy first met James McCord, in their joint functions as coordinators of so-called security for the convention.[78]

They laid plans to have internal counterrevolutionary violence go on, which they would blame on the New Left. Then they would declare martial law. In other words, a right-wing paramilitary conspiracy, perhaps even beyond what Nixon wanted, started to take shape in response to planning for San Diego. It got so heavy, according to Jeb Magruder, that the convention was pulled out of San Diego. The Administration couldn't handle it.[79]

There might have been other reasons. Maybe the trip to China guaranteed Nixon's reelection and they thought they didn't need any convention violence, or it wouldn't help them, and there could have been other factors. Magruder said they made up a big lie and peddled it to columnists Evans and Novak and California Governor Ronald Reagan. They pretended it was logistic problems or an embarrassment with ITT's gift to the convention planners.[80] The spectacle of demonstrators coming to San Diego forced them to shift to Miami.

## 1972

The paramilitary conspiracy shifted from the west coast to the east coast, from the paramilitary right in southern California to the Cuban paramilitary organizations. We'll never know what

---

[78] Gordon Liddy (1930–) and James McCord (1924–) were two of the Watergate scandal conspirators.

[79] Jeb Stuart Magruder (1934–2014) was the Deputy Director of the Committee to Re-elect the President, and a Watergate conspirator. He spent seven months in federal prison for it.

[80] Harold Geneen, President of International Telephone and Telegraph Company (ITT), gave four hundred thousand dollars to the Republican San Diego Convention Planning Committee. On February 29, columnist Jack Anderson revealed the contribution and linked it to ITT's interest in a favorable Justice Department ruling on an antitrust suit.

would have happened in San Diego. Also, we'll never know what would have happened in Miami, because it was partially or completely aborted by the Watergate arrests of June 17, 1972. We can assume a real clash was coming that would have made Chicago 1968 seem mild by comparison.

The next big upsurge, in the middle of the planning for San Diego, was the mining of Haiphong Harbor in North Vietnam in May 1972. I believe there were more militant demonstrations in that one month than any previous year and there was a deliberate choice to take them out of the media. I don't mean more numerically, but more militant in the sense of people now adopting the tactic of Mayday of the year before—blocking streets—and applying it locally. Over a hundred cities saw the phenomenon with actual disruption resulting, in some cases for as long as a week. There was also heavy repression. Two people were shot in Albuquerque. Several hundred people were arrested and probably a large number were expelled from universities or suspended.

I think the Russian summit broke the back of that. It's not clear where things would have wound up had it been otherwise. Much of the antiwar climate in America was because of fear it would lead to a bigger war. When the Russians let Nixon come to Moscow, it broke the fear and the impetus for big demonstrations disappeared.

If there had been no Moscow summit, I think there would have been the biggest demonstrations in the history of the country in May-June 1972, and Washington, D.C., would have been paralyzed from at least one day to a week. I remember at the time there was a push to go to Washington like I have never experienced. I felt like everybody was getting ready in one week to be in Washington by the thousands. I would say seventy-five thousand people or more, perhaps two hundred thousand, three hundred thousand or more would have come to Washington and at the least engaged in tactics leading to mass arrests. If it hadn't been for the Moscow summit, the war might have ended. The price of the war would have become too great.

One, détente, which was important to people in business and liberals, would have been lost.[81]

Two, there would have been fear of a confrontation in Haiphong Harbor.

Three, the disruption at home would have been the final straw. It would have been the biggest and the most permanent disruption in the spring, leading towards the election. McGovern might well have won the election, with Nixon sent into a tailspin by having failed to achieve détente, failed to end the war, and failed to restore order at home, which was his big promise. "Peace abroad, peace at home."

So, we lost the most profound opportunity we ever had to have a test with them finally. Maybe we could have ended the war on our terms, the thing Kissinger was the most hysterical about preventing. This was before there was a draft peace agreement. I'm not sure the Vietnamese would have introduced a draft peace agreement in August if they didn't think Nixon was the sure winner anyway. With no negotiations, no détente, no peace in America, McGovern, even with Eagleton, would have given Nixon a good run.

## Effects of the Peace Movement

In summary, the effects of the peace movement can be defined by categories, though we need to do more research.

First, the effect of the peace movement on institutions was great. It contributed to the withdrawal of the armed forces, out of necessity. It contributed to the ending or suspension of the draft. It transformed the Democratic Party in its policy and structure in a reform direction. Remember, the 1968 Chicago confrontation was the immediate cause of the McGovern

---

[81] "Détente" means the easing of hostilities between nations, and usually refers to U.S.-Soviet or U.S.-China relations.

Commission to reorganize the Democratic Party, which led to reform groups winning power in the Party in 1972, which led to their being able to nominate McGovern.

It had an enormous impact on almost all professions, and even the transformation of people like Jane Fonda or Daniel Ellsberg or Benjamin Spock, people who were pro-war or apolitical. People who had been given the highest rewards by American society were more attracted to the antiwar movement than the rewards.

Public opinion polls show this. We went from being a fringe to a majority, with seventy-two percent of the American people saying the war was a mistake, and sixty-three percent saying it was morally wrong. It was the first war in American history opposed by a majority of the people.

The people's opposition to the antiwar movements was interesting to watch. From the early phase, there was hostility to antiwar demonstrators, and support for the president during every escalation, even though a growing number of people said they had doubts. By the end of the direct American involvement, the majority of the people said the peace movement had valid questions, the war was morally wrong, they did not support the mining of Haiphong, and they especially did not support the Christmas bombing of Hanoi. By the end of that phase of the war, the American people had completely reversed their opinions. Pollster Lou Harris concludes the peace movement "succeeded beyond its wildest dreams."

Throughout the war, we made escalation of the war more difficult.

We created contradictions between groups in the establishment, who had the actual power to, for instance, change the Democratic Party or the Congressional majority which started the war and by 1972 was willing to end it. We made it necessary for the Peace Agreement to be signed. Henry Kissinger said in late 1972, "This is it. We cannot go on another four years like this. We have to sign."

Of course, this was always complementary with world forces. The Indochinese resistance and world solidarity movements made our effect possible.

The effects will last into the future. The experience of the antiwar movement, more than any other movement, re-created the existence of an anti-imperialist American left. There was no left before this started, and afterward, there was. It was mainly because of the war, although other issues did it as well.

Secondly, the re-created left has a certain legitimacy in the public mind, especially on issues of government secrecy, deception, war, who was right about the Vietnam War and amnesty.[82] There is also respect for people who went to jail or took risks or who lost their jobs or had to change their careers. This legitimacy has potential in American society for years to come, just as those who fought and won World War II won legitimacy in the postwar period, the critics of this war will win some degree of legitimacy after it.

Third, we accumulated an enormous body of experience and skill that was not there before. It will be there as long as people who went through the antiwar movement still know each other and relate. It's been the policy of the government, of course, to eliminate the body of skill and history so there will always have to be a new left because it has no precursor, no experience. It has to start from the beginning. We have prevented that this time. There is a living body of experience that goes on through other organizational forms.

## Indochina Peace Campaign

Now, a brief history of the Indochina Peace Campaign (IPC), prospects for the future, and strategy:

---

[82] "Amnesty" refers to the issue of whether the government should give an official pardon to people who violated military draft laws or who deserted while in the military.

IPC began as an incipient idea in late 1971 in classes I taught in Los Angeles. It specifically began in the spring of 1972, was galvanized by the sudden Easter Offensive of March 30, 1972, which made the Vietnam crisis a sudden and major one for the American people and the left. The date is less important than the social origins, and the process out of which IPC came.

The people who decided to form it had a multitude of notions. Mostly, of course, we were concerned about Vietnam and Indochina.

We were also reacting to several things happening on the left. Part of it was a lack of any day-to-day work or organization about Vietnam. Part of it was lack of non-rhetorical education about Vietnam since the teach-ins of seven years ago. And the left did not identify with Vietnam. It put down antiwar work and did not turn to Indochina for any political inspiration or ideas. There seemed to be a connection between the left abandoning its Vietnam work and its political isolation. The isolation was reflected in sectarianism and internal struggles going so far that they no longer had any meaning except in the life of the people affected. They had no social impact anymore. We felt the existing antiwar organizations could not correct any of these problems.

The National Peace Action Coalition (NPAC), the Trotskyist organization, was only interested in demanding the United States leave, and only interested in mobilizations. The function of its local committees was to get people to come to the mobilizations. The local committees did not do outreach work. From local to national levels, there was no education about Vietnam, because the inner group in the coalitions, the Trotskyists, were against educating about Vietnam. They didn't agree with the Vietnamese revolution for deep sectarian political reasons.

The New Left antiwar groups were more attached to the second big coalition, the People's Coalition for Peace and Justice (PCPJ), headed by the traditional radical pacifist groups, the Communist Party, and some liberal antiwar groups. It had much the same problem of having an exclusive focus on mass mobilizations alone, not recognizing that many people felt frustrated with mobilizations. It did not have an educational or community program for between these mobilizations, and in their way diluting any emphasis on Vietnam because of organizational opportunism. Since public interest in Vietnam was declining, they felt you shouldn't organize around Vietnam. In other words, instead of working harder and fighting to restore public interest to Vietnam, they felt the only way to keep the organization alive was to add more issues and more constituencies. It was not philosophical, like, "We believe in all these issues, and here's how they're tied together." It was opportunist: "How can we get blacks into the coalition? By getting the Southern Christian Leadership Council. How can we get Puerto Ricans? By relating to the Young Lords. How can we get welfare in? By relating to welfare rights organizations."

The organization became a body of organizations, each with their specific interest and only with a partial interest in Vietnam. The effect of this, of course, was to blur the Vietnam focus. It was almost impossible to deepen any focus on Vietnam because you would then run abreast of differences between the organizations about what to say. We call this a least common denominator result.

It happened daily. I always wondered why at these rallies, the speaker would get up and say, "We didn't call you here for just one rally. We know it's frustrating. This is to show our numbers. We have an ongoing program, and this is only one event. You must go back to your communities and organize." Then no one would go back to their communities to organize. It was almost to a point where you would blame yourself.

There was an organizational reason for this. The controlling groups within the coalition, in fact, opposed, for organizational reasons, the growth of a local day-to-day Vietnam-oriented movement.

To put the best light on it, they thought, if you wanted to join a left organization, you should join us, the Communist Party or one of its allied groups, or our Trotskyist organization, or our Student Mobilization Committee.

To put a worse light on it, they were threatened by the possible emergence of a mass movement organized in day-to-day community work about Vietnam. In their meetings, they opposed turning their coalitions into day-to-day community-based coalitions. What held them together was only the agreement to have a rally at a certain day, with certain slogans, with certain speakers. Of course, you could call for action after the rally, but each group in the coalition wanted to have its own action. The welfare mothers would go back and organize themselves. The Communist Party would do what it does, and so on.

No group would go away from the demonstration saying, "We are organizing a membership group around the ideas expressed during the rally. Join us, and we'll do community work for from six to nine months."

Within the coalition, there were political parties and political groups that did not want to see the emergence of any new membership groups. I don't think they had anything to fear if they had emerged, but they did fear it. In other words, they didn't know how to relate party-building to mass movement-building. Rather than take a chance on it, they stuck to their narrow organizational existence and didn't welcome the emergence of anything new. Since the New Left-type of people were against organization on some deep level, they couldn't do it either.

IPC was also a response to a new situation, the Easter Offensive, and the contradictions in the establishment producing a presidential candidate running on an antiwar platform. Now we could say we were no longer a fringe group. We were the majority of Americans from all walks of life. We could unite around a demand to end the war, which hadn't been true in 1968 and 1969. In other words, IPC was a response to the feeling there was a new opportunity to change the Vietnam policy of the government, rather than protest it.

So, in 1972, we formed, mostly as an educational group, the Indochina Information Project, to put together slide shows and graphic materials, and digest the Pentagon Papers into a readable form. Marin Marcus and others here were involved.

When the offensive started, we changed from being an educational group to a mobilizing group and chose the name, "Indochina Peace Campaign." We still didn't have a clear idea about a program. Over the summer, we chose to build a national network around the tactic of having a big campaign through which we would get all our educational materials—the graphic exhibition, the slideshow, a *Pentagon Papers Digest*, and our leaflets—into the hands of many groups all over the country, combining it with a speaking tour. That's where Jane Fonda, Holly Near and I got together.[83] We decided to ask George Smith, who had been a POW, to join the tour and give a humanizing talk about the Vietnamese.

The strategy was to build an independent antiwar effort to take advantage of the contradiction between McGovern and Nixon, and the offensive, which was bringing Vietnam to the forefront. We hoped one result would be a tangible increase in McGovern's success because we thought that would put pressure on Nixon to end the war or lose the election.

On the other hand, we didn't trust McGovern or his campaign enough to endorse it fully. Only a year before we had heard McGovern say Vietnam wouldn't be an issue in 1972. So, we declared our independence from electoral politics at the same time we were working to influence politics. This gave us a broad base. We also made coalitions with other existing groups. There

---

[83] Singer-songwriter Holly Near joined the 1971 FTA (Free The Army) tour led by Jane Fonda and Donald Sutherland, performing for GIs opposed to the Vietnam War.

was a difficult time with PCPJ, which saw us as a threat. We made a good coalition with Medical Aid to Indochina, which Bill Zimmerman was involved in starting, and thought many of the same things about organizing.[84]

The election came and went. Nixon won forty-nine states, and there was a draft Peace Agreement on the negotiating table. There was a lot of pessimism plus a feeling the war might be over soon.

We had a conference in early December 1972 in Detroit. About two hundred people came to various parts of it. The main thing coming out of the conference was a decision to maintain IPC, going from *ad hoc* to established. The main issues were over whether it should turn into a multi-issue organization, and whether it should be democratic in the sense that people would elect the leadership, or whether it should be single-issue and still an alliance of groups getting together around a common program and might build more of a structure in the future.

These were intense debates, compared to the meeting we're in now. Andy Truskier remarked to me in the middle of it, "You know, this is the first attempt by the movement to have a meeting since the split-up of SDS. People are approaching it with great fear and trembling that there would be a renewal of bloodletting and destruction. It is amazing the meeting is happening as well as it is." It was a hopeful sign to all us movement cripples that a meeting could even happen. That shows people were at a low ebb. It did happen, and there was a feeling of opposition to a multi-issue approach given what we had been built around this kind of a single-issue approach for nine months and having seen the multi-issue approach dilute Vietnam work into almost nothingness. We didn't want to recreate SDS. We were building on what we had. No one had any bright ideas about what it would be.

---

[84] Bill Zimmerman joined the IPC Resource Center in Santa Monica, California in 1974. He organized the Assembly to Save the Peace Agreement in Washington, January 25 to 28, 1975. Later, he managed Tom Hayden's 1976 U.S. Senate campaign and worked closely with the new Campaign for Economic Democracy.

We could not have formed the organization at a worse time. Two and a half weeks later, Hanoi was being bombed, which nobody could have predicted. Maybe the agreement would be signed and maybe it wouldn't. Nobody expected this cataclysm, and when it came, we were poorly equipped to deal with it.

We had some meetings, some contact with other antiwar groups, and helped to get underway the January 20 demonstration, the last of the great peace demonstrations in Washington. It was called by the skeleton of what remained of all the groups. It was huge, testifying to the deep feeling against the bombing of Hanoi, the betrayal of "Peace is at hand," and because a lot of people felt they were humiliated being away during Christmas and unable to respond. The group that grew the fastest then was Medical Aid for Indochina, which gathered almost a half-million dollars from ads.

We opened our office in Santa Monica on January 27, 1973, the day the Peace Agreement was signed. It was a leap of faith that the war was not over. We were putting our money down to back it up.

Then began the most difficult period. It was like going from an *ad hoc* network doing a speaking campaign and small-scale intense research, writing, and production of resources, into learning how to be an organization with relations with a lot of local groups. There was a war-is-over psychology, the POWs came home, and essentially the other peace groups folded, even though they didn't announce it.

I believe NPAC, the Trotskyist group, secretly decided to fold. At any rate, it didn't appear again, even in local form, as far as I can tell. It was a big strategic error on their part, and it certainly got one headache away from us. I believe they decided there wasn't any more mileage in the peace issue. They weren't interested in it for the sake of Vietnam. It was a question of running a big organization and mobilizing and getting people to join their party. Since there was no great potential for that, they just folded.

PCPJ didn't fold, but its death began. As we had correctly analyzed, they were afraid to push too hard. They were friendlier to us. They weren't interested in Vietnam. They were interested in mobilizing a left peace movement. Since the new situation would prevent any mass mobilization, there was no basis for a coalition, so they started to decline.

We poked around the office. If you want a colorful graphic history of the period, you could speak to Jane Fonda, Marin Marcus, or me. It was bad. We were figuring out what to do.

We had another national meeting, early in 1973, in Detroit. It was after the signing of the Peace Agreement, and we had the advantage all the way through this of following a correct line:

In the spring of 1972, we said the offensive is going to have a big effect on the election.

After the election, we said if the Peace Agreement is signed, it will only be because of public pressure.

After the Peace Agreement was signed, we said, "It's been signed, it's a great victory, but it will not be carried out, except by the combined forces that made it be signed in the first place."

Early, before it was signed, we knew the Saigon political prisoners would be the foremost area of violation of the Agreement.

If you see the minutes of the meetings and what we resolved, you'll see there were no big incorrect evaluations or predictions leading us down a blind alley. They were all, more or less, correct. Of course, you can have a correct line, but in a sinking situation like the spring of 1973, it might not help you much.

What did happen was Watergate. It became the basis for a resurgence of hope. The Senate Watergate hearings began in May. We knew this was going to be a big issue and had already analyzed it as a direct byproduct of the war. It was going to create a big crisis that would probably lead to the collapse of the Nixon

Administration and would change the balance of power so the "Watergate opportunity" would emerge.

We had a big meeting in June in Cleveland. Some people came from Boston and other places and said, "Maybe we should change IPC somewhat to have a campaign for democracy, including Vietnam, and also take Watergate into account." The feeling was so pessimistic and low, in other words, that we would not be able to keep this Indochina thing going. Other people felt different things about Watergate. After a lot of discussions, we finally took a middle position that we had to continue the Indochina struggle, the Peace Agreement was going to be violated, Cambodia, for heaven's sake, was still being bombed, and Watergate gave us an opportunity to have an impact. Sure enough, it began to come true, to materialize in close votes in the spring and summer to cut off the bombing of Cambodia.

Out of the summer meeting, and out of these Congressional votes came a strategy paper aimed at uniting the antiwar movement around building a broad campaign we called finally the "United Campaign" formed in October in Ohio.

We were forced to do a lot of thinking, first about why Indochina would continue to be an issue. With help from the Swedish antiwar movement, we arrived at the notion that Indochina was a focal point. We had been getting at this for a long time, and it finally gave us a more ideological way to look at it. The clash between imperialism and national liberation was taking its most extreme form in Indochina.

The Peace Agreement didn't settle that, so the clash would continue. If you looked back twenty years, you would see these ups and downs of the struggle in Indochina. There were always times when people said the war was over and then it would escalate again and then there would be a decline and then an escalation.

We took the view it was a focal point, and we should bring the broadest possible strength to bear against this weak link in the American empire.

We were happy to do this anyway, not for ideological reasons, but for reasons of movement experience. We wanted to do mass work. We wanted to feel we were relating to a majority of people. Indochina gave us the opportunity to feel this was a revolutionary, principled issue, an anti-imperialist question, something the left ought not to abandon, and at the same time a question that would allow us to feel at home with a majority of the American people. The decade of confrontation in America had created a new coalition, a new majority feeling against it. There were mixed reasons for being against it, but now we could go from confrontation to the fruits of confrontation, the opportunity to mobilize majority sentiment to force a change in the policy, go from protest and resistance to power.

It was an exciting ideological notion and much in keeping with what people wanted to experience. They wanted to boomerang back from a feeling of isolation and difficulty.

It went in extreme directions. People were sporting American flags on their lapels, doing everything possible to snap back. People were starting to spell "America" with a "c" instead of a triple "k." Holly Near had this song, "Oh, America, I now can say your name, without feeling bitter, without feeling shame."

There was something both ideological and emotional about this feeling. I don't know about the newer people, but those of us who were veterans of these previous several years felt they had at last reconnected with the positive energy they had lost somewhere. They had gained many things during the bad period. It wasn't that it was all bad, it just felt like this was a great opportunity.

Out of the summer came the plan to have another tour in the fall, this time with Bob Chenoweth and Jean-Pierre Debris.[85] It

---

[85] Bob Chenoweth was a U.S. Army Sergeant in Vietnam, working as a helicopter door gunner, when he was shot down and captured in 1968. During his five years as a POW, he became an opponent of the war. In 1970, Frenchmen Jean-Pierre Debris and Andre Menras, both twenty-

was great to find this pair of people who had prison experiences in Saigon and Hanoi and could deal with this issue of whether the war was over and the treatment of Saigon political prisoners. The tour was an organization-building effort and a way to keep the issues alive. We had a strategy again. This time it wasn't to keep the war in the forefront between McGovern and Nixon. It was to rally people, to break through with the idea that the war was not over and lay the organizational basis for ending it by putting pressure on the government. At the end of that tour, we had the United Campaign meeting in Ohio, which formed a coalition of a new type. Instead of the former coalitions which consisted of groups of organizations with their own interests, this was to be a coalition in which people would put their organizational identity aside and enter around principled agreement on a program and a campaign as activists, whether they came from a church group, or a left group or IPC or what have you.

It was a remarkable experience. People did not relate to each other at that meeting as blocs of people, like "Oh, that's the Indochina Resource Center speaking" when somebody spoke.[86] There were some rivalries and bloc tendencies, but overall, we formed a coalition of a new type. There is a much higher level of communication and working relationships between the people in the several groups than ever existed in past coalitions.

When we have United Campaign meetings, we'll have in the room people from the American Friends Service Committee (AFSC), Coalition to Stop Funding the War, Indochina Resource

---

nine-year-old teachers in Saigon, climbed a monument outside the National Assembly. They unfurled an NLF flag and scattered Vietnamese-language leaflets urging peace. They spent two-and-a-half years in Chi Hoa prison.

[86] The Indochina Resource Center was founded in 1971 to inform the American people, legislators, and the media about the war in Indochina. It was closely affiliated with Project Air War and the Indochina Mobile Education Project.

Center, IPC, and others, and they relate to each other as individual activists rather than as blocks of people.[87]

The coalition accepted a radical view of Indochina, and the initiative of the radicals was restored. Many groups joined the coalition to be part of it even though they had many other priorities. They were happy to be part of the coalition in which IPC would carry the main burden and not be threatening. IPC was the only group exclusively concerned with Indochina, the only group primarily concerned with building a broad united front or campaign, and the only group interested in building chapters and in involving new people. Instead of being accepted in paranoia and fear, it's accepted on a principled and open basis.

To sum up: A key to our success has been having an identity with the political direction of the Indochinese people, and at the same time seeing that direction is good for the American people because it brings about peace and democracy.

Our strength is having a political line to help us see through difficult periods and see opportunities like Watergate far in advance of others. The main thing is to perfect ways to discuss our political line, deepen it, and adjust it. It is what gives people a perspective and a basis of work. It's not abstract. It says you put pressure on here for this reason.

Organizations are held together among other things by having concrete work, a task, and having certain things that are out of bounds, not important to discuss, that could be discussed in other organizations. When they're in an IPC meeting, people know the boundaries, what the consensus is, and what the plan is.

It's much easier to keep unity in such a framework, than, in an SDS framework in which they could decide in 1968 racism was the focal point and stop working on the war and start working

---

[87] The American Friends Service Committee (AFSC) is a Quaker organization founded in 1917, which operates service, development, and peace programs throughout the world. The Coalition to Stop Funding the War was founded in January 1973 in Washington DC, with thirty-three organizations cooperating on a common legislative strategy.

on racism, and then in 1969 decide Lin Piao's notion was correct and go underground. In these kinds of organizations, everything is open, and any possible program or ideological direction is open to whoever is the majority at the meeting.

### The Future

About the future, we're still in the interval Kissinger wanted.[88] At the end of it, coming soon, the United States is going to have to give way, through the pressure of Congress, or there's going to be an intensification of the fighting.

Indochina is still a focal point and will flare up again. The evidence for this is the relative scale of the American commitment there, that a real revolution is nearer there than anywhere else, and that our policies are weaker there than anywhere else.

Whether this happens this year or in the 1976 election, I don't know. I would say the United States under Ford and Rockefeller is more likely to remain more hardline on Indochina than it is to decide to cut their losses and turn to other priorities and take the best deal they can get in Cambodia and South Vietnam.

I can't imagine too many reasons why they would change unless the overall crisis of the economy is so great, and the policy in Indochina so hopeless, they decide it's better not to have the Indochina burden on their back approaching the 1976 election. We can't rule it out. We always need to think of many possibilities. That's remote but conceivable, and that's what I would propose to Ford if he wanted to know how to stay out of trouble.

The reason it is more likely they'll stay in trouble is the usual: they don't know the trouble they're in. They always believe they can devise a new formula. They didn't think Cambodia would last this

---

[88] Nixon and Kissinger wanted a "decent interval" of time between the withdrawal of U.S. forces from Indochina and the collapse of the U.S. client regimes in Saigon, Phnom Penh, and Vientiane.

long after the bombing, yet here it is one year after the bombing stopped, and Lon Nol is still in power, Thieu is still in power, and all their critics are made to appear to be fooled once again.[89]

The image of a guarantor is still important. The United States has identified itself with both Saigon and Phnom Penh and therefore feels it cannot let these regimes fall to revolution. There has not been a revolution directly against American imperialism since fifteen years ago in Havana. Since then the United States has not yielded to any revolutionary force inside or outside the country. It might allow something to happen in a country where we're not directly involved, like South Yemen. It is firmly opposed to any change in any countries where we have interests.

The other reason I think the government will be hardline is South Vietnam and Cambodia remain a revolutionary threat to American hegemony in the Pacific. The economic interests of the United States have increased in the Pacific since 1972.

We have to include the possibility of a Vietnamese offensive in our range of possibilities, sooner or later, without depending on it. In other words, in addition to a political evolution towards victory, we also need to have a military scenario, involving the collapse of Phnom Penh or Saigon, and a big crisis about whether the United States should re-escalate.

The Vietnamese call this a "final uprising." Key to their revolutionary theory is that the process of revolution doesn't end with a whimper, but with a bang, a flare-up, a great cascade of people into the streets. I see no reasons why this will not take place again. I believe they are making every plan for this to happen if there is not a political solution possible.

If there were a war between the Soviet Union and China, it would likely stop the Vietnamese from launching an offensive.

---

[89] Lon Nol (1913–1985) became President of Cambodia after a U.S.-backed coup d'état against Cambodian Prince Norodom Sihanouk in 1970. He fled Cambodia on April 1, 1975, as the opposition Khmer Rouge army approached the capital of Phnom Penh. He went to Indonesia, and then Hawaii, before settling in Fullerton, California.

In the case of an offensive, our organizational response would change, obviously, to a level of nationwide militant mobilization. We must always have it in the back of our minds. The level we're working on might suddenly be transformed overnight. Many of us might have to move immediately to Washington or other key parts of the country, to get people to rise against the re-escalation of the war, to force Congress to prevent the Executive from carrying out its plans.

In the meantime, single-issue work around the war is possible. The Indochina Resource Center proves it, the Stanford students prove it, and people like Jane and David Barton prove it.[90] There are many examples of dedicated people doing successful antiwar work. This proves we don't have to change our focus to do good work, just learn from these people how to do it.

At the same time, we always need to relate to trends. We related to the election in 1972, we related to the Watergate crisis of the last year, and we're now in a period when we must relate to a new set of trends at a time when it's hard to glimpse what they are. It's fortunate we're meeting just after Nixon has resigned, instead of the week before. It's unfortunate we're only meeting two weeks after. The left is bad at making predictions, so you need to be hesitant about predicting anything. The left certainly did not predict itself in the sixties. It's best to make predictions based on a lot of information.

Some trends are obvious. The American commitment to Vietnam has been reduced from when it was thirty billion dollars a year, and Indochina is no longer a point of red-hot friction between the United States and the Soviet Union, so we're in a period of the re-emergence of the contradictions of 1960 to 1963 on a much higher level.

---

[90] Jane and David Barton, workers with the American Friends Service Committee, reported on the brutal treatment of prisoners in Quang Ngai province, South Vietnam.

## The History of the Antiwar Movement

In the last twelve years, blacks have achieved the right to vote, and one thousand blacks have been elected to office. A movement has been radicalized and learned an enormous amount about the system and organizational skills. Public opinion is drastically different. You could almost say the American people's opinions recorded in Lou Harris' book are opinions SDS advanced as a tiny minority in 1962.[91] Imperialism, in an all-around sense, is weaker because of the initiative of the Indochinese people, the growth of the Third World, and the growth of the non-aligned nations. That's what I mean by the domestic contradictions of the early sixties reappearing in the mid-1970s, with imperialism weaker and the forces for domestic priorities and peace stronger.

If so, we have to relate to it as the reality of the times, partly because to succeed in cutting off aid, you have to be able to mobilize many organizations and many forces moving in the direction of liberal to left-wing populism.[92] To cut the aid, a Congressional action, you need mass support to prevent a re-escalation when Saigon or Phnom Penh falls. To defend against the right-wing reaction, and to teach the lessons of the war, you need a broad base. That's why we need to relate to the trend towards populism in the United States.

What can we contribute to the populist trend? One thing we can contribute is an anti-imperialist and an Indochina perspective.

Nineteenth-century populism was against monopoly capitalism. It still seems to think the bogey-man is the domestic robber barons and the oligopolists. Monopoly capital, however, has been transformed by imperialism into the structure of the multinational corporation. This is a new phenomenon brought

---

[91] Louis Harris, *The Anguish of Change* (New York: W.W. Norton and Company, 1974).

[92] "Populism" is sometimes used to refer to proto-fascist appeals to public prejudices. Here, Hayden uses it in the original sense, from the Populist movement of the 1890s: favoring democratization of the government and the economy. See Anton Jäger, "The Myth of Populism," *Jacobin*, January 2018.

on by the weakness of imperialism and its need to escape the restrictions of the American labor movement, consumers, and regulatory laws. It now serves as an international force.

Those who control the multinational corporations control the American economy. These corporations require a high defense budget to protect themselves from the world. The American economy is, therefore, a war economy, geared only for the preservation of the multinational corporations' prerogatives throughout the world and increasing in Asia.

Populism is no longer, therefore, fighting against domestic monopoly control and the misallocation of resources in this country. It is fighting against an international empire built for the multinational corporation which requires an economy whose first, and foremost, objective is spending for war. This is an entirely new situation.

Anti-imperialism is a necessity for the new populism. It is not simply a radical idea imposed by the desires of anti-imperialists. Populism as an idea and a force must become interested in the question of peace. It is structurally necessary for its growth because the American economy is no longer domestic. It has been internationalized. It is no longer servicing the corporation alone. It is servicing the military, which is servicing the corporation. In the age of the multinational corporation and the war economy, populism must become anti-imperialist.

So, we can relate on a principled basis to populism with something to say, not simply get them to do something about Indochina on the basis of guilt.

The second thing we can contribute is an idea of how the American system works. Populism still believes in an anti-trust philosophy and in using the government to regulate the economy. It doesn't consider the growth in the power of the executive, the CIA, what we know as the militarized state.

To reform American power in a populist direction, you must understand the entire apparatus of rule created through the Cold War to fight communism, revolution, and disorder at home. The

## The History of the Antiwar Movement

antiwar movement can update populism's knowledge, which now consists of the idea of breaking monopolies and big trusts.

The third contribution we can bring to populism is the importance of highly organized and educated people. You must build, if not a cadre organization, at least a nucleus of people who are prepared to take on the state and don't hope for the goodwill and generosity of the ruling elite to hand down reforms. The history of populism is a history of wonderful, vast, mass single-issue movements around economic reform that didn't produce lasting radical organization.

In that way, we can contribute to the building of a majority-based new American left that is populist, anti-imperialist, and organized for a long struggle.

Populism is a main trend, unless there is a war between Russia and China or the United States starts a new war, in the Middle East for example, or suddenly re-escalates the war in Indochina in the next year. All of which I think are possibilities, not probabilities.

However, you must remember what happened the last time populism reared its head: the escalation of the war in Vietnam. It may not happen again this time because the people are stronger and imperialism is weaker. It is not in a position to start a new war to escape the people at home.

I view imperialism and war as an attempt by the establishment to escape the rising strength of the American people, not simply to find new markets. You wouldn't look for new markets if people let you run all over them at home. The political reason for war and imperialism is to reduce class conflict, by providing jobs and foreign enemies. Without a war, class conflict will intensify at home. When you don't have a war to fight, you have to come home and face the people.

We're now in a period when there are no foreign enemies. How can the Vietnamese NLF be our enemy when we shake hands with Mao Tse-tung? For the first time in thirty years, the

American people are not being told a Communist threat encircles them.

This is a big problem for the government. It has undermined the rationale for its politics of the last thirty years. This contradiction was clear for Nixon. He was forced into détente on the one hand, saying it's OK to go to China, and he also wants to use the old scare tactics at home against his enemies, saying they're Communist, pro-Communist, Hanoi sympathizers, and liberals who will bring about communism.

The lesson Nixon had forced down his throat was you can't accept détente and the implications of the Nixon Doctrine and try to keep Cold War politics going at home. Therefore, the American people can now look for who their real enemies are. In this period the strength and consciousness of the people can grow like wildfire. The question is whether the government can find a way to divert them. It will be difficult for the government to find a new war.

Maybe we should take a break and have the evening to discuss this. I feel embarrassed the sun has gone down.

# Chapter 4

# Indochina and the American Power Structure

## August 28, 1974

*Tom Hayden also gave this talk at the Indochina Peace Campaign Organizers School. The beginning of the tape is lost, so there is no transcript. In 2014, however, Hayden restated the key initial points from contemporaneous notes.*

The system does not operate independently. It interacts with social movements, and we need to understand how. Only three crises have challenged the U.S. system as a whole: Civil War, Great Depression, and Vietnam War-Watergate.

Most Americans, including most progressives, accept the premise of political pluralism. "Political pluralism" is the view that we live in a system of countervailing powers where, if one group becomes too dominant or extreme, other groups react to restore the equilibrium, known as the "vital center." There is considerable evidence for pluralism, including the fall of Nixon. It is not just a smokescreen. Activists should participate fully in the arenas of pluralism.

We also recognize a power elite and the technicians of power operating on their behalf. [93]

---

[93] "Power Elite" was coined by C. Wright Mills, identifying the elite with the dominant economic, political and military institutions of the society. C. Wright Mills, *The Power Elite* (New York: Oxford University Press, 1956). See also G. William Domhoff, *Who Rules America?* (New York: Prentice Hall, 1967).

We can take advantage of conflicts within the ruling class, but we must not depend on them. The power elite will only act on our behalf if it is also in their interest. The ruling class has a hard, reactionary wing, sometimes called "hawks" or "Cowboys," and a more flexible wing made up of corporate liberals, sometimes called "doves" or "Yankees."

Conflicts within the ruling class arise from issues of war and peace, economic crises, pressure from social movements and lesser differences. These conflicts can result in concrete progress, repression, or co-optation (meaningless reform).

03

*As the transcript begins, Hayden has just finished describing what he called the "first crisis" over U.S. policy in Vietnam in 1963 and 1964.*

There was a prowar lobby. The United States did not get into this through thousands of small decisions made by thousands of men stretching back to 1945 until one day there was a Vietnam War. This was the mistaken theory of the sophisticated left. Nor did it happen through Presidential decisions, which is Daniel Ellsberg's theory. There's some truth to the Ellsberg theory, of course. No President since the fall of China in 1949 could "let a country go" without being destroyed from the right. It's wrong, though, to say one President after another passed on the Vietnam commitment doing just enough to stay in there, but not enough to get out until, finally, it grew into a war.

Our whole experience as activists shows things don't happen that way. There are power groups who fight for a decision. They fight for a policy to go one way or another. Some win and some lose, and the war in Vietnam is no exception. It would be an enormous intellectual and political breakthrough to start seeing the Vietnam War in those terms rather than as happenstance or Presidents or the logic of imperialism. We can contribute an activist's theoretical approach to the Vietnam War.

As we get to Watergate and what's now going to happen to us under Ford, Rockefeller, and Kissinger, you'll see the enormity of being able to know interest groups are doing this.

## Crisis: 1967–1968

There was a crisis in 1967 and 1968, by which time we had 550,000 troops in Vietnam and were spending thirty billion dollars a year. As the Vietnamese are always telling us, each step of escalation meant a failure of a policy. They never saw the escalation of the war as coming from American strength—they always saw it coming from weakness.

We need to assume the American power elite saw this as well and discussed it. Someone would say, "Another one hundred thousand troops should do the job." Someone else would say, "Alright, let's do it," and sign the paper. Over time, as the casualty figures and the infiltration rates remained high, with no end in sight, some started asking, "What is the actual possibility this new increment of troops would turn the tide in Vietnam?"

They said that for several reasons: All this was beginning to have an effect at home on public opinion and the growth of the peace movement. The American military was overextended, undermining its ability to fight a war elsewhere. The cost—thirty billion dollars a year—was a fantastic money outflow. The effect on America's image—being over there, brought to a standstill by a small, poor country. And, finally, there was a little hysteria along Wall Street. Investment capital was starting to seek a haven outside the country because of market opportunities opened by the flow of American dollars abroad to service the growing American military commitment. There was a rise in speculation, a sign of danger.

The domestic reflection of this was inflation, which started in 1966. Public opinion was key because inflation could have been dealt with better if Johnson had taxed the American people for the war. He couldn't tax the American people for the war, though, because he thought Congress wouldn't go for it. That was his error early on: he could get people to agree to escalate, but not to pay.

The inflation built into the 1965 escalation has now brought us to worldwide inflation. It didn't just consume America. It consumed the European banks and everybody who had the poor luck to have to accept American dollars as they started to become less valuable.

For the first time in the Cold War, there was a major split in the ruling class, greater than the Truman-MacArthur split.[94]

Among the first to see it was Stuart Symington, a self-made electronics millionaire, a U.S. Senator from Missouri, and an expert on economic and defense policies. As far as the Senate is part of the establishment, he would be the Senator at the top. In his memoirs of turning against the war, the hopelessness and the war's cost, including moral damage to the U.S. image, was decisive. He was raised to have an image of capitalism and democracy going hand in hand, fighting fascism in World War II for the sake of democracy.

A like-minded member of Symington's generation was Robert McNamara, Defense Secretary for Presidents Kennedy and Johnson. No one is more of a corporate liberal than McNamara. In the early sixties, we, from Ann Arbor, were always told you couldn't criticize Bob McNamara and his wife since they've done so much for the community in health, mental health, community development, and civil rights. There were several University of Michigan faculty who said in 1961 that McNamara going to Washington gave us an ear to the Pentagon. They could never figure out why McNamara became this monster. Maybe he was neither the charming liberal nor the monster. Instead, he played a certain role, first at Ford Motor Company and then at the Pentagon.

---

[94] During the Korean War, President Harry Truman fired U.S. Commander General Douglas MacArthur (1880–1964) for refusal to respect the authority of the President.

In 1967, Robert McNamara decided to have somebody start putting together the Pentagon Papers study. He chose civilian militarists, so-called "best and brightest" young men who did not come up through the armed services. Instead, they came up through Harvard and the RAND Corporation to work on questions of national security.[95] They took a tough line on national security and served as a civilian counterweight to the generals. They could look through the budget and argue, "No, we don't need this missile, and I can tell you why."

In other words, the generals were able to get their way with everything, because how could Lyndon Johnson know a missile from a schmissile? He had no expertise.

McNamara's little revolution was to bring these young men into the Pentagon. They were dovish in that they had no qualms about cutting losses if it looked like a policy was going nowhere. They were not committed to expanding the war for the sake of defense industries. They were hardly on an anti-communist global crusade. They were used to wheeling and dealing with different kinds of communists, leftists, liberals, as well as conservatives. Leslie Gelb, now the *New York Times* defense correspondent, was put in charge of the Pentagon Papers project. He was one of Kissinger's graduate students at Harvard. In 1960, Mort Halperin was another graduate student under Kissinger. He was later an advisor to Daniel Ellsberg's legal defense team and now works for the Brookings Institution. These people fell into the flexible category.

They were put in charge of this study. McNamara's assistant, John McNaughton, is found in the Pentagon Papers expressing doubts about the war, for example, whether it is all worth it because of public opinion, or because there was no end in sight.

McNamara's experts decided on a cost basis the war was wrong.

---

[95] The RAND Corporation was created in 1948 as a spin-off from the Douglas Aircraft Company in Santa Monica, California. It is a think tank whose name comes from the phrase "research and development."

We played a role here. The demonstration on the Pentagon in October 1967 is the first big demonstration mentioned in the Pentagon Papers as something hurting the U.S. image, and a precursor of vast civil disorder coming. The Joint Chiefs of Staff decided they had to allocate one or two divisions for possible use in a civil war at home.

One response to the domestic turmoil was for the establishment group becoming antiwar to seize political power by the conventional route of a presidential campaign.

One of those who sought a candidate was Allard K. Lowenstein, the President of the National Student Association early in the 1950s. Every year he plugged away at preventing the NSA turning to the left and the streets. He always organized the moderate alternative to civil rights, SNCC, SDS, and draft resistance. He may not be a CIA agent, although one needs to assume he is. He works exactly according to what one would imagine being the plan of a CIA agent or a person in the clothing of a flexible member of the ruling class, and a principal organizer for the ruling class of youth in the political arena. The New Left saw him as their absolute nemesis and hated him more than anyone else.

In 1967 he came and spoke as a representative of the Dump Johnson movement. He also had easy access to South Vietnamese Third Force figures like General Duong Van Minh.[96] He was

---

[96] Duong Van Minh (1916–2001), also known as "Big Minh," led the 1963 military coup against Ngo Dinh Diem. On Minh's order, Diem and his brother were assassinated. "Third Force" refers to "non-violent political and social forces that attempted to play the role of intermediaries," between the National Liberation Front and the U.S.-installed Saigon government, including non-communist republicans, students, urbanites, lawyers and influential Buddhists and Catholics. Sophie Quinn-Judge, *The Third Force in the Vietnam Wars: The Elusive Search for Peace 1954–1975* (New York: I.B. Taurus, 2017).

always visiting them, then coming back and commenting on the moderate opposition to President Nguyen Cao Ky.[97]

Anyway, he led the Dump Johnson movement and electrified almost everybody except SDS. In a few months, thousands of people signed up. This was the summer of 1967 when *Ramparts* magazine revealed the CIA had been financing the National Student Association for twenty years.

At that point, the head of the National Student Association advisory body was twenty-five-year-old Sam Brown. He was then picked as the Dump Johnson wonder boy and led the Get-Clean-for-Gene McCarthy movement up to New Hampshire in the fall and winter of 1967.[98] He presided over the meetings that supposedly cleaned the NSA of any CIA taint. He played a junior Lowenstein role, but history will probably push him somewhat to the left. He took the Get-Clean-for-Gene movement to Chicago in the summer of 1968. He organized the 1969 Moratorium. He was Averell Harriman's hero and was on the cover of *TIME* magazine, always touted as the effective youth leader, instead of you-know-who and all those people.[99]

Senator Eugene McCarthy announced he was running for President in November 1967. His explicit reason for running was to end the war and to provide an alternative to the irregular channels of political activity youth were involved in, to create a political alternative within the system which could achieve some change.

He is characteristic of this wing of the establishment and its agents or friends and many sincere-minded people. They are as concerned with the domestic structure of life as they are with

---

[97] Nguyen Cao Ky (1930–2011) was Prime Minister of South Vietnam from 1965 to 1967.

[98] "Get-Clean-for-Gene": Many campaign workers for Senator Eugene McCarthy cut their hair and dressed up before campaigning door-to-door.

[99] ". . . you-know-who and all those people" refers to Tom Hayden and SDS.

foreign policy and wars because they know foreign policy begins at home. You need to have the consent of the governed. You need to have national unity, stability, and a sense of participation rather than war plus repression, which they could see coming. They favor imperialism plus democracy, not war. They think there's a way to work this out and it may just be possible. It would involve a lot of illusions and a lot of luck. They stand as ferociously for what we call conventional democracy as they stand for economic imperialism.

Then came two extraordinary events. The first was the Tet Offensive, beginning on January 30, 1968, labeled a "very near thing" by General Earle Wheeler, Chairman of the Joint Chiefs of Staff. The second, peaking in March 1968, was a severe economic crisis, brought on in large part by Vietnam War spending. The United States was staggered militarily and went broke at the same moment. What happened next was a rapid body blow, a peaceful coup d'état against Johnson.

On February 29, Defense Secretary Robert McNamara stepped down, and Johnson asked Clark Clifford to become Secretary of Defense. It was an amazing choice, where some of the accidental nature of the dynamic came into play. Johnson had every reason to believe Clifford was a hawk. He was a Washington corporate lawyer and a legendary figure. He was Mister Big, who could fix anything for anybody. He had done so since the early 1940s when he came to Washington as assistant to the President's Naval Adviser and then became White House Counsel for President Truman. He was the Democrats' chief economic and defense advisor and, as much as anyone, the architect of the entire Cold War. His law firm, Clifford & Warnke, represents a range of big multinational corporations, and if he's not a CIA agent, his partner Tom Finney is.

Jane Fonda and I had the opportunity to meet Clifford recently. As you now know, he's against aid to President Nguyen Van Thieu. He recounted the story of his conversion. He had seen in 1967 the United States was diplomatically isolated. Since we didn't have an imperial ideology to hold countries together, they were falling away. Clifford's closest friend, Symington, told him at length why he thought the war was a military and economic fiasco.

Clifford's first task was to ask for a review of the Vietnam policy. He spent many hours listening attentively to Leslie Gelb and other advisors tell him the war is not going well, we are not pacifying South Vietnam, the cost is going to be higher, and the time is going to be longer.

In the wake of the Tet Offensive, the Joint Chiefs of Staff, through William Westmoreland, proposed to pour more fuel on the fire.[100] Six months before the November election, they wanted 206,756 new troops, for a total of 731,756. Public opinion polls showed Americans in heavy numbers no longer believed we were winning the war or that we even could win the war. And the cost of the new troops would have been staggering.

The civilian defense people gave the information to Teddy and Bobby Kennedy, who leaked it to the *New York Times*. On March 10, it was on the front page of the *Times*, under Neil Sheehan's byline. His article shook Congress, the media, and official Washington. This was the first great leak and whoever did it must have been intoxicated with success because it led to a series of events which reversed the whole Johnson policy overnight.

Public opinion crystallized against it, and Congress was not going to finance this escalation.

## The Wise Men

Clark Clifford called in a group known as the "Wise Men."

In the Pentagon Papers we discover that at a key point of decision-making in the history of the Vietnam War Johnson reached outside of the elected government, outside of the cabinet,

---

[100] William Westmoreland (1914–2005) was Commander of the U.S. Military Assistance Command Vietnam from 1964 to 1968. He was relieved of duty four months after the January 1968 Tet Offensive.

to call in something that would have had C. Wright Mills jumping out of his grave, screaming, "I told you so."

They take the wraps off. No more democracy, no more talk of pluralism, no more reference to the electorate or the cabinet, Presidential forms of decision-making, or all this nonsense fed to millions of American college students over the years about how decisions are made.

The Wise Men are so powerful the Pentagon Papers authors didn't have access to any original documents for the meeting. They had to rely on a later newspaper clipping giving some of the events. None of the documents put before the Wise Men, and none of the debate is in the Pentagon Papers. All we know from the Papers is they met.

The group included George Hall, a top corporate attorney; Arthur Dean, Rockefeller interest group; Dean Acheson, Rockefeller interest group; Matthew Ridgeway, U.S. Commander in the Korean War; Maxwell Taylor, former Chairman, Joint Chiefs of Staff; Cyrus Vance from Yale, a New York corporate lawyer and the above-ground Kissinger of the Johnson Administration; McGeorge Bundy, head of the Ford Foundation, National Security Advisor to Johnson and Kennedy; C. Douglas Dillon, Rockefeller interest group and Treasury Secretary; and General Omar Bradley, the first Chairman of the Joint Chiefs of Staff.

The Wise Men first got together for dinner with Dean Rusk, the former Kennedy-Johnson Secretary of State, and the Rockefeller Foundation; Clark Clifford, Defense Secretary; Averell Harriman, roving Ambassador and representative of all these corporate interests; Earle Wheeler, Chairman of the Joint Chiefs of Staff; Richard Helms, CIA Director, whose family is interlocked by marriage with the Rockefellers; Paul Nitze, Deputy Defense Secretary, also in the Rockefeller group; Nicholas Katzenbach, Undersecretary of State, corporate lawyer from Yale; and William Bundy, Assistant Secretary of State for East Asian and Pacific Affairs, former CIA analyst, son-in-law of Dean Acheson, Truman's Secretary of State, and brother of McGeorge Bundy.

## Indochina and the American Power Structure

Then they had three people give presentations on the current situation, just like we do, at the beginning of the meeting—like Paul Ryder did last night.[101] Who they were is interesting.

One was Philip Habib, Deputy Assistant Secretary of State for East Asian and Pacific Affairs and linked to the Bundys, CIA, and Rockefellers, and is now the Ambassador to South Korea. He delivered an unusually frank briefing, telling this group the Saigon government was much weaker than they had been hitherto led to believe.

On the other hand, they had Major William DePuy, the Joint Chiefs of Staff expert in counterinsurgency. He came from the Marines into the Joint Chiefs and favored "rock 'em, sock 'em" counterinsurgency programs in South Vietnam.

Then you had George Carver, a CIA analyst who writes for *Foreign Affairs* as an Asia expert, without identifying himself as CIA. He gave the Agency estimates.

There was a dispute between DePuy and Carver—that is, between the Pentagon and the CIA—over the enemy's strength. The Pentagon said the enemy was weak and debilitated, and the CIA said the enemy was as strong as ever. One argued for more troops, and the other argued it wouldn't make any difference. It was two to one, Habib and Carver versus DePuy.

They then adjourned for the evening. The members of the cabinet and elected government met with the Wise Men to discuss what they had heard. In the morning, they continued discussions among themselves and then invited President Johnson into the room. Not the cabinet, not other elected officials, just LBJ and the Wise Men for lunch.

It was a social affair with no business transacted during the meal. At the end of the meal, the advisors delivered their verdict to the President. The verdict was that was it. The cost had become too high—militarily, economically, and in the disunity of the

---

[101] Paul Ryder was on the national staff of the Indochina Peace Campaign in Santa Monica.

American people. Johnson was surprised and shocked, according to this account. He expected these people to stick with him against all his enemies.

The myth is he then brooded and maybe brought in his family. And that Johnson told no one of his decision. That instead he said he was planning a usual war speech to mollify his domestic critics. Although he was afraid he couldn't get the new troop request, he was going to stick it out right through his re-election. He had different people writing different speeches for him and then, just an hour or two before the speech, he happened to show somebody a final draft. He pulled out this page from his pocket and said, "Here, look at this." It was the paragraph saying he would not run for re-election.

This story flies in the face of all history.

I think he was visited. He started to have visits from trusted friends and allies, slowly putting the screws on. Then, of course, he was allowed to go through this process of deciding to quit.

It was the same with Nixon. We now know this was a key for Haig and Kissinger, who pulled off the coup. You need to make sure the President thinks he is deciding not to run because then there won't be a counterreaction later.

The people who go in to deliver the final blow are the oldest, most trusted friends, advisors, and listeners. It was in Clark Clifford's character to be the one to go to Johnson and advise him to resign. The president then talked himself into believing this was for the good of the country, and that he was above politics. He would do this.

The Wise Men were the same group that advanced the escalation of the war in 1963 and 1964, advanced the de-escalation of the war in 1967 and 1968, and brought about Vietnamization.

The Wise Men did not advise withdrawing from Vietnam. Some of them probably did feel South Vietnam wasn't worth it and even if we lost it to communism, it would not decisively affect the balance of forces. In the main, though, they wanted to stay in

Vietnam at a reduced cost. This made them vulnerable to the slogan "peace with honor," the idea that a non-humiliating withdrawal would have to be arranged, with Thieu staying in power. As a part of the ruling elite, they probably believed Hanoi would be happy to have the punishment lifted and the troops withdrawn, leaving Saigon in control of the South. After all, hadn't this been done before?

I'm not saying they are completely crude, vicious men. Some of the costs they were concerned about were the generation gap and agony in their own families. Some of them probably did think the war was immoral. In their minds, it was not being fought for a moral cause like World War II. It was being fought for a complete ass. At least a million people had been killed already. Some of the Wise Men probably did have some conception of limits on how far you go. McNamara certainly raised this in his secret memos. Was this much destruction worth what it was doing to our image in the world? It was a cost-oriented decision by the same men who, four years before, escalated the war.

## The Nixon Doctrine

Thus entered the Nixon Doctrine, which was not Nixon's Doctrine. He simply inaugurated the same doctrine the Wise Men had dictated to LBJ in 1968—and had previously been the Kennedy Doctrine.[102]

The Nixon Doctrine began with a consensus by the summer of 1969 to continue the war at a lower cost. Nixon and Kissinger didn't think they were going to have to continue it for four years.

---

[102] Vietnamization was the stated doctrine of all six Vietnam War presidents—Truman, Eisenhower, Kennedy, Johnson, Nixon, and Ford. It means, in Richard Nixon's words, ". . . we shall furnish military and economic assistance when requested in accordance with our treaty commitments. But we shall look to the nation directly threatened to assume the primary responsibility of providing the manpower for its defense." (President Richard Nixon, speech on Vietnamization, November 3, 1969).

I think they believed they could get a deal from Hanoi and the Soviet Union and they soon found out there was no deal possible on terms acceptable to them.

Then the question became how to extend the war while seeming to reduce it until you could get a deal. Nixon's plan had five parts.

First was to eliminate the hardcore resistance wing of the antiwar movement right away. There was a rapid escalation in the number of FBI agents assigned and a series of indictments in the spring of 1969, especially the Panthers and Chicago Eight.

The second was the eighteen-year-old vote.

The third part was the elimination of the draft.

The fourth part was troop withdrawals, maybe a few thousand at a time.

And fifth was to adopt the rhetoric of representing Middle America against the liberal establishment. Here the class split became clear. The Ted Kennedy, Averell Harriman, and Clark Clifford wing was critical of the failure to find a settlement in the spring of 1969, and they became antiwar critics by the summer. Nixon decided to unleash Agnew and himself and isolate Kennedy, Harriman and Clifford as snobs. The first speech using the words, "I speak for Middle America against all these liberals," was given by Nixon in October 1969 at the time of the great Moratorium orchestrated by the liberal Democrats.

The final step was détente. Nixon made the decision to open relations with China when the Soviet Union closed the door. In the spring of 1969, Kissinger told the Russians, including Soviet Ambassador Anatoly Dobrynin in Washington, there would be an escalation of the war if the Soviets didn't pressure Hanoi to settle on U.S. terms. Kissinger offered no concession like letting North Vietnamese troops stay or a coalition government. Instead, he said Hanoi ought to be happy for us to withdraw our troops. There'll be a decent interval, and then if the fighting resumes, we'll be out of there. If this doesn't happen, there will be an escalation, which might bring the Soviet Union into a humiliating confrontation in Haiphong harbor.

The Soviets said no, they couldn't join in an American deal at the expense of Hanoi.

Then Nixon told Kissinger to start negotiations with China, which began in the summer of 1969. This was the secret weapon. If the Soviet Union wouldn't go for a deal, the United States was going to start tickling and irritating the one thing in the world the Soviet Union was afraid of, China overcoming its isolation and becoming a greater world power, and perhaps linking with the United States.

The primordial Soviet fear is of encirclement. Soviet foreign policy is guided more by the goal of preventing imperialist encirclement than of supporting revolution. Having Western Europe on one side and China and Japan on the other is a most important consideration for them because of what it means if there's a war. They lost twenty million people in World War II.

Détente came directly out of the failure of Nixon and Kissinger to achieve a solution in 1969. They decided to put the screws on Russia by loosening the screws on China. There had been talk long before of recognizing China. The actual decision to begin, however, came out of frustration at failing to get a Vietnam settlement through Moscow.

In 1969 the establishment group that triggered Johnson's overthrow now found themselves facing a contradiction with Nixon and Kissinger.

On the one hand were Nixon, Kissinger, the Republican Party, most of the business establishment who sought peace with oil if not peace with honor as the outcome and all those corporate forces who believed Nixon and Kissinger were getting out. On the other hand was the Democratic Party, the political-financial establishment, much of the media and wide sectors of public opinion. Because of the Tet Offensive, the decline of Johnson, and Nixon running as a peace candidate, it had now become legitimate to stand for peace. There was now a revolutionary element on this more liberal side of the spectrum, provoking the contradiction by its existence, the factor of domestic turmoil, confrontation, polarization, and alienation.

In 1969 it became clear the same differences, perhaps between new forces, would reappear. The 1969 Moratorium was the first time the more flexible wing of the ruling class urged people to go into the streets. They were now taking their quarrels out of the cabinet rooms and boardrooms, and even beyond the channel of electoral campaigns. Now it was the streets, the Moratorium, financed by the liberal Democrats, with Harriman and Cyrus Vance among the chief spokespeople. It was even willing to make fragile and tenuous alliances with the more left antiwar forces and try to lure the base of SDS to support the Moratorium.[103]

After Nixon invaded Cambodia in spring 1970, the atmosphere was unbelievable. Nixon lost his senses and mentally collapsed under the pressures. The people we consider to be the right wing of the Watergate element—Bob Haldeman and John Ehrlichman—also went bananas. Kissinger moved into the White House and became the organizer of White House morale. Four of Henry Kissinger's aides quit. Kissinger told them they represented the cowardice of the bleeding-heart liberals of the eastern establishment.

This is how complex these things get. Kissinger in the sixties was a doubter on Vietnam, favored Vietnamization and had great misgivings about whether the United States should escalate with

---

[103] On July 7, 1969, Nixon told aides public support for the war would hold "until about October" referring to the planned demonstrations for the fall. He ordered preparations for Operation Duck Hook, to include mining Haiphong harbor, bombing dikes throughout the North and bridges at the Chinese border, and saturation bombing of Hanoi, possibly including nuclear weapons. On September 10, Kissinger told Nixon, "The pressure of public opinion on you to resolve the war quickly will increase—and I believe increase greatly—during the coming months." With this and Hanoi's defiance of his threats, Nixon cancelled Operation Duck Hook. See Tim Weiner, *One Man Against the World* (New York: Henry Holt and Company, 2015).

more U.S. troops. In the new contradiction, which had shifted leftward along the spectrum, he was now the fanatic.

You can't quite say what influences people to act this way. Was he now just a Rockefeller agent? Or had his egomania led him to an identity with the policy and he lost track of where he was? He was the key man in the Cambodian invasion. He was getting up in the morning in the White House, berating the staff, "We are the President's men! We are the President's men!" The President was in the bedroom. The twenty most prestigious members of the Harvard faculty, people whom you would not even consider to be liberal, descended on Kissinger's office and told him he had a responsibility to resign. He gave them a long philosophic lecture about why he could not and would not resign. He never left the White House during this period.

Another example of the intensity of the contradiction: The political ramifications which had been felt in the McCarthy and Kennedy campaigns and at the 1968 Democratic Party Convention were now showing up in Congress. For the first time in the history of the war, during the Cambodia period, Congress acted against the Executive branch, putting a sixty-day limit on the invasion.

## The Pentagon Papers

The next moment of intense aggravation of the contradiction was in 1971—the Pentagon Papers case.

All these contingencies flow one from another. If Congress had acted the year before, there might not have been a Pentagon Papers. If Kissinger had acted the year before instead of escalating, or if Humphrey had won the election, it might have been different. These are ascending levels of intense activity within the ruling class in a no holds barred, anything goes climate building up over Vietnam.

People at this level were now willing to go beyond legal demonstrations to take illegal action against their government for the first time. The GIs had already done it.[104] Now it was a combination of defense intellectuals, former CIA people, with the secret backing of liberal Democrats and some liberal Republicans like Pete McCloskey, and in the forefront, the *New York Times* and the *Washington Post*.[105] These were the forces who released the Pentagon Papers and were one side of the Watergate contradiction.

Against these forces were the Administration and most of the corporations. The Administration was now willing, for the first time in American history, to inaugurate prior censorship of the press. These are fundamental blows. Only assassination is a higher level of inter-ruling class rivalry. You now have people saying to one another they need to go beyond bourgeois legality and conventional democracy and wage war against each other outside of the constitutional system. Always saying they're within it while their tactics stretch it. We violate this law. They violate that law.

The group that released the Pentagon Papers in 1971 was now going to rally behind Edmund Muskie to run for president in 1972. Muskie was ahead in the polls against Nixon. Muskie's foreign policy adviser was Clark Clifford, and his defense advisor was Clifford's law partner, Paul Warnke. His foreign policy intellectuals were Leslie Gelb and Morton Halperin, the authors of the Pentagon Papers study. A secret supporter was Daniel Ellsberg.

One important thing about the Pentagon Papers is what they do not reveal.

---

[104] Marine Colonel Robert Heinl wrote, "The morale, discipline, and battleworthiness of the U.S. armed forces are, with a few salient exceptions, lower and worse than at any time in this century and possibly in the history of the United States. By every conceivable indicator, our army that now remains in Vietnam is in a state approaching collapse, with individual units avoiding or having refused combat, murdering their officers and noncommissioned officers, drug-ridden, and dispirited where not near mutinous." (*Armed Forces Journal*, June 7, 1971).

[105] Pete McCloskey (1927–) was a Republican Congressman from California from 1967 to 1983.

First, they show no concern for the Vietnamese people, which demonstrates calculations on the higher level are generally cold-blooded. There are a few agitated remarks by Robert McNamara and John McNaughton about children or what people will think or what it is doing to our morality.

Second, it whitewashes the CIA. This is circumstantial evidence that the mainstream CIA was instrumental in the release of the Papers. By now it had become linked to the Clifford group and the establishment group on the peace side of the contradiction. If you read the CIA documents, especially as the *New York Times* interprets them, it makes it seem like the CIA knew all along the United States couldn't possibly win this war.

A multitude of other documents show the CIA advocated the escalation of the war and a rapid escalation of the bombing for a quick victory—short of using the atomic bomb—holding down the economic costs, inflation, and the balance of payments crisis. This is consistent with the idea that CIA and corporate interests are linked.

The CIA tolerated the release of the Pentagon Papers. We know, for instance, police agencies knew Daniel Ellsberg was carrying them around in a box for a year. They did not move on him. Someone was preventing his apprehension, this character carrying these papers in a box on airplanes and spilling them to Congresspeople. Everyone active at the higher organizational levels of the peace movement knew a guy was running around with a box overflowing with top-secret documents.

Third, there is no economic factor in the Pentagon Papers. They don't let you in on what the corporate elite think. Groups like the Wise Men set the overall policy, and then the planners implement it. These are not the documents of the ultimate deciders. There's no reference to the deciders. These Papers are the documents of the planners.

People often say the Papers have an amoral tone. The purpose of the policy is never stated. It just seems to be there for its own sake. It leads people to a technocratic analysis, like, "These men are Albert Speers" as though Albert Speer didn't work for a Nazi world.[106] As though technocrats—power mechanics who don't have any purpose except to kill, wipe out, and push aside—are running the world.

I believe these technicians are dangerous, but they are technicians in the service of the establishment. They do not carry out their programs for no reason. It is for the sake of larger goals which, of course, they don't even have to discuss because they aren't setting the goal. They are merely the agent of achieving the goal.

Periods of decision-making are murky in the Pentagon Papers. This shows either the men who wrote them didn't know how decisions were made or they did know and are covering up. If you read about the period of the overthrow and assassination of Ngo Dinh Diem, or the 1964 election, or how the United States got into the war earlier, you'll find you can't grasp what it is. You may think, "These guys aren't clear, or maybe they're defensive." I think it means the authors of the documents are covering for their higher-ups and they can't tell what was happening.

This is as ferocious a split as ever happened in the history of the Cold War. From the release of the Papers to the Ellsberg trial, Nixon attempted to impose censorship and secured a conspiracy and espionage indictment against Daniel Ellsberg and Tony Russo. His plan to indict fifteen or twenty other people only failed for lack of evidence. He engaged in character assassination, and asked the CIA for help in burglarizing Ellsberg's psychiatrist's office. He also attempted to link the Pentagon Papers with the New Left and the Muskie campaign, and even Alger Hiss.[107] All

---

[106] Albert Speer (1905–1981) was the First Architect of Germany from 1934 to 1942, and then German Reich Minister of Armaments and War Production from 1942 to 1945. He was convicted by the Nuremberg Tribunal and served twenty years in Spandau Prison in Berlin.

[107] Alger Hiss (1904–1996) was a high-ranking State Department official in the Franklin Roosevelt Administration who was later accused of being a

## Indochina and the American Power Structure

the enemies were to be wrapped together in one left-wing conspiracy directed from some Communist center.

The other side had establishment actors breaking the law, breaking national security regulations, conspiring at the highest levels to release information against the law, and accepting conspiracy charges. To protect Ellsberg and the release of the Papers, the CIA went so far as to have their top psychiatrist, Dr. Bernard Malloy, write a profile concluding Ellsberg might be ego-involved because he's a man approaching forty, worried about what his life is all about, but all-in-all he was a patriot. They said there was no reason to doubt his patriotism. This was the CIA's position on someone who had dropped a thirty-year bomb load of state secrets, which just happened to make the CIA look good.

I don't think it just happened. I think it's either a conspiracy or converging interests between the top CIA people, the Pentagon Papers conspirators, the Clifford group, the liberal Democrats, the *Washington Post*, the *New York Times*, and whatever other vested interests we don't know about yet.

This showed up in the trial. It would be interesting for Paul Ryder to tell you who the witnesses were—Paul put the defense together in large part. On one side were high-level Ellsberg witnesses who started the war. On the other side were people linked to the Nixon Administration. Aside from a few antiwar defense witnesses, the trial was between these two elements of the establishment.[108]

---

Soviet spy. Little-known California Congressman Richard Nixon used the case to launch himself into the Senate.

[108] Prosecution witnesses in the Pentagon Papers Trial included Gen. Alexander Haig, nine days from being named White House Chief of Staff, Lt. Gen. William DePuy, Brig. Gen. Paul Gorman, and Fred Buzhardt, General Counsel, Defense Department. Defense witnesses from the Kennedy and Johnson Administrations included McGeorge Bundy, Theodore Sorenson, John Kenneth Galbraith, and Arthur Schlesinger, Jr. Defense witnesses from the antiwar movement included Noam Chomsky,

## 1971 to 1972

I want to remind you of certain moments in the 1971 to 1972 conflict.

The trip to China ended an era. It sent the China lobby and all those who started the Cold War into the establishment trash can. It was the last in a series of moves against them, going back to Truman versus MacArthur, Kennedy versus Nixon, Kennedy at the Bay of Pigs, Kennedy's American University speech, the refusal to use the atomic bomb on Hanoi, Johnson being ushered out of office, and Kissinger coming into the government.

The right sees this as a long history of a liberal-corporate elite which has an ultimate converging tendency with the Soviet Union. The widely-held John Birch Society view was these bankers would take over both the Soviet Union and the United States and purge America of its free enterprise tradition and its right wing.[109]

Howard Hunt said as he watched the trip to China on television, he was filled with hate.[110]

It didn't mean the end of the establishment at all. They saw it as a way to open new markets, end the war in Vietnam, get leverage on the Soviet Union and, above all, consolidate power at home.

---

Howard Zinn, Tom Hayden, Senator Ernest Gruening, Don Luce, and Richard Falk. Other witnesses on both sides testified to technical issues such a fingerprints and the government's classification system.

[109] The John Birch Society was founded in 1958 by Robert Welch (1899–1985). The group was a vehicle for Welch's views, including that President Dwight Eisenhower "is a mere stooge or that he is a Communist assigned the specific job of being a political front man." He estimated Communists controlled sixty to eighty percent of the United States.

[110] Howard Hunt (1918–2007) was a CIA officer involved in a string of covert actions including the overthrow of the democratically-elected government of Guatemala (1954) and the Bay of Pigs invasion of Cuba (1961). After Anthony Russo and Daniel Ellsberg released the Pentagon Papers, Hunt was hired as one of President Nixon's "plumbers" to prevent future leaks.

## Indochina and the American Power Structure

The trip to China prevented the corporations from bolting to the Democrats in 1972. They were worried about the war and Clifford could have brought them around. The trip to China, which opened the period of détente, settled whatever fears or qualms most people in business had about the danger of a war with the Soviet Union or China growing out of the Vietnam War, and tyranny and repression at home becoming necessary because of this escalation. Aside from those fears they would prefer a wide-open Republican administration full of businesspeople and all the privileges businesspeople get from it. That move sealed their alliance with Nixon for the next period.

Clifford must have felt frustrated, whatever he represents, because he couldn't get traction by winning over a large segment of the business community.

There were a couple of points where it was close, though.

One was the May 1972 crisis over Haiphong, which threatened to become a war with Russia. Many businesspeople and most of the National Security Council opposed mining Haiphong harbor.

Henry Kissinger opposed it, too. His main interest was securing détente with the Soviet Union. He didn't believe the mining was worth it if the Russians would pull out of the summit.

Nixon and John Connally, representing the most aggressive right-wing oil interests, put it on the line in the cabinet meetings and, essentially argued you are not a man if you don't do this.[111]

Kissinger got on board as soon as he saw the Moscow summit was still on. He was all smiles when the Russians came over the next day to be photographed with Nixon in the White House and

---

[111] John Connally (1917–1993) was a protégé of Lyndon Johnson, a Democratic Governor of Texas, and the Treasury Secretary under President Richard Nixon. Connally became a Republican in May 1973. After Vice President Spiro Agnew resigned in October 1973, Nixon wanted Connally to replace him. Connally would have had a tough time getting approved by the Senate, though, so House Minority Leader Gerald Ford got the job.

say, "Of course the summit is still on." That increased Kissinger's confidence in Nixon's guts, and he became a real defender of this bold stroke.

At the time, Nixon said, "The whole establishment is against me." He gave a similar speech several times in his career. This time, I think he was right. You need to go back to this notion of activists within the ruling class trying to bring everybody this way or that way. He was then losing an enormous amount of support that he could only recover if he could get the Russians to agree to let him come to Moscow. He gambled and won. You need to see it as a dynamic. His winning ended demonstrations in America and solidarity for Vietnam. It severely hampered the North Vietnamese offensive. We must credit Nixon with having taken the gamble, which the ruling class much respected. Everybody else was ready to cave out of fear.

Of course, it set up a new contradiction which destroyed him not so long afterward.

He said the same thing about the December 1972 bombing of Hanoi. He said it was the loneliest decision he ever made. I believe this is true. If anybody made it with him, it was Kissinger, who got his guts together after seeing in May that Nixon could pull it off. Apart from him, I'm not sure anybody favored the bombing of Hanoi. I'm not sure even the Joint Chiefs of Staff did.

Maybe Nixon's personal friends did, such as Robert Abplanalp and Bebe Rebozo.[112] Nixon had individual business supporters, just like we do, but Rebozo doesn't pull much weight in the ruling class. That's all Nixon had out there on the yacht besides his family.

I want to pose a question about what happened then. Nixon pulled that off, even though the majority of the American people

---

[112] Robert Abplanalp (1922–2003) became wealthy as the inventor of the plastic aerosol valve in 1949. Charles "Bebe" Rebozo (1912–1998) was a Florida banker. Both men provided financial and political support to Richard Nixon throughout his career.

opposed the bombing—or any escalatory move—by a decisive margin. All of America's allies opposed it. Congress opposed it and probably would have stopped it if Nixon hadn't done so himself before they got back to Washington. Still, Nixon, in one sense, pulled it off.

## Watergate

Yet, in the third week of March 1973, when the POWs were coming home, James McCord told Judge John Sirica there was a high-level conspiracy suppressing facts in the Watergate case.[113] In this way, the return of U.S. soldiers, including POWs, from Vietnam was connected to the decision to open the Watergate case. Forces in the ruling class that had used the war against Nixon now switched to Watergate.

If they had done it before the Peace Agreement, they would have been accused of destroying the internal stability and structure of the United States while we had troops in South Vietnam and POWs in Hanoi. With them back home, the establishment could inaugurate a new struggle against Nixon.
The same forces who favored the release of the Pentagon Papers, sponsored the Moratorium, and threw Johnson out of office, were now going to eliminate Nixon. But not Kissinger.

We can speculate that after Nixon won his decisive victory in 1972, they feared if he stayed in power you would see a return of the aggressive right wing of the establishment that had been pushed out through détente, the trip to China, and all those things Nixon regarded as necessary compromises to maintain power. The consequence would be a return to domestic turmoil and disorder, including extra-legal moves against other elements of the establishment.

---

[113] John Sirica (1904–1992) was Chief Judge for the U.S. District Court for the District of Columbia, where he presided over many of the Watergate scandal trials.

When Jane and I interviewed Clark Clifford, he pointed at his window, from which we could see the White House, and said, "The people down there who have taken over the government do not believe in our form of government."

We could say, "Since when does Clark Clifford believe in our form of government?" I think, though, he does believe in our form of government in the literal sense of trying to retain both the corporate enterprise as the pivot of the economy and constitutional democracy as the political framework, to maintain a balance between profit and order. He thinks to make inroads against political democracy—in the limited sense we have it—would bring about disorder, possibly a right-wing coup d'état, fascism, and possibly World War III. This is a firm position of this element of the ruling class. That's why they think Nixon was against our form of government.

They believed a coup d'état had taken place against constitutional democracy and they had to move against him. They believed the only solution was a counter-coup d'état staged on many levels to restore the form of government they thought was most suitable to the American people and American interests.

In their minds, "American interests" is identical to corporate interests. They think our good way of life has been a byproduct of this corporate system. They understand the corporation has some problems, like greed or plundering, but when it gets out of hand, the government can check it. They are pluralists and believe in private corporate enterprise combined with political democracy.

They were threatened with fascism, maybe in a step-by-step process, by what they perceived to be the curtailment of normal liberties, the normal framework of doing business, which would ultimately lead to disorder and a right-wing coup. They were in a pretty good position to know. By "they" I mean the mainstream CIA, corporate liberals, main economic establishment, Democratic Party and, finally, the Republican Party and the *New York Times*, *Washington Post* and the rest of the mass media which is controlled by the main financial interests of the country.

They have essentially succeeded, in a brilliant stroke, in recovering power, esteem and authority, without any sense on the part of the American people that there has been a coup from the right followed by a coup from the left within the establishment.

## Looking Forward

Gerald Ford and Nelson Rockefeller represent a closing of differences within the establishment among those who remain after the big purge. They represent a reopening of the system to the liberals who no longer have to fear being put on enemies lists or losing prerogatives. They represent a recovery of support for the center as reflected in the position Ford has taken on amnesty, a centrist position meant to locate himself between two positions and bring together as much as possible from them. They represent a repair of relations with Congress. They represent a restoration of business confidence, if not in the economy, in the means of managing the economy through the government because there are certain key things the government can do.

The big losers are the Cold War conservatives. They made their bid at various levels: paramilitary police, secret agents, and financial contributions. They came to power, but a counter-attack destroyed them. They still exist. I wouldn't say they're in the woodwork, but now they have to recoup for a long time.

On the other hand, the restored establishment has problems.

Republican losses and Democratic gains in November mean perpetuation of forces demanding certain changes in foreign and domestic policy.

Vietnam is still a simmering problem which can reopen the whole contradiction again at any time it renews itself in the form of an offensive or the fall of Phnom Penh or Saigon.

Economic problems are serious and have gotten out of hand by the government over the last two years. So much so it is not clear there can be a restoration a businessperson or a worker would consider normalcy to the economy.

Their biggest problem is the consciousness of the American people, created by the experiences of the last fifteen years. It has been an unbelievable change, and the new occupants of the White House must face it.

## Chapter 5

# Patterns in the Way People Struggle

September 26, 1976
Keene, California

*Tom Hayden delivered this talk to people who had campaigned for his nomination as the Democratic candidate for U.S. Senate from California, including Cesar Chavez (1927-1993), leader of the United Farm Workers. Hayden had lost to John Tunney in the primary, and Tunney was soon to lose to Republican S.I. Hayakawa in the general election. Out of the 1976 Hayden campaign came a new grassroots organization, the California Campaign for Economic Democracy. The talk took place at La Paz, the organizational headquarters of the United Farm Workers, in Keene, near Bakersfield, California.*

〜

No matter how different struggling people are in their geography, race, or class, beneath the differences, there are universal laws. It's a matter of faith that there's one world, one set of dynamics, and one way people deal with and go through this world.

Oppressed people will always look like they are asleep to everyone from their oppressors to the experts observing and writing about them. For example, for thirty years people wrote that farm labor could not be organized into a union. They said it was impossible because nationality and language divided the workers and there was a big turnover. This is a universal pattern. It can make you give up.

People who seem asleep awaken at the most unusual times. No one ever correctly predicts when people will rise, as with the Filipino farmworkers whose action brought Cesar Chavez in 1965, the first farmworker strikes in the San Joaquin Valley, California, labor strikes of the 1930s, civil rights movement in the South, or the way the southern liberation forces in Vietnam started. There has always been a spontaneous mass outbreak, usually before anyone expected it. You wait for it to start somewhere and it happens somewhere else.

Without organization and leadership, no spontaneous struggle will ever sustain itself. It will run out or be crushed. In dead times and live times, quiet times and animated times, there is a need for an alert, sensitive organization that doesn't try to come in and steal and control all the energy, and instead comes in to give some shape and wisdom to people who are starting to move.

That is why in the United Farm Workers nobody thinks they were born yesterday. There is a sense of history and identity many of us in this room do not have because we are cut off from whatever our radical ancestors were. Not so in any successful mass movement. Like Cesar just said, if you try and fail ninety-nine times, you try again. That has been the history of the farm labor struggle over the last 125 years in California.

Their history has been of trying to organize and organize and organize. There have been bloodbaths and slaughters that haven't even been recorded. Without the history of organization, there would never be any hope for spontaneous struggles.

It is important that the organization not lay a heavy hand on the movement and that it accumulates information and wisdom from the past to apply to the present. If you don't have an organization to do that there will be no history. If you don't have a history, you're always starting over.

A lot of people like starting over. They feel it makes them new in human history to come along and start a struggle. The opposite is true. You have been so cut off from your world, you're living in a self-centered situation.

It's nothing to brag about that you're the New Left, or the new this or new that because it means the previous left was destroyed. It's better to have a hand-me-down quality, and organization is the only hand-me-down thing we have.

Have you seen the book *North from Mexico* by Carey McWilliams?[114] It is a great social history. In the end, after going through the whole miserable story of this part of the country, he says there isn't much hope. There is this guy, though, named Fred Ross who's organizing something called the Community Service Organization.[115] McWilliams says change might come only through efforts like this.

Fred Ross had to go for many years organizing what seemed to be failures, and then he found Cesar Chavez, who, at the time, looked like anybody else you might organize. From there, things started to pick up.

How would you like to be in the Central Valley before there was a farmworkers union, before there was a boycott, and before anybody heard of any of this? You'd have to live with a college education that told you farmworkers couldn't be organized, and a white guy wandering around the Central Valley looking for one person to start an organization—in an area which has a history of complete repression and failure.

This organizing approach is rare. You could sit back and say, "It's happening because of the dynamic of history. It's objective conditions." There is truth to it, and it's usually what you say later. You say, "It came about because the time was ripe." But when the time is ripe, nobody knows it's ripe, and everybody is

---

[114] Carey McWilliams, *North from Mexico: The Spanish-Speaking People of the United States* (Santa Barbara, California: Praeger Publishers, 1949).

[115] See Gabriel Thompson, *America's Social Arsonist: Fred Ross and Grassroots Organizing in the Twentieth Century* (Oakland, California: University of California Press, 2016).

saying it's not ripe. You are crazy because you're trying to do something impossible. The only way the time becomes ripe is when you make it so. You run the risk of being ahead of your time, of madness, of repression. There is no other way to determine whether the time is ripe except for somebody to be the historical agent to make it so. This is what an organizer does.

Universal Methods

There is a lot of talk about house meetings in the union. It's a small group meeting. The meeting is put together by an organizer, and the other people do not usually have any prior experience. This is one of the best ways to build an organization.

Many people like us who are activists would like to create an organization of people who already have our consciousness, people who are already like us. We develop little circles. We do outreach work, but there's a real gap between the little circle and the mass.

That's not the way to proceed if you take up the path of organizing house meetings and small group meetings. It's completely the opposite.

What you do is build an organization of organizers who bring in fresh people constantly—people who have no previous organizing experience, who are not scarred with the history of the left, or the history of other organizations, but marked with the scars we all have as Americans.

The organizer must choose a life of discomfort unless you are some strange extroverted freak who loves being among strangers all the time. Most people don't. It's tiring and extremely hard. Just as you get a group organized, as you begin to form friendships, start to enjoy yourself, you might even fall in love—and you're bogged down. What you must do, which is psychologically hard, is to leave your friends, just leave them. Not in your mind, leave them, and go to an entirely new area—it

## Patterns in the Way People Struggle

might be a ranch, a block, or an office — and start all over again after having gotten this whole group of people together out of nothing.

Start over again, walking up to people you don't know, and with whom you only have about thirty seconds to strike up a relationship. You must convince them to let you talk to them, and then to let you use their house for a meeting of people you're going to bring who they don't know, in cities full of crime. People will think you're just a sophisticated criminal, or at the end of your rap, that you're going to ask for money or there's going to be some trip laid on them. You must overcome that in a minute and get your way into the conversation and through the door. Then, after an hour, you go on to the next person and do this incessantly until you have enough people to have a meeting.

An organizer's rule of thumb is you must talk to fifteen people to get one to come to a meeting. To have a meeting of ten, you must talk to one hundred and fifty people. How many people want to do that? It's psychologically hard, yet this is the only way to build an organization that gets deeper and deeper into the community and involves the people with the problems.

All other kinds of organizations are just organizations of organizers, radicals. They're not organizations of consumers or workers or tenants. You can't figure out a solution to the problem, though, unless you organize the people who have the problem.

The organizer usually doesn't have any problems except dealing with pain and frustration. The only people who can say where the shoe pinches are the people wearing the shoes. They can tell you where it hurts and where the solution lies.

Unless you're a saint or a dreamer you can't expect people to do this. It calls for an organization of organizers to give each other support, or else you'll never survive the ordeal of having to go out and continually do this.

183

Relate to people where they are instead of where you are. Not entirely where they are, though. If somebody says, "I want to stop busing and keep those people tied up in South Central," you can't say "Right on" and then hope you can add a little social analysis or something.

There's got to be a line. Too often, the organizer is so conscious of wanting to change everything in the world they want to organize everybody into all those changes. That's a disaster.

For example, Tom Starkey raised the question of nutrition yesterday at the clinic in Delano.[116] The answer from the doctor was "Cesar would like to organize everybody to be a vegetarian, but you have to walk a fine line." Then you are running against ingrained eating habits that don't necessarily have anything to do with the principal focus of the struggle, which is to improve working conditions, the contracts, and so on.

Vietnam is divided, with lots of minority people. Historically there was no way to unify people against the French or Americans or anybody else unless you could get the majority people to get along with the minority. The minority had different habits and were looked down upon by the majority. One of the things they did was chew betel nut all day long. Their teeth were black. They thought it had a hygienically positive effect. The majority thought it was unhygienic and uncivilized, too.

Nevertheless, Ho Chi Minh sent people to work in the minority areas and told them they had to file and blacken their teeth with betel nut and be prepared to spend twenty years. They were not going to fight people on the question of betel nut. They were not going to go in and insist everyone have white or black or yellow teeth. They were going to "relate" to that.

Have tactics that give a lot of people a little to do. Most people work and have good reasons why they can't be full-time

---

[116] Tom Starkey would become a leader of the Campaign for Economic Democracy chapter in Santa Cruz, California.

organizers. That doesn't mean they don't want to work with the organization when they can, and organizers must provide that work.

In a boycott, for example, when you go up to people on the street and ask them not to eat grapes, the question never leaves them. You haven't done anything to make them take on an extra burden. You're asking them to lessen their burden by not eating one kind of food. You're not asking them to do much, just putting the question inside them. They are personally involved, not just supporting other people who are doing the work. They are doing the work by not eating grapes, and they see them every time they go to the market.

Values are abstract. If you ask people to go from individual competition to cooperation and don't give them a way to do it, it seems like a 180-degree shift in their lives. They don't know what they're supposed to do.

Most people are not like St. Paul on his horse getting hit by God's insight, dropping to the ground, and getting up a radical Christian. It doesn't happen. For those who do change like that, it doesn't last long. They're some of our most eloquent speakers and some of our most brilliant media stars. And they last about as long as a shooting star. Nobody can be changed in an instant if they've been made into what they are over twenty to thirty years.

There must be alternative institutions to give a concrete picture of the values you're talking about. A medical clinic or a consumer co-op is not abstract. It's concrete. Through participation in it, people can get new values.

United Farm Worker institutions are not institutions in themselves. They are part of a union struggling for its survival. What we have in the cities or the college towns are counter-institutions. They started with the best of intentions, with a lot of idealism and euphoria. Then they bog down, because what they're doing is providing service for a community, and that makes people passive. They don't remember there was a riot, there were hearings, there was a commission, and then the authorities decided to give you the money to start your co-op institution. Only the initial leadership remembers they created the free clinic out of struggle. For later generations, five years later, the free clinic is just another institution to rip off personally or get something from.

Almost no institutions in California can remain an alternative unless they're tied into a movement that stands for and is trying to create an alternative. Otherwise, they dwindle.

This mistake was repeatedly made in movements other than the farmworkers movement—creating new institutions as if somehow, they would then change the community. The new institutions soon start to serve the oppressor unintentionally.

If you have terrible health care, people are going to get angry about it and revolt, unless you have a free clinic that takes care of people who come and ask for help. Soon the free clinic, which was supposed to be an alternative, instead becomes at best like a service station, and at worst a buffer between the community and the real power structure. People start complaining about the free clinic not taking care of their problems when they should be blaming the whole structure which makes a free clinic necessary. In the union, there is an attempt to make these things go hand in hand.

## Nonviolence

Most of us don't consider ourselves to be nonviolent, or we associate nonviolence with a certain religiosity, or we think it's just a tactic. I don't want to talk about the moral philosophy here. I want to talk about the role of nonviolence in building an organization.

Last night, someone asked the speaker, "Through the bleak times, what did you do to stay together?" Mack Lyons described the example of Cesar's fast in early 1968, when the student movement, the black movement, and the antiwar movement were all becoming violent.[117] They were becoming immersed in, at the least, confrontation with police over the right to demonstrate. Tremendous repression followed.

The farmworkers were in that atmosphere of confrontation. There was enormous frustration in the movement. The growers were cheating and using violence. In early 1968 when most of the world was going up in violence—from the Tet offensive in Vietnam to college campuses and black ghettos—it was likely this movement would drift in the same direction.

When Cesar fasted, you don't have to think of it being based only on religious philosophy. If you read *Cesar Chavez: Autobiography of La Causa* by Jacques Levy, you know Cesar thought the movement was getting out of hand.[118] In response to frustration, people were moving toward violence without any thought about whether it would help build the movement or destroy it. It was just what the growers wanted.

Things were getting out of hand, so Cesar stopped eating. He didn't kneel and tell everybody he was fasting for religious reasons. He just said there must be a stop to analyze what we're doing and where we're going. He told people he had stopped eating. There is no better way to stop than to stop eating. That turned the whole situation around. It got people to focus on why he was doing it, and there were all kinds of side discussions about it.

More importantly, it got back to the question of creating a way to re-examine where the organization was going before it went off in a direction that was not planned and not thought through and might well be bankrupt and destructive. That's an example of the relation between nonviolent action and organizational health.

---

[117] Mack Lyons (1941–2008) was an organizer for the United Farm Workers, a member of the UFW Executive Board, and led the union's political work.

[118] Jacques E. Levy, *Cesar Chavez: Autobiography of La Causa* (New York: W.W. Norton Publishing Company, 1975).

If you look over the last fifteen years, there was a healthy, growing mass movement in America from 1960 to 1965. Millions of people were involved in the civil rights, student, and antiwar movements. In the case of the civil rights movement, there was majority support for the right to vote in the South. These movements were deeply influenced by nonviolence, coming from Martin Luther King, Jr. Almost nobody in them believed in nonviolence as a religious philosophy, but they accepted nonviolence because the leadership felt it was the only way to get mass support.

From 1967 to 1972, state violence and repression grew. All we could remember was people being killed, street confrontations, organizations being broken up by indictments, and leaders going to jail. Maybe there was no relation between violence and nonviolence on the one hand and organizational health on the other. Maybe it was just happenstance things turned out that way. I'm not clear in my mind.

Sometimes things in the world are achieved through violence. There's no need, though, to debate violence versus nonviolence. There are certain things about nonviolence, at least in the way the farmworkers use the phrase, which we should do some deep thinking about regarding organization building.

## Creativity

There is no shortcut. When you're frustrated, the solution is not the destruction of property or taking the life of an individual oppressor. The solution is to find a creative act which will turn the tables and get things going again. Creativity is the answer to frustration and is an important organizational principle.

It doesn't have to be individual creativity. You don't have to go off and try to think up the answer. Often the answer comes from the people.

When things were at a most frustrating point in the United Farm Worker's history, like when the big strikes were going on

## Patterns in the Way People Struggle

and on and on, Cesar at one point went to a mass meeting and said, "I know you're frustrated. You want to change direction, but ideas come from people. I know if I were you, I would try to think of an idea to get us through this situation."

Sure enough, three women who were loyal pickets and had never opened their mouths came to him a couple of hours later and said, "You wanted ideas. We're not challenging your leadership." He thought they wanted something. The problem, in this case, was in dealing with workers who were inside the ranch, who never had to come out. Going in to meet the workers, you'd get busted, beaten, and sent off to jail. The women said, "What about having an altar in a car outside the gate and having a vigil." He said, "That's it. There's more than one way to skin a cat, backward and forward. You can't go in, so we have to get them to come out." They started a vigil and succeeded. All the farmworkers came out.

The only way to bring about change is when the people who want change have the power to make it happen.

This also affects work. Here we are in a quiet place, La Paz. It means 'peace.' We know the farmworkers work harder than almost anybody. Farmworker organizers probably not as hard as farmworkers in the field, but they work hard. Still, there don't seem to be bad vibes which you see around other movement offices or electoral campaigns when people are at the height of the struggle. There seem to be good vibes. People work so hard you'd think they'd be going crazy and taking it out on each other.

The problem is how, when you're in a violent situation, and Teamsters are standing five feet away, challenging your virility, your strength, your integrity, egging you on. How do you deal with a whole upbringing that says you're a coward if you don't hit back? How do you overcome that and come back stronger? How do you discipline yourself to let someone beat you and beat you and beat you? It's not easy. You must force yourself to learn how to do it. If you think you can do it just because the cause is glorious, because it is exciting, you couldn't possibly make it. You must undergo training to accept self-sacrifice.

It may also be why there have been no factional splits which have torn the union apart. Every other organization we know about has split. I don't think nonviolence will guarantee there will be no splits or no violence. These attitudes, whether we call them nonviolence or a healthy mentality attitude, may be why the leaders of the union are unified. The unity consolidated, as far as I can find out, after the first fast.

Unity

You can't possibly have a successful struggle without organization. You can't succeed organizationally without unity. And confrontational violence may have raised the stakes faster than people could handle. It may have contributed to psyching out a lot of people, putting them on a nervous edge where factionalism became commonplace.

Whatever the truth of these connections, the practical consequences of the United Farm Workers' nonviolence have been enormous. They have always retained mass support, and it's grown. They have never alienated the great mass of moderate voters. They have always acted in ways just short of breaking the law or going over the edge into violence.

Only through nonviolence has the United Farm Workers been able to avoid the pattern of every single other organization in the last fifteen years. Organizations reach a certain point, then a conspiracy charge is leveled at them, leadership is taken away, and the movement tries to defend the leader. You're no longer fighting for peace or social justice. You're fighting against repression and the freedom of political prisoners.

The Black Panthers, for example, spent six million dollars on bail from 1969 to 1971. For what? Not to get a single person a free breakfast or a job, just to keep certain leaders out of jail. Cesar says when you go on the defensive, and you're struggling to free political prisoners, your mass following declines somewhat because people only follow a movement when they get something out of it. There's no job or an improved living condition for the average person. The base of support goes down until you get back on track.

You can't predict in advance whether you can succeed in the struggle. Still, there cannot be any success unless you have a group of people unified among themselves, who have a sense of community, are able to reach many, many people around their immediate grievances, organize those people into an organizational base, and work harder than anyone else, setting an example of courage and humanity and principle.

## Belief in Change

In the antiwar movement, people often asked, "Why do you go on?" or asked, "Are you an optimist or a pessimist?"

If you're a painter or an artist or an observer of reality you could be either an optimist or a pessimist and still create something meaningful. If you're trying to change conditions, though, if you're trying to improve the world, then you can't possibly take a pessimistic detached position. You must be an optimist, whether or not there's evidence to justify it. How can pessimists improve things? The only things brought about through pessimism are enjoyable cocktail parties, social relationships, discussion groups, games between people, and incessant conventions.

There must be another attitude brought to things. The most important thing if you want to change the world is to believe in change. And belief cannot be based on proof. It must be based on faith. I don't think people can sustain themselves with sociological statistics which prove change is possible, with Harris polls, or with theories which explain why change is inevitable. I don't think people can live that way. They must have something more.

It goes back to this question of nonviolence. I must say, at the risk of being misunderstood, it goes to the question of religion. If you don't have religion, I don't think you can continue. I don't mean institutional religion. I don't even mean a belief in God. You must have a belief that humanity can improve. That belief can't be proven any more than you can prove whether a God exists. It's a matter of how you choose to nourish, sustain, and conduct yourself, and relate to other people. It's a matter of what faith you adopt.

It's probably the most fundamental thing in the history of the farmworkers, or any movement. Even movements that don't believe in God believe things are going to get worse. We're going to have terrible troubles. We may not see each other or make it through together. People are going to die. People are going to be arrested. People are going to fail, burn out. People are going to discover awful things about each other. In the end, people are going to win. That's what I mean by faith.

If you don't have that kind of faith, it's impossible to win because material conditions are not enough to bring about social justice or a new reality. You must have faith which, when it's organized, increases your strength.

## When the Police Come with Clubs

When the police come with clubs, they see the farmworkers singing. They're not singing to throw the police off balance. They're singing to increase their strength against the increased strength of the oppressor. Otherwise, you'll fall victim to fear. The only way to overcome the fear of death or any other fear is to increase your spirit. The only way is to have faith you can rely on to get you through those moments. That's hard.

Many of us come from movements where to be moral is considered wrong. You aren't supposed to talk about morality. We're supposed to be hard people. Tough. "We only talk about economics." There must be a reason people who talk about economics are in the universities or are not successfully building mass movements. I think the reason is that people do not live by bread alone.

*Chapter 6*

# What Is the Hardest Question We Face Now?

August 19, 1977
Hell, Michigan

*SDS held a reunion in 1977 at the University of Michigan Fresh Air Camp in Hell, Michigan, near Ann Arbor. At the outset, Al Haber (1936- ), the first President and first Field Secretary of SDS, raised the question that is the title for this talk. In his remarks, Hayden proposes an answer.*

CB

What do we want to achieve in the years ahead? The discussions here about whether there will be something apocalyptic like war, fascism, or revolution, are real questions, of course. At the same time, we cannot organize around them or assume any of them will occur. The other option that seems to be theoretically open is a peaceful, gradual evolution from one social system to another. Since that has never occurred, we can't assume it will happen here. What we must conceive of is complicated—to work within the system as far as possible while realizing there may be limits we don't even know about in theory.

We are talking about a historical period often trivialized or diminished in left theory into a concept of the "transition to socialism." I have always been more interested in the transition part than the socialist part because I don't know if I will ever live in a socialist society. I do know I will live in the transition. My children will grow up in it, and almost everything that happens in my life will happen then.

No one has described this period in detail. Calling it a "transition" sounds like a shortcut or something you go through—like a tunnel from darkness to light. Or it is seen simply as a period of struggle without institutional form. If there is such a thing as a "transition to socialism," it could be one hundred fifty, one hundred, or seventy-five years.

Within this murky area short of a total revolutionary transformation, and long enough to encompass our lives, certain things must be achievable. On the policy level, this could include a substantial degree of decentralized public control of industry, basing our energy sources on solar energy, de-escalation of the arms race, a foreign policy of nonintervention, extension of equal opportunity and rights, improvements in public health and education, and making the executive branch more accountable, particularly the intelligence agencies.

To be able to win these objectives assumes we can win a significant degree of state power, even if having control of the state does not mean we have full economic power, or power to abolish prejudice overnight. It does mean electing a president, ten or fifteen senators, one hundred or one hundred fifty members of Congress, twelve governors, five hundred members of state legislatures, and one thousand to five thousand city officials and union officials.

To not talk about this possibility would be to accept political failure. We could have successful lives in other ways, yet still fail in a task I think is possible. We used to talk about "revolution in our lifetime." We should also talk about failure in our lifetime and reform in our lifetime.

Getting from here to there is the question. It doesn't happen naturally, or through pressure, or through civil disobedience and demonstrations, or through local organizing, or through anything short of an attempt to win power on a national level through a combination of electoral, union, and community organizing. We must deal with gathering political power. That means trying to take over the Democratic Party and changing it, which seems unrealistic, or forming a new party, which seems unrealistic, or developing a political force in the twilight zone between those two alternatives, which does seem realistic even though not theoretically sound. This is the famous pragmatism of the New Left.

In any case, we need to solve five equal and interrelated problems in dealing with power: program, leadership, organization, unity, and spirit.

I don't know if these problems can be solved. We must have great ambition and be modest about American history. It reveals a pattern of great social movements arising, achieving some or all of their aims, splintering, and then falling apart without creating political parties or mass organizations.

On the whole, we have not had a good history of permanent movements or third parties. There have been brief periods for the Socialist Party, and someone could make a similar case for the Communist Party. Whether the abolitionists of the last century or the antiwar movements of the 1960s, they are followed by long periods of decline and apathy before another great movement comes along. If something beyond that is going to be possible, these problems must be solved.

How were these problems approached in the sixties? What were the pitfalls and what could have been done differently?

## Program

I'm not talking about the rigid "correct line-ism" people often fall into when they are searching for a program. I'm not talking about a program of organizing against all the symptoms of capitalist society on behalf of a total alternative, but more about a limited program based on an analysis of the world.

By way of example, let's say we are entering a new period. What does it mean for us? In 1963, we made a start in a little-known document called, "America and the New Era," which was quite correct, though it did not anticipate ten years of the Vietnam War in which the American establishment would try to delay the new era from arriving. Now it has. In this era, American power is somewhat on the decline, rather than the ascendancy. If this is true, many things that held the country together won't be in play in the future. We won't have increasing affluence. We won't have new frontiers in which to expand. We won't be able to police the world. The former key to American stability was to buy off opposition and insurgent groups, and that is becoming harder because there is less to go around.

Traditional welfare liberalism will turn into what Jimmy Carter and Jerry Brown represent: a socially liberal force and a more conservative austerity in economic matters.[119] This is not because they are themselves Scrooges. Instead, they perceive it as necessary for a system with declining affluence. If you want to preserve the privilege of the rich, you must take it from the poor and the middle class as well.

A program should come from analysis such as this. In other words, it needs to define what stage of history we are in before going on to say what is possible. Often in the past, we would put forward ideas and demands we thought were possible, because we wanted them to be possible without any concept of limits. If we took it literally, we would have to trash Eugene Debs for not supporting the legalization of marijuana in 1919.[120] When we

---

[119] Jerry Brown (1938–) was the Governor of California from 1975 to 1983 and from 2011 to 2019. He also served as California Secretary of State and Attorney General, and Mayor of Oakland.

[120] Eugene Debs (1855–1926) was a founder of the International Workers of the World (IWW) and the American Railway Union, and a five-time Socialist candidate for U.S. President. He spent two years in prison for opposing U.S. entry into World War I.

look backward in history, we always celebrate people for what they did where they were. We often don't think the same way about contemporaries.

If we are in such a stage, liberal welfare state economics will not work. At the same time then, we must have a program which neither the New Deal nor socialism fulfills. That is why we speak of economic democracy.

We are talking about a program to be struggled for during a period in which monopoly capitalism and liberal solutions are failing, and in which there was enough strength on their part and enough weakness among the socialists to make big change impossible. Still, there is a tremendous effort by consumers, environmentalists, and labor, all struggling for more say over the means of producing and distributing the pie.

A program must also have a way of reaching a majority, which is possible if the middle class is in trouble. In earlier days it might have been necessary to mobilize the poor without enough allies to constitute a majority. Now, though, it may be possible to mobilize a majority if someone can find the right consciously reformist formulation. We ought not to be ashamed of the word "reformist." For people to posture that there is nothing between now and revolution makes no sense and will be promptly dismissed as such. The questions are "What is a reform that advances?" and "What is cooptation?"

Boston Mayor James Curley was reelected from jail on the program, "If we cannot redistribute the wealth, then let's redistribute the graft."[121] Being able to serve day-to-day interests is the minimum definition of reform. Lunch on the table is a reform for a lot of people. To deliver it creates an opportunity to talk about other things.

---

[121] James Michael Curley (1874–1958) was a four-time Democratic Mayor of Boston, Massachusetts.

At the same time, a program must create models that give you a taste of the future or a taste of the dream. Two things are required here: concepts different from prevailing capitalist concepts—a struggle in the realm of ideas—and showing people those ideas are practical and can be tested and achieved. It could be an integrated children's camp or electing the mayor of a large city and running it in a cleaner and fairer way than any other city in America.

We used to talk of alternative institutions. The problem is there is only one system, not a system and its alternatives. Alternative institutions tend to pass away as the system adopts the alternative. Or the alternatives hold out for independence and lose their money. Either way, it's not much of an alternative after a while. We must think of alternatives growing from within the system.

Lastly, we must overcome the left's ambivalence about electoral politics. Behind that is a larger ambivalence about the system. It is the chronic strategic problem of the American left which is in a capitalist society with democratic political institutions.

To consider the state, as left theory traditionally does, to be nothing more than the "executive committee of the ruling class" is to miss about one hundred years of the development of the state. On the one hand, the capitalist class controls the state, and on the other hand, the state acquires more and more workers because of the demands for social service and labor laws. The state is not only them. It is also us. To think of the state simply as an agency of repression to abolish following the creation of a new state is nonsense that has plagued the left for a long time.

You don't have to give up left theory to say parts of the state have to be neutralized while others are strengthened, and other agencies created to take care of things the state is not now allowed to control, such as capital investment. That view leads you to include electoral politics somewhere in your outlook on how to bring about change. The case for electoral politics should follow from a theory of what the state is.

Also, you need the practice of electing people who do not become co-opted shortly after that. There must be proof in practice somewhere in the country that it is possible to carry out any of these theories.

## Leadership

The idea that we do not need leadership came from our ambivalence as middle-class people about opening a Pandora's Box of leadership after we shut the old box of pursuing success. It was much easier to say you don't need leaders than for five male honchos to sit in a circle saying, "Let's one of us be the leader." People do not want to do it for ethical reasons and psychological anxiety. It was played out not just as a moral or political concept, or a philosophy of anti-elitism. People were trying to get away from the things we were trained for but did not know what to put in their place. There was also the fear of being swallowed up in the release of all the old bogeymen if the questions were out front.

Also, there was the concept of "rotating leadership" which, if you think about it, is entirely mechanical. No one would want to rotate Ho Chi Minh out of the presidency of Vietnam. No one would want to rotate people who are doing a good job. We thought rotation was good in itself. When someone was good at what they did, they felt ethically and structurally obliged to leave. People would be placed in jobs because they had to be, not because they were qualified or ready. Then they would fail, and no one could say why because the theory was anyone could lead.

We tended to undercut leadership. As we conferred leadership on someone, we would immediately undermine them psychologically, guilt-trip them, create structures, and leave them confused about what they were authorized to do. They could not lead creatively, only report to the group. No one going to the national level felt they were entirely justified in what they were doing.

Beyond this, a lot of leadership was terrible, and it reinforced the idea that leadership itself was no good. Whether it was because we were immature, still acting out of old achievement orientations, or because there was no old left or adult reform movement, it resulted in bad, egotistical leadership patterns. We took on issues before we knew who we were.

One of the most interesting or bizarre cases of this was when SDS elected a national secretary on the program of ending the New Left. When I read in *New Left Notes* that Rennie Davis and I should not be followed in Chicago because we were "New Left," I knew something was profoundly wrong. Many people chose leaders to reflect their view that the New Left was some immature trip they had been on.

Few in the New Left were against the leadership of Castro, Ho Chi Minh, Malcolm X, or Cesar Chavez. We only seemed to have difficulty with the concept when it got to us. So, if there must be leadership, what holds us back and how do we move on it?

People have a legitimate psychological need for leaders. It is not just infancy or immaturity. I don't think I'm an infant or immature anymore, and I have a psychological need for leadership. For example, if Rachel is an expert on childcare and I'm not, and we are in an assembly, I'm not going to study childcare to catch up with Rachel. If I trust her, I'm going to ask her how I should vote on childcare, because I trust her judgment for a chemical mix of reasons having to do with her expertise and character.

This is the normal way we make judgments, on the facts and the character of the person telling us what we are hearing. If everyone here stood up and argued to an audience for the necessity of socialism, how would I as a member of the audience know who to believe? I wouldn't. It is difficult to know what to make of any proclamation on paper. Everyone from President Carter on down can write good words, so the only way is to get beyond the words. You need to know something about who is talking to you. What is their character, history, practice, background, and record?

If there can't be healthy leaders, you can write off change. Any mass movement will be taken over by sick leaders because we all know that in mass movements people can move to the top quickly and unpredictably.

Leadership should be based on expertise, some measure of humility and the ability to listen. Leaders should have a sense of their destiny and a daring that makes them troublesome and upsetting. There is ambiguity between leadership reflecting what people want and leadership being slightly erratic, bolting, making leaps forward that are difficult for an organization. There must be accountability and leadership training to stabilize or control problems. There is also the question of personal responsibility for your leadership. Nothing can make you accountable if you don't want to be.

American society is based on the idea that if you build enough fences, enough checks and balances, you can check personal greed. That is impossible because the greedy are the ones who design all those fences. Maybe we did not spend enough time on people making themselves better, instead of inventing structures to keep them from being worse. There needs to be moral self-discipline and a conscious attempt to improve yourself. Otherwise, you always get the contradiction of wayward and bizarre leadership patterns coming out with merely a paper structure to contain and control them. Even if the structure is pretty good, you never resolve the question of leadership because you always need to beat it down after electing it. This poisons possibility.

## Organization

People went through two extremes in the sixties: spontaneity and mechanical foreign models.

Spontaneity is a key force, and anybody in an organization should be humble in the face of it. Often, people take new directions spontaneously and organizations race to catch up. However, there was too much belief in spontaneity. People came to ruin on that one.

Foreign models also had crippling results. The guerilla model is hard to apply in the United States. Vanguard Bolshevik models came out of societies where the old order was smashed, and the Bolsheviks created a new state.

The new interest in Eurocommunism models has a problem.[122] It is good because they are the only example of left political parties functioning in political democracies. Eurocommunist and socialist parties, however, are based in countries with more of a class tradition than ours. A lot of the Communist Party leaders have their stature not because they are communists, but because they are patriots. They resisted German occupation and earned their credentials for generations to come. In the United States, the capitalist government earned their credentials by joining the war against Germany. If we think we can leap from where we are to a full-blown Italian-style political party, it could be devastating because we have no strong labor base and no current potential for a mass party with five or ten million votes independent of the Democratic Party.

We need organization because it is a way to raise consciousness. When there are no tables on campuses, consciousness goes down. When there is no union organizer in the shop, it goes down. It is the only way to make sure victories we win are implemented, like when the farmworkers got labor legislation in California. If they were not organized as a union, the labor legislation would not be carried out. They are the only agency to do it.

If people believe there is something larger than themselves that is going somewhere, they are more likely to commit

---

[122] Eurocommunism was a trend among Western European communist parties, especially in the 1970s and 1980s, to pursue a democratic road to socialism, to become independent of the Soviet Union, and to democratize their internal functioning.

themselves. Their organization becomes the seed of an alternative society where you get an education, make your closest friends, and where your family grows up. If it is not there, you will become more like the system merely by being under its daily pressures.

A struggle to get an organization back together must proceed. One of the elements in it is visibility, not organizing quietly for some long-term goal. You need to make a splash, have an impact, either by the number of votes you get or the polarizing effect you have. You need to be in the media, known to people, and not just a patient, base-building, long-haul invisible association. You need to have names, programs, symbols like the farmworkers' flag, and you need to operate on almost all levels.

One thing we are working on in California is a way of affiliating people with our organization at whatever level they happen to be. Maybe a mass membership of twenty thousand people who will send in dues and participate peripherally in programs. Another level of activists will come to chapter meetings and carry out programs in the community. Others will be full-time people whose whole life is building the organization. The coalition should work in many areas at once: Democratic Party, labor, professions, and single-issue movements.

Social dynamics are such that things are always breaking out or starting spontaneously in different areas. We need to deal with it the way water deals with going down a hill. It moves in the direction dictated by the lay of the land.

Sometimes we had paper coalitions or coalitions at the top that were used for the media. Coalitions at the bottom are more important, though. If I have a press conference with Cesar Chavez, it looks like a coalition. There is a world of difference, though, between us talking, and California Campaign for Economic Democracy (CED) members who only speak English meeting with farmworkers who only speak Spanish. The coalition must be threaded together locally. This is one reason we have a camp, to start with the next generation—thirteen-year-olds—and integrate them into the coalition, two hundred every summer. Over five years, that's a thousand young people approaching twenty years old. There are many other ways.

We also need training schools like the Midwest Academy.[123] There is a need for something like "repair shops" for our organizations.

Finally, we need a hard core of fanatics. I don't know any other word for it, and this is not a popular word. It is the difference between, on the one hand, the full-time organizer with gleaming eyes and, on the other hand, people who want to raise families and still participate.

You need a fanatic element for economic reasons. There is a lot of money in this society, but not for organizing. If you can get money for organizing, which is like one in a million people, even then it is limited.

Fanaticism comes in when full-time organizing requires doing without economic security. It often involves collective living to save money. Many people can't keep this up indefinitely. Often, they get channeled into areas where they can get foundation money, so they aren't doing what they really should be doing.

Fanaticism can bring other problems. It was bad, for example, during the ERAP period of SDS when people, including me, were guilt-tripping anybody who wasn't willing to drop out of what they were doing and organize. That was an immature way of dealing with a real problem.

## Unity

Often our politics reversed the Chinese idea of uniting the many against the few. In our case, "the few" was us.

---

[123] The Midwest Academy, an organizing school based in Chicago, was founded in 1973 by Heather Booth (1945–), an early SNCC volunteer and participant in Freedom Summer.

Often this was because we could not stand our allies. They were always to the right of us. Often, they could not stand us either because we were the new kids on the block upsetting the apple cart. We managed to isolate ourselves as a left-wing force and stayed out of coalitions because they seemed too bureaucratic or too top-down, too deadening, cutting off the radical edge. Or the notion of unity was false and militaristic. We had a revolutionary siege mentality. "We don't have time to discuss your particular problem. We know it is important. See us in the twenty-first century. As for me, I'm in the trench."

None of these things were entire fantasies, because guns were blazing, and war was going on. But that kind of unity was not satisfying or lasting. We need to learn how to unite uneven struggles.

We can overcome one psychological obstacle by forgiving each other for our sins. While it is a good practice, it is hard to carry out. Nevertheless, understanding we are all sinners is a key to coalitions and unity.

The old SDS approach of moving by consensus rather than parliamentary or factional rules makes sense. If you have a fifty-five to forty-five split in a meeting, you decide as a group of fifty-five not to go ahead until more of the forty-five are convinced it is all right. If it is eighty to twenty or seventy to thirty, go ahead, so long as there is a way of showing genuine feeling for the twenty or thirty. Postpone decisions if it seems like you can only make them by damaging unity.

Time is a problem. Most countries like ours have one capital in the middle, such as Stockholm or Paris. In this country, we have multiple capitals and nerve centers. SDS wasn't a national organization. We were mainly in the Midwest and East Coast relating to things happening in the South and West.

In California, there are big cultural, logistic, and geographic differences between San Diego and San Francisco. You need time.

We used to say we are going to have a statewide meeting Friday through Sunday. Most people will need to drive, and they get there late Friday and leave early Sunday to get back to work. They only really function from about ten o'clock Friday night to Sunday morning. The working papers, agenda, and resolutions to be delivered on Thursday instead arrived on Friday just before the meeting. The group organizing the conference is determined to get those resolutions through and the people getting there are more likely to be set on sharing experiences and meeting friends. Inevitably, even with a fully democratic process, they are rushed.

There is no solution except not to have those kinds of meetings. You have to say we will have the meeting next year and the working papers will come three months beforehand. Or we will have local and regional meetings before a statewide meeting.

Speaking of foreign models, the Communist Party in Vietnam has a party congress every five years. The western press says it is a totalitarian rubber stamp because there is no dissent. Why? Because it happened before the conference. It went into many cell, local, and regional meetings, causing numerous rewrites of the draft. By the time the big meeting happens it is a chance for everybody to get together and hold hands and clap and sing and stomp and have a good time. They affirm something without feeling they are arriving and have one-and-a-half days to settle the affairs of the world and perhaps provoke a split and destroy their organization. They don't do crazy things like that.

We tended to set up meetings as if there was going to be a battle. If there needs to be one at all, let's fight it out for a few years, achieve a consensus, and then have a meeting to affirm our consensus.

Lastly, and I think this meeting reflects it, we did not deal with the personal undercurrents people were feeling. We overpoliticized everything. I was talking to someone here who recalled old SDS meetings where things like a floor fight or an argument were only on the surface. During this all-too-rational conversation

## What Is the Hardest Question We Face Now?

about whether to hold demonstrations against the war, what was going on was some man felt attracted to a woman, and the threat factor was so great to him, it influenced the way he voted, even though none of this could be admitted.

Is Jeff Shero here?[124] Something I read in the SDS book startled me. There was a meeting where I was supposed to speak about "What is the agency of change," or something, and you were going to debate me. I don't remember the debate exactly, something about the New Guard vs. the Old Guard. The book said this is how Jeff won his "spurs" for Prairie Populism.[125] This is a small example of the infinite number of examples of pain people have been through at this level.

It can't be combatted by just saying, "I know what you are feeling." In our organization, we have an organizer training process going beyond ideology, program, and organizational skills. We also have seventy-two-hour, ten-person encounter sessions where people say who they are, how they got into the movement, what are their biggest personal problems, how they intend to overcome them, and why they are in the organization. Other people are assigned to assume they cannot tell the truth about these things. This forces people a little bit beyond telling all the false stories we tell to make ourselves look good or, more likely, to keep ourselves from being hurt by having to reveal something we hope nobody notices. It is usually something everybody has noticed for several months or years and never told us about.

These are not ominous sessions which are trying to destroy people's character or reshape their personality. Nor are they separate from politics. At the same time, we have people role-play

---

[124] Jeff Shero, now called Jeff Shero Nightbyrd, was SDS Vice President from 1965 to 1966, and was later a Yippie.

[125] See Robbie Lieberman, Prairie Power: *Voices of 1960s Midwestern Student Protest* (Columbia, Missouri: University of Missouri Press, 2004).

door-to-door organizing, press conferences, or things that will put a stress on their ego, performing some task in which they discover they are embarrassed to do it even though they are among friends. Gradually, over time, we start to learn we are usually afraid of our friends knowing what they already know about us, which is liberating. Then they can go into ideology sessions, and then into organizing schools. We've found that if we start with ideology, it opens the old game plan with people expounding on all their little theories and everyone else knowing behind all the talk there is something else at play.[126]

### Spirit

Karmic or religious forces, idealism, whatever words you choose: one problem is that left theory is atheist and materialist.

If a problem for the left is to translate "theories" into society creatively, it must both go through the door of patriotism—which some have not yet done—and the door of religion. I don't mean institutional religion. I mean we need to appreciate how people can be motivated by what amounts to a religion.

The early New Left, the healthiest movements and people in the last fifteen years, believed in morality, had a sense of humor and enough sociability to clasp hands and sing. And then came a time when people believed moral outrage was naïve.

The psychology worked like this. If you are morally outraged, it means you are new to politics and ready to be seduced. Moral outrage was a rung on a ladder which led upward from the heart to the head and then something beyond. If you said, "I am morally outraged that children at this moment are being buried alive in Vietnam," someone who was more sophisticated would call it "guilt-tripping" and "out of touch with reality." To become

---

[126] For a critique of the use of encounter groups by Cesar Chavez in the United Farm Workers union, see Frank Bardacke, *Trampling Out the Vintage: Cesar Chavez and the Two Souls of the United Farm Workers* (Brooklyn, New York: Verso Press, 2012).

## What Is the Hardest Question We Face Now?

a leftist, you had to take a step above raw emotions and into the world of the mind. Then you said, "The war in Vietnam is not a mistake. It is the logical outgrowth of a system of imperialism."

This was the only ladder of opportunity. The desire to be taken seriously by other people required closing off the feelings that were the basis of your involvement. It became impossible to involve other people on that basis. From there it was one step to the isolation of only being able to involve other "serious" political people.

It's good Dave Dellinger is here. Lately I've become, more or less, dedicated to nonviolence. I say "more or less" because I feel as I did fifteen years ago—something is lacking from each ideological stance: socialism, pacifism, and anarchism, to name the three most current when I was young. I am a political person, and a political person should not be entirely satisfied with those ideologies.

For example, I don't believe the Vietnamese have been made more vicious by their use of violence. I don't agree with those who say they would have won their revolution through nonviolence. I believe, for reasons I don't understand, they somehow became more human even though they were engaged in violence.

However, I also feel the healthiest movements in my lifetime have been explicitly nonviolent in the broadest sense of church gatherings and people singing "We Shall Overcome," as well as in the tactical sense of people not letting themselves be drawn into direct violence. These include the Southern Christian Leadership Council, early SNCC, the draft resistance to some extent, and above all the United Farm Workers, the only movement of the last fifteen years that has continued.

All these movements had certain things in common, like a charismatic leader and a concrete issue, such as Jim Crow at the lunch counter or lack of a union to protect them in the fields.[127]

---

[127] "Jim Crow," a term which may have come from a minstrel show character, refers to white supremacist state laws passed after Reconstruction creating different rules for blacks and whites.

The thing they had in common is nonviolence and its discipline to see the system, not other people, as your enemy. You need to see the people you are against as potential friends, or at least not your future enemy. It forces you to be creative because you rely on the positive side of people. And it has a material power. When people are facing a police attack and are about to be beaten, they sing or hold on to each other. They conquer fear they could not possibly deal with without that spirit.

Nonviolence counteracts a lot of egotism and manhood problems that would otherwise—and in many cases did—send people off on suicidal confrontations. Nonviolence can create the moral and emotional equivalent of going to war, channeling the psyche in a less destructive direction. It saves lives, leaders, and organizations.

Let me conclude. People don't live by bread alone. The desire for freedom and love motivates them. Connecting self-interest to the liberation of your spirit is something we haven't yet solved. If we had dealt with these problems, it would be the social foundation around which the structure of a political party could form.

I am a devotee, not a critic, of the earliest SDS. We had a winning psychological and political outlook. Much of it, to be sure, was associated with being junior achievers, conditioned to win. To eliminate the junior achiever psychology, though, is not to create a loser mentality which often started to prevail. It is crucial to reconstruct ourselves around the belief that what we want to do is win, rather than existentially enjoy and suffer through failure. A desire to win political power without it being a trip must be a central psychological task for people. Otherwise, you know the answer to Al Haber's other question last night, "What is the point in carrying on?"

I see no point in thinking about dead people or people in jail. They did not sacrifice in order to lose. They gave their lives hoping somebody will make use of their example to carry their ideals into reality. The living have that obligation.

# A Vietnam Peace Movement Chronology
# 1945 – 1975

*The list below is a small fraction of local, national, and international activity protesting and resisting the Vietnam War.*

## 1945–1953 Harry S. Truman, U.S. President

World War II ended when Japan surrendered on September 2, 1945. Within hours, Ho Chi Minh declared Vietnamese independence. Within days, President Truman ordered U.S. troopships to begin carrying U.S.-armed French troops to recolonize Vietnam. Within weeks, the first American protest of the Vietnam War occurred on November 2, 1945, when crew members objected to the use of troopships to "subjugate the native people of Vietnam."

The United States supplied the French with money and arms throughout the war. In 1951, the Truman Administration delivered to French forces in Vietnam the first shipment of napalm, a jellied petroleum weapon that melts human skin and suffocates its victims.

## 1953–1961 Dwight D. Eisenhower, U.S. President

In 1954, the French army surrendered to Viet Minh forces at Dien Bien Phu. The Geneva Agreement which followed temporarily divided Vietnam into North and South along the seventeenth parallel, pending nationwide free elections in 1956. North Vietnam was led by Ho Chi Minh, and South Vietnam's president was Ngo Dinh Diem.

It was common knowledge Ho Chi Minh would easily win a free election. With Eisenhower's backing, Diem announced in 1955 there would be no nationwide election. This decision caused the Vietnam War.

During 1960, Eisenhower's last year in office, three organizations came into being: The National Liberation Front of South Vietnam (NLF), Students for a Democratic Society (SDS), and the Student Nonviolent Coordinating Committee (SNCC). The next year brought the new Women Strike for Peace.

### 1961–1963 John F. Kennedy, U.S. President

With the Diem regime near collapse, Kennedy ordered a twenty-fold increase in U.S. personnel, from eight hundred to 16,300, the beginning of U.S. combat air missions, indiscriminate bombing in the countryside, spraying of Agent Orange defoliant, dropping napalm bombs on villages, and the building of concentration camps.

Despite this, the Saigon regime was still too weak to prevail against the NLF in the countryside and the Third Force in the cities, especially the Buddhists. On June 11, 1963 Buddhist monk Thich Quang Duc immolated himself to protest the Diem regime, shocking the world. Two weeks later, fifteen thousand Buddhists demonstrated for peace in Saigon. Diem declared martial law and arrested fourteen hundred Buddhists.

After Ngo Dinh Diem began to make peace overtures to North Vietnam, a U.S.-backed military coup overthrew him. They assassinated him the next day, November 2, 1963.

**War Resisters League** protests the war at the U.S. Mission to the United Nations in New York. (September 21, 1963)

**Three hundred protesters** picket a speech by Saigon's Madame Ngo Dinh Nhu at the Waldorf-Astoria in New York City. (October 9, 1963)

## 1963–1969 Lyndon B. Johnson, U.S. President

1964 – 23,000 U.S. forces in Vietnam

**Malcolm X denounces U.S. policy** in Vietnam, predicts U.S. defeat. (April 3)

**First draft card burning**, by twelve men in New York. (May 12)

**President Johnson announces fictitious attacks** by North Vietnam on U.S. Navy ships in the Gulf of Tonkin. Congress quickly gives Johnson a blank check for escalation, 416-0 in the House, 82-2 in the Senate. (August 1964)

**Weekly Times Square Vigil Against the War** begins in New York City and continues until 1973. (October)

**Vietnamese Buddhist leaders begin a hunger strike** to protest the war. (December 12)

**First coordinated peace protests** across the country. (December 19)

1965 – 184,300 U.S. forces in Vietnam

**Alice Herz, founder of Detroit Women Strike for Peace, immolates herself.** (March 16)

**2,500 students attend the first Teach-In** on the Vietnam War at the University of Michigan. (March 24-25) Thirty-five other campuses follow.

**SDS holds first national antiwar demonstration** in Washington DC with twenty-five thousand attending. (April 17)

**Women Strike for Peace members** Mary Clarke and Lorraine Gordon visit Hanoi for meetings with Vietnamese women and Prime Minister Pham Van Dong. (May)

**UC Berkeley teach-in** reaches thirty thousand students with a broadcast to 122 colleges. (May 21-22)

**McComb, Mississippi civil rights leaders** declare, "Negro boys should not honor the draft [and] mothers should encourage their sons not to go." (July)

**Assembly of Unrepresented People** peace sit-in at the White House, 356 arrested. (August 9)

**Rev. Martin Luther King, Jr.'s first statement** against the Vietnam War. (August 12)

**Clergy and Laity Concerned About Vietnam** founded. (October)

**Eighty cities worldwide** hold first International Days of Protest against the Vietnam War. (October 15-16)

**Twenty-five thousand people join the antiwar demonstration** in Washington DC, organized by the Committee for a Sane Nuclear Policy (SANE). (November)

**Quaker Norman Morrison immolates himself** at the Pentagon. (November 2)

**Celena Jankowski immolates herself,** South Bend, Indiana. (November 9)

**Roger Allen LaPorte immolates himself,** New York City. (November 10)

**Thirty thousand at a rally in Washington DC** hear Coretta Scott King, Dr. Benjamin Spock, and Carl Oglesby. (November 27)

**Des Moines, Iowa, high school** suspends students for wearing black armbands. The Supreme Court later rules for the students in the *Tinker v. Des Moines* case. (December 16-17)

**Tom Hayden, Herbert Aptheker, and Staughton Lynd** travel to Hanoi to meet Vietnamese leaders and return released POWs to the United States. (December 28)

1966 – 385,300 U.S. forces in Vietnam

**SNCC opposes the Vietnam War.** (January 6)

**Julian Bond expelled** from the Georgia legislature for opposing the Vietnam War. (January 10)

**Fulbright Senate Hearings televised live** nationwide, question Administration officials about the Vietnam War. (January 28-February 18)

**2,500 from Women Strike for Peace** March on the Pentagon. (February)

**Muhammad Ali refuses to be drafted**: "Take me to jail." (April 23)

**In the Gallup Poll, forty-three percent** of those with an opinion say it was a "mistake sending troops to fight in Vietnam," up from twenty-nine percent in March. (May)

**Bertrand Russell International War Crimes Tribunal** hearings begin in Sweden. (May 2)

**In Aviso, California,** four women, two from Women Strike for Peace, two from the Women's International League for Peace and Freedom (WILPF), stand in front of a forklift moving napalm bombs to a loading platform, bringing operations to a halt. (May 25)

**Fort Hood Three announce** they will refuse orders to go to Vietnam. (June 30)

**National campaign begins against Dow** Chemical for producing napalm weapons. (August 8)

**SDS challenges Defense Secretary** Robert McNamara to debate the war at his Harvard speaking appearance. McNamara declines. (November 7)

**GOP picks up three Senate seats** in midterm elections, two of whom ran against the war. (November 8)

**The U.S. Supreme Court votes 9-0** to reinstate Julian Bond to the Georgia legislature. (December 5)

## A VIETNAM PEACE MOVEMENT CHRONOLOGY

**1967** – 485,600 U.S. forces in Vietnam

**The Resistance organization founded.** (March)

**Martin Luther King speech against the war** to three thousand people at Riverside Church in New York City. (April 4)

**Spring Mobilization demonstrations**: Four hundred thousand in New York, one hundred thousand in San Francisco. 158 draft cards burned in New York. (April 15)

**Vietnam Summer**: Seven hundred local projects nationwide, with twenty-six thousand volunteers and five hundred paid staff, canvassing door-to-door, counseling on draft resistance, holding teach-ins, conducting local demonstrations, and disseminating antiwar literature. (June-August)

**Vietnam Veterans Against the War** (VVAW) founded. (June 1)

**Ten thousand demonstrators clash** with riot police outside a $1,000-a-plate fundraiser for President Johnson in Los Angeles. Fifty-one arrested. (June 23)

*The Bond*, **the first antiwar GI newspaper,** established. There would soon be 768 such newspapers. (June 23)

**Florence Bennett immolates herself** in Los Angeles, California (October 15)

**1,400 draft cards burned** nationwide in one day. (October 16)

**Baltimore Four:** Father Philip Berrigan and others pour blood over military draft records. (October 27)

**Dow Riot at the University of Wisconsin Madison** over the chemical company's napalm production. (October 18)

**One hundred thousand March on the Pentagon,** 683 arrested. Protests across Europe, Japan, Australia. (October 21)

**Erik Thoen immolates himself** in Sunnyvale, California. (December 4)

**Stop the Draft Week,** New York City. 263 arrested at a New York induction center. (December 4-8)

**Peace demonstrations in forty Swedish towns,** violent clashes in Stockholm. (December 20)

## 1968 – 536,100 U.S. forces in Vietnam

**First antiwar GI coffeehouse,** the UFO, opens outside Fort Jackson near Columbia, South Carolina. Coffeehouses spread to bases across the country. (January)

**Tet Offensive** by NLF/North Vietnamese begins throughout South Vietnam, forty-four provinces, five major cities. Within a month it yields the highest U.S. casualties of the war: 543 killed, 2,547 wounded in one week. (January 30)

**Joint Chiefs of Staff (JCS) Chairman** Earle Wheeler asks Johnson for 206,756 more troops for Vietnam. (February 27)

**Antiwar presidential candidate** Eugene McCarthy gets 42% of the New Hampshire primary vote against Johnson. (March 12)

**Robert Kennedy enters the presidential race** as an antiwar candidate. (March 16)

**My Lai Massacre:** U.S. Army unit kills 504 unarmed Vietnamese civilians. (March 16)

**Ten thousand protesters rally at the U.S. Embassy in London.** Two hundred arrested, eighty-six injured. (March 17)

**Ronald Brazee immolates himself** in Syracuse, New York. (March 19)

**President Johnson tells JCS Chairman** Wheeler he won't get more troops. (March 22)

**President Johnson announces** he won't seek reelection, halts the bombing of North Vietnam, calls for peace talks. (March 31)

**Catonsville Nine, led by Father Daniel Berrigan and Philip Berrigan,** burn draft files at a Selective Service office in Maryland. (May 17)

**National Draft Card Turn-In Day:** One thousand cards returned. (April 3)

**Columbia University revolt** begins. Building takeovers. Seven hundred arrested. (April 23)

**Federal court convicts** Dr. Benjamin Spock, Reverend William Sloan Coffin and others of conspiracy to aid draft resisters. (June 10)

**Police riot** against ten thousand antiwar demonstrators at Democratic Convention in Chicago. (August 28)

**Presidio Mutiny sit-down protest** by twenty-seven military prisoners in San Francisco. (October 14)

**Eight hundred thousand across Japan protest** the U.S. war in Vietnam. (October 21)

### 1969–1974 Richard M. Nixon, U.S. President

1969 – 475,200 U.S. forces in Vietnam

**Antiwar protests at inaugural** for Richard Nixon. (January 20)

**Chicago Eight indicted** for conspiracy to riot at the Democratic convention. (March 20)

**Canada says it won't ask immigrant applicants** about military status. (May 22)

**Brown University gives Henry Kissinger an honorary degree.** Two-thirds of graduating class turn their backs to him. (June)

**David Harris arrested for refusing draft**, serves a fifteen-month prison term. (July 16)

**More than one million people** participate in the Vietnam Moratorium. (October 15)

**President Richard Nixon cancels Operation Duck Hook** for fear of the reaction by the American public and the peace movement. It was to include mining of Haiphong harbor, saturation bombing of Hanoi, bombing dikes, air strikes against passes and bridges on the Chinese border, and the possible nuclear bombing of Hanoi. (November 1)

**Forty-hour March Against Death**: Fifty thousand people read names of war dead at the White House. (November 13)

**250,000 protest war in Washington DC and two hundred thousand in San Francisco.** November 15)

1970 – 334,600 U.S. forces in Vietnam

**Mutiny on the U.S. merchant ship** *Columbia Eagle* transporting napalm bombs. (March 14)

**Nationwide actions including blocking Manhattan induction center.** 182 arrested. (March 19)

**National student strike called** to protest U.S. invasion of Cambodia. 536 campuses shut down. (May 2)

**National Guardsmen kill four students** at Kent State University, Ohio. (May 4)

**One hundred thousand protest in Washington, DC**, 413 arrested. One hundred fifty thousand protest in San Francisco. One hundred thousand people demonstrate for peace in Melbourne and every Australian state capital. (May 8)

**George Winne self-immolation,** La Jolla, California. (May 11)

**Police kill two students** at Jackson State University in Mississippi. (May 14)

**President Nixon attends Reverend Billy Graham's evangelistic crusade** in Knoxville, Tennessee. Three hundred people carry signs saying, "Thou Shalt Not Kill." Forty-nine are arrested. (May 28)

**Thirty thousand-person Chicano Moratorium** against the war, Los Angeles. Police arrest 150 and kill four, including *Los Angeles Times* reporter Ruben Salazar. (August 29)

1971 – 156,800 U.S. forces in Vietnam

**Tonkin Gulf Resolution** of 1964 repealed. (January 12)

**Cooper-Church Amendment** prohibiting reintroducing U.S. ground forces into Cambodia becomes law. (January 5)

**VVAW Winter Soldier Investigation** of U.S. war crimes. (January 31-February 2)

**Free the Army (FTA) tour of U.S. bases** begins, led by Jane Fonda and Donald Sutherland. Twenty-one shows, with sixty-four thousand GIs attending. (February 16)

**VVAW Operation Dewey Canyon III** in Washington DC, returning medals to the U.S. Capitol steps. (April 19-23)

**175,000 march in Washington DC,** another 150,000 in San Francisco. (April 24)

**Mayday civil disobedience in Washington DC.** Ten thousand troops, including four thousand from the Army's 82nd Airborne Division, and five thousand police. 12,614 people arrested, the largest mass arrest in U.S. history. (May 1-3)

*New York Times* **begins publishing the Pentagon Papers** leaked by Daniel Ellsberg. (June 13)

**Evict Nixon protest** in Washington DC. Three hundred arrested. (October 26)

**VVAW occupies the Statue of Liberty.** (December 26)

**Justice Department indicts** Daniel Ellsberg and Anthony Russo for espionage. (December 29)

1972 – 24,200 U.S. forces in Vietnam

**Washington DC sit-down protest.** 240 arrests. (April 15)

**Anti-ROTC protest** at the University of Maryland. Eight hundred National Guardsmen enter the campus. (April 17)

**Protests across the country erupt** against President Nixon's mining of the port of Haiphong, North Vietnam. Mass marches, silent vigils, traffic-blocking sit-ins. Most prominent were demonstrations in New York City, Syracuse, Rochester, New Paltz, and Binghamton, New York; Albuquerque, New Mexico; Boulder, Colorado; Oxford, Ohio; Chicago and Champaign-Urbana, Illinois; Palo Alto, San Jose, Santa Barbara, and Berkeley, California; Minneapolis, Minnesota; Madison, Wisconsin; Gainesville, Florida; New Haven and Westport, Connecticut; St. Louis, Missouri; New Brunswick, New Jersey; Baltimore, Maryland, and Amherst, Massachusetts. (May)

**People's Blockade at the Pentagon.** 224 arrests. (May 22)

**People's Blockade at Leonardo**, New Jersey Naval Depot. 36 arrested. (June 10)

**Ring Around Congress,** led by singer Joan Baez. Two thousand women and children encircle the Capitol in a peace protest. (June 22)

**Jane Fonda tours North Vietnam** to bring attention to the U.S. bombing of the dikes, an international war crime. (August)

**Three thousand protest** at the Republican Convention in Miami, led by Vietnam veteran Ron Kovic. (August 21-23)

**Indochina Peace Campaign national speaking tour** begins, reaching ninety-five cities with four speeches a day. (September 3)

## 1973 – 50 U.S. forces in Vietnam

**Coalition to Stop Funding the War** founded in Washington DC, with thirty-three organizations cooperating on a common legislative strategy. (January)

**VVAW march, 85,000 people**, from Arlington Cemetery to Lincoln Memorial. (January 21)

**Secretary of Defense Melvin Laird announces** the end of the military draft. (January 22)

**The Agreement on Ending the War** and Restoring Peace in Vietnam is signed in Paris by all parties to the war. (January 27)

**U.S. POWs released**, return to the United States. (February 12-March 29)

**Last U.S. combat troops leave South Vietnam.** (March 29)

**South Vietnamese President Nguyen Van Thieu visits** Richard Nixon at San Clemente, California. IPC leads protest. (April 2-7)

**Charges against Ellsberg and Russo dismissed** due to Nixon Administration misconduct in Pentagon Papers case. (May 11)

**The Case-Church Amendment becomes law**, prohibiting further U.S. military activity in Indochina without prior Congressional approval. (July 1)

**IPC national speaking tour** with Jane Fonda, Tom Hayden, Jean-Pierre Debris, Bob Chenoweth, Holly Near, Jeff Langley. (September 16-October 15)

**International Days of Concern and Action** for South Vietnamese Political Prisoners: Boston, Chicago, El Segundo, Berkeley, San Francisco, Palo Alto (September 17-23)

**Actions in Seattle, Eugene, Portland, and San Francisco** demand U.S. end aid to Saigon. (November 16-17)

### 1974

**VVAW occupies Saigon office** in Washington DC, six arrested. (January 25)

**White House sit-in**, sixty-two arrests. (March)

**Community for Creative Nonviolence members pour blood on files** at the Vietnam Overseas Procurement Office, Washington DC, four arrested. (April 12)

Ten thousand attend IPC Rally at Kent State, Ohio, hear Dean Kahler, Daniel Ellsberg, Julian Bond, Jane Fonda, Holly Near, Ron Kovic. (May 4)

American Friends Service Committee tiger cage vigil and fast begins at the U.S. Capitol. (July)

## 1974–1977 Gerald R. Ford, U.S. President

### 1975

Tiger Cage replica at United Nations in New York. Twelve arrests. (October 1)

Draft resister David Harris, seven other Americans in IPC protest at U.S. Embassy in Saigon, arrested, deported. (January 24)

Five thousand people at Assembly to Save the Peace Agreement in Washington DC. (January 25-27)

VVAW seizes Saigon Consulate in San Francisco. (January 27)

Sit-downs during White House tours. Sixty-two arrests. (March)

President Ford and Henry Kissinger meet with Senators to ask for more war funding to counter the Spring Offensive and Uprising. NY Senator Jacob Javits said, "I will give you large sums for evacuation, but not one nickel for military aid to Thieu." (April 14)

U.S. war in Vietnam ends. Vietnam is reunified. (April 30)

## 1962–1975

# The Human Cost of the U.S. war in Vietnam

| | |
|---|---|
| Vietnamese dead | 3,800,000 |
| U.S. military dead | 58,220 |
| Vietnamese refugees | 10,000,000 |
| South Vietnamese orphans | 300,000 |

*The deaths and casualty tolls continue to rise. For example, since the end of the war, more than forty thousand Vietnamese have been killed by unexploded ordnance.*

# INDEX

In the following index, "n" refers to a footnote. "84n6" means footnote 6 on page 84. "Passim" refers to scattered references within a given range of pages, as in "79–102 passim."

Abplanalp, Robert, 174
Acheson, Dean, 160, 161
Action Faction, 117
AFL-CIO, 11n10, 11n12
Agent Orange, 214
Agnew, Spiro, 123, 164, 173n111
Albuquerque, New Mexico, 129, 223
Algeria, 47n37
Ali, Muhammad, 217
All-African People's Revolutionary Party, 48n38
Alpert, Richard (Ram Dass), 68n46
alternative institutions, 74, 75, 185, 200
American Federation of Labor, 11n10
American Federation of State, County, and Municipal Employees (AFSCME), 108n61
American Friends Service Committee (AFSC), 142, 143n87, 146n90, 225

Americans Committed to World Responsibility, 3
Americans for Democratic Action, 13
American University, Washington, DC, 172
*America's Social Arsonist: Fred Ross and Grassroots Organizing in the Twentieth Century* (Thompson), 181n115
Amin, Jamil Abdullah al-, 112n66
amnesty, 132, 177
Anderson, Jack, 128n80
*Anguish of Change, The* (Harris), 147n91
Ann Arbor, Michigan, 3–4, 6, 38n28, 154, 195. *See also* University of Michigan
anti-communism, 11n12, 13n13, 40, 82, 85, 104, 148, 150, 155, 163
anti-imperialism, 22n20, 98, 132, 141, 147–149
antiwar movement. *See* peace movement
Aptheker, Herbert, 35, 216

# INDEX

Assembly of Unrepresented People, 216
Assembly to Save the Peace Agreement, 137n84, 225
Atlanta, Georgia, 5, 35
Atlantic City, New Jersey. *See* Democratic National Convention: Atlantic City 1964
Avakian, Bob, 121
Aviso, California, 217

Baltimore Four, 218
Bank of America. *See under* Santa Barbara
Bardacke, Frank, 210n126
*Barron's Weekly*, 115
Barry, Marion, 16n15
Barton, Jane and David, 146
Beat Generation, 1, 7, 13
beatnik, 14, 30
be-in, 68
Bennett, Florence, 218
Berkeley, California, 20, 22, 28, 70, 109, 115, 215, 216, 223; Hayden in 1960, 1–2, 5; Hayden in 1969, 30, 61, 69, 71, 73–74, 122, 125; See also Free Speech Movement
Berrigan, Daniel, 42, 220
Berrigan, Philip, 218, 220

betel nut, 184
Binh, Nguyen Thi, 110
Birmingham, Alabama, 64, 98
Black Hills, South Dakota, 83, 84
Black Panther Party for Self-Defense, 6, 46, 47, 48n38, 75, 111, 112; arrests and trials, 123, 164, 190
Black Power, 23
*Black Skin, White Masks* (Fanon), 47n37
Bond, Julian, 16, 107, 217, 218, 225
*Bond, The*, GI newspaper, 218
Booth, Heather, 206n123
Booth, Paul, 108
Boston, Massachusetts, 140, 199, 224
Boudin, Kathy, 63
Bradley, Omar, 160
Bratislava, Czechoslovakia (now Slovakia), 38, 110
Brazee, Ronald, 219
Brewster, Kingman, 123
Brown, Edmund G., Jr., "Jerry", 198
Brown, Edmund G., "Pat", 51n39
Brown, H. Rap (Jamil Abdullah al-Amin), 112

INDEX

Brown, Sam, 157
Brown University, 220
Buddhists, 43, 156n96, 214
Bundy, McGeorge, 106, 160, 161, 171n108
Bundy, William, 160
Burchett, Wilfred, 36, 8n7
Buzhardt, Fred, 171

cadre organization, 25, 37, 73, 103, 149
California Campaign for Economic Democracy. *See* CED
Calvert, Greg, 108
Cambodia, 140, 144, 145; Kissinger role in, 166, 167; Congressional response to, 140, 167, 222, public response to, 68, 123–125, 127, 221
Carmichael, Stokely (Kwame Ture), 47, 48, 110, 111, 112
Canada, 220
Carter, Jimmy, 198, 202
Carver, George, 161
Case-Church Amendment, 224
Castro, Fidel, 111, 202
Catholic resistance, 122
Catonsville Nine, 43n31, 220

CED (California Campaign for Economic Democracy), 137n84, 179, 184n116, 205
*Cesar Chavez: Autobiography of La Causa* (Levy), 187
Chaney, James, 21
Chavez, Cesar, 179–181, 187, 202, 205, 210n126
Chenoweth, Bob, 141, 224
Chicago Eight, 38n28, 43n31, 70n47, 122, 123, 124n76, 164, 220
Chicago, Illinois, 38, 223, 206n123. *See also under* Democratic National Convention; Chicago Eight
Chicano movement, 2; Moratorium, 222. *See also* farmworkers; United Farm Workers
Chi Hoa prison, Saigon, South Vietnam, 141n85
China, 36, 39, 45, 121n72, 150, 152; and Soviet Union, 130, 145, 149, 164, 165; Nixon trip, 128, 172, 173, 175. *See also* détente
Chomsky, Noam, 99n55, 171n108

231

## INDEX

*Choosing War: The Lost Chance for Peace and the Escalation of War in Vietnam* (Logevall), 101n55

CIA: and National Student Association, 6–11, 156–157; and Vietnam policy, 43, 156–161

CIO (Congress of Industrial Organizations), 11

civil rights movement, 3–4, 7–8, 12–21 passim, 30, 36, 43n31, 46n34, 47, 53, 57, 62, 66n45, 85, 96–100, 108, 154, 156, 180, 188, 216. *See also* freedom rides, Freedom Summer, Mississippi

Civil War, 152

Clark, Joseph, 10

Clark, Ramsey, 122

Clergy and Laity Concerned about Vietnam, 216

Cleveland, Ohio, 63, 140

Clifford, Clark: 1968 election, 116; 1972 election, 173; and Pentagon Papers, 168–169; as Secretary of Defense, 158–162; and Watergate, 164, 168, 169, 176

Coalition to Stop Funding the War, 142, 223

Coffin, William Sloan, 220

Cold War, 39, 42, 96–97, 148; Cuban missile crisis, 18; establishment divisions, 116, 150, 154, 158, 170, 172, 177; old left and, 10, 13; *Port Huron Statement* and, 85; Robert Kennedy views, 50

*Columbia Eagle* merchant ship, 221

Columbia University, 46, 59, 61, 115–117, 127, 220

Columbia, South Carolina, 219

Committee to Re-elect the President, 128n79

communism: 35, 40, 85, 148, 150; and New Left, 8, 13, 22n20, 37; and Vietnam, 41, 82. *See also* anti-communism, Communist Party USA, Eurocommunism

Communist Party USA, 61n43, 101–103, 133, 135, 197, 204, 208

community control of police, 29, 71

Community for Creative Nonviolence, 225

Community Service Organization, 181

## INDEX

Congress for Cultural Freedom, 11
Congress of Racial Equality (CORE), 21n18
Connally, John, 173
Cooper-Church amendment, 222
cooptation, 23, 61, 62, 70, 92, 116, 199
cowboys, 152
Cuba, 36, 53, 54, 96, 128; Bay of Pigs invasion, 172n110; Fidel Castro and Stokely Carmichael, 110–111; Hayden visit to, 58–59; missile crisis, 18–19. *See also* Guevara, Ernesto
Curley, James, 199
Custer, South Dakota, 83
Czechoslovakia, 38n29, 46, 110

Daley, Richard, 90
Davis, Mike, 105n58
Davis, Rennie, 38, 49, 58, 71, 110; Chicago 1968, 60, 61, 118, 119, 202
decent interval, 144n88, 165
Dean, Arthur, 160
Debray, Regis, 45, 117
Debris, Jean-Pierre, 141, 224
Debs, Eugene, 198

Dellinger, David, 42–43, 58, 71, 100, 102, 211
democracy, 91, 154, 158, 159, 168, 176; economic, 137n84, 179, 199, 205; and IPC, 140, 143; Oglesby speech, 105; participatory, 68, 69; revolution for, 97; and SDS, 69
Democratic National Convention: Los Angeles 1960, 1–4; Atlantic City 1964, 12, 21, 22, 26; Chicago 1968, 46-71 passim, 89, 91, 102, 107, 115–123 passim, 127, 129, 130, 157; Miami Beach 1972, 29. *See also* Chicago Eight
Democratic Party, 11, 12, 16, 48, 60, 77, 98: prospects for, 90–91, 130, 131, 197, 204, 205; and Vietnam, 99, 116, 118, 165, 176; *See also* Democratic National Convention, realignment
Democratic Republic of Vietnam (DRV). *See* North Vietnam
Democratic Socialists of America, 10n9
Des Moines, Iowa, 216

# INDEX

Department of Defense: Joint Chiefs of Staff, 156–159, 160, 161, 174, 219

DePuy, William, 161, 171n108

détente, 130, 150, 164, 165, 173, 175

Detroit, Michigan, 110, 137, 138, 215

Dewey Canyon III, 125n77, 222

Diem, Ngo Dinh, 7, 156n96, 170, 213, 214

Dien Bien Phu, Dien Bien Province, Vietnam, 88, 213

dikes, 90, 166n103, 221, 223

Dillon, C. Douglas, 160

Doar, John, 18

Dobrynin, Anatoly, 164

Domhoff, G. William, 151n93

Dong Ha River, Quang Tri Province, Vietnam, 81

doves, 32–34, 45, 76, 152

Dow Chemical, 120, 217, 218. *See also* napalm

draft, 28, 60, 164, 224; resistance to, 30, 39, 73, 106–112, 114, 130, 156, 162, 211, 215–220, 225

Dump Johnson, 107, 156, 157

Duong Van Minh. *See* Minh, Duong Van

Dutschke, Rudi, 59, 115

Dutton, Fred, 50, 53

Eagleton, Thomas, 130

Easter Offensive, 133, 135

Economic Research and Action Project. *See* ERAP

Ehrlichman, John, 166

Eisenhower, Dwight, 105, 163n102, 172n109, 213, 214

elections, 50, 85, 213, 214; in 1964, 107; in 1966, 217; in 1968, 51, 116, 120, 162, 167, 219; in 1972, 1, 84, 86, 87, 91, 128, 130, 136, 137, 139, 146; in 1976, 144, 179. *See also* Democratic National Convention, Republican National Convention

Ellsberg, Daniel, 18, 225; and Detroit riots, 110; presidential decision-making views, 152; Pentagon Papers release, 44, 108n60, 155, 168–171, 172n110, 222; trial, 107n60, 171, 222, 224; transformation, 131; *See also* Pentagon Papers

El Segundo, California, 224

empire, 83, 112, 138, 146; and civil rights, 95–96; Che Guevara speech, 45n33, 109; imperialism, 47, 101, 103, 123, 138, 143, 145, 147, 150, 156, 209; and liberals, 102–104; Carl Oglesby speech, 102–104; and populism, 145–148. *See also* anti-imperialism

ERAP, 38n29, 206. *See also* Newark

establishment, 2, 65, 66, 74, 147, 152; liberal wing, 8, 12, 14, 20, 36, 112, 155; McGovern role in, 83; Robert Kennedy, Martin Luther King role in, 51; choosing New Left leaders, 68; reaction to New Left, 107; technocrats and, 168; divisions within, 121, 129, 133, 154, 163, 164, 167, 169, 172, 173, 174; prospects, 90, 171, 174, 175, 196. *See also* power elite, pluralism

Eurocommunism, 202

Falk, Richard, 170n108
fanaticism, 165, 204
Fanon, Frantz, 47
farmworkers, 2, 5, 24, 178, 179, 184-187, 190, 202, 203. *See also* United Farm Workers, Chavez, Cesar
fascism, 11, 152, 174, 193
FBI, 16, 64, 65, 111, 162
fear, 141, 190, 210
Federal Correctional Institution, Long Beach, California. *See* Terminal Island
final uprising, 143
Findley, Tim, 1
Finney, Tom, 156
Fischer, Louis, 40n30
Flacks, Richard, 1–91 passim
Flint, Michigan, 11
focal point, 77, 94, 96, 138, 141, 142
Fonda, Jane: and Clark Clifford, 156; FTA tour by, 134, 220; and Indochina Peace Campaign (IPC), 1, 79, 137, 221, 222; transformation, 79, 129; visit to North Vietnam, 221
Ford Foundation, 33, 158
Ford, Gerald, 142, 151, 161n102, 171n111, 175, 223
Ford Motor Company, 152
foreign models, 201, 202, 206
Fort Hood Three, 215
*Fortune* magazine, 78, 113

235

# INDEX

Foxborough, Massachusetts, 80n52
France, 43, 49, 61; student–worker uprising, 45, 57. See also Paris, Mendes–France, Pierre
Freedom Farms Cooperative, 26n23
freedom rides, 5n3, 47n38
Freedom Summer, 16n15, 204n123
Free Speech Movement, 20, 113n69
Free The Army. See FTA
Froines, John, 122
FTA tour, 134n83, 220
Fulbright, J. William, 215
Fullerton, California, 143n89
*Furtive War, The* (Burchett), 8n7

Galbraith, John Kenneth, 170n108
Gallup poll, 215
Gelb, Leslie, 153, 157, 166
Geneen, Harold, 126n80
Geneva Agreement, 211
Germany, Nazi, 57, 61, 168
Gide, Andre, 40n30
Ginsberg, Allen, 13n14
Glenn, John, 50n39
Gold, Ted, 61n44

Goldberg, Arthur, 103
Goldwater, Barry, 14, 21
Goodman, Andrew, 20–21
Gorman, Paul, 169n108
Graham, Billy, 219
Great Depression, 149
Green Berets, 7
Green movement, 57n42
*Greening of America, The* (Reich), 74n48
Greensboro, North Carolina, 5n3
Gruening, Ernest, 37, 169n108
Guatemala, 90, 170n110
Guevara, Ernesto "Che", 45, 109, 115
Guinea, Republic of, 47n38
Gulf of Tonkin incident, 19n17, 37n27, 213, 220

Haber, Al, 4, 6n6, 9–12, 193, 210
Habib, Philip, 159
Haig, Alexander, 160, 169n108
Haiphong, Vietnam, 79, 127–129, 163, 171, 219, 221
Haldeman, Bob, 164
Hall, George, 158
Halperin, Mort, 153, 166

## INDEX

Hamer, Fannie Lou, 26. See also Democratic National Convention: Atlantic City 1964

Hanoi. *See* North Vietnam.

Harriman, Averell, 41, 42, 155, 158, 162, 164

Harrington, Michael, 10, 13

Harris, David, 218, 223

Harris, Louis, 145

Harvard University, 16, 153, 165, 215

Hayden, Tom. *See* University of Michigan; SDS; Mississippi; Newark; North Vietnam; New Left; Democratic National Convention: Chicago 1968; Berkeley; Indochina Information Project; IPC; CED

Hawaii, 143n89

hawks, 32, 33, 74, 97n55, 150, 156

Hayakawa, S.I., 177

Heinl, Robert, 166n104

Helms, Richard, 158

Helsinki World Youth Festival, 8

Herz, Alice, 213

Hiss, Alger, 169

Hoffman, Abbie, 68, 69

Hoffman, Anita, 68n47

Hoffman, Julius, 87

Hoover, J. Edgar, 64

House Un-American Activities Committee. *See* HUAC

HUAC (House Un-American Activities Committee), 5, 8

Huggins, Ericka, 121

Hughes, Richard, 32, 33, 34

Humphrey, Hubert, 4n2, 11–13, 21, 22, 85, 90, 116, 167

Hunt, Howard, 170

*I.F. Stone's Weekly*, 19n17

imperialism. *See* empire

Indochina, 84–87, 90, 125, 131, 138–142, 144–147.

Indochina Information Project (IIP), 134

Indochina Mobile Education Project, 140n86

Indochina Peace Campaign. *See* IPC

Indochina Resource Center, 140, 144

Indonesia, 143n89

induction centers, 107, 217, 219

IPC (Indochina Peace Campaign), 1, 93, 107n63, 130–142, 159n101, 222, 223

International Days of Concern and Action for South

237

# INDEX

Vietnamese Political Prisoners, 222
International Days of Protest, 214
International Student Travel, 8
ITT (International Telephone and Telegraph Corporation), 126n80
IWW (Industrial Workers of the World), 196n120

Jackson State University, Jackson, Mississippi, 123, 219
*Jacobin* magazine, 145n92
Jäger, Anton, 145n92
Jankowski, Celena, 214
Japan, 5, 41, 163, 211, 216, 218
Javits, Jacob, 223
Jim Crow, 96, 209
John Birch Society, 170
Johnson, Lyndon, 44, 96n54, 104n59, 120n74, 152, 153; 171n111; 1964 election, 11n12, 21, 83; 1968 election, 48, 49, 58; Dump Johnson, 105, 112, 114, 118, 154–157, 163, 170, 173; Vietnam War, 35, 36, 79, 97, 151, 161n102, 169n108, 213, 216, 217; Wise Men, 157–161
Justice Department, 52n40, 120n74, 126n80; and civil rights, 16, 18; and Pentagon Papers, 220. *See also* FBI

Kahler, Dean, 223
Katzenbach, Nicholas, 158
Kennedy, Edward, 51, 157
Kennedy, John, 18, 52, 98, 99, 51n39, 53n40, 98n54; 1960 election, 3–7, 85, 172; assassination of, 15, 85; and civil rights, 16, 18; Vietnam, 35, 99n55, 105, 154, 160, 163, 214
Kennedy, Robert, 18, 49–55, 99n55, 114, 159, 219; assassination of, 4, 62, 85
Kent State University, Kent, Ohio, 125, 221, 225
Kerouac, Jack, 13n14
Khanh, Nguyen, 38n29
King, Coretta Scott, 216
King, Martin Luther, Jr., 3, 51, 107, 111, 188, 216; assassination of, 59, 62; Riverside Church speech, 107, 218
Kissinger, Henry, 76, 153, 155, 160, 162; Cambodia crisis, 166, 167, 172, 220, 225; China-Soviet

238

Union, 164, 165, 173, 174; Vietnam Peace Agreement, 130, 131; Watergate, 175. *See also* decent interval

Klonsky, Michael, 119, 121

Knoxville, Tennessee, 221

Koestler, Arthur, 40n30

Korean War, 11, 36n26, 39, 51n39, 154n94, 160, 161

Kovic, Ron, 223, 225

Krassner, Paul, 70n47

Kresge, S.S., 5

Ku Klux Klan, 21n18

Kurshan, Nancy, 70n47

Kurtz, Carol, 109

Ky, Nguyen Cao, 157

Laird, Melvin, 224

Lake Arrowhead, California, 95

LaPorte, Roger Allen, 216

Latin American Organization of Solidarity. *See* OLAS

Lau, Ha Van, 110n64

leaders, 24, 26, 44, 71, 137, 180, 190, 201–203, 212; in European Communist parties, 204; and old left, 13, 78; picked by media, 70; in SDS, 49, 60, 61, 71, 72, 73, 100, 115, 117, 126; and repression, 188, 190

League for Industrial Democracy, 10, 12

left. *See* old left; New Left

Lenin, V.I., 10, 115, 119n70

Leonardo, New Jersey, Naval Depot, 223

Levy, Jacques, 187

Lewis, John, 16n15

*Liberation* magazine, 43n31, 71

Liddy, G. Gordon, 128

Lieberman, Robbie, 209n125

Lin Piao (Lin Biao), 47, 144

Livermore, California, 2

Lodge, Henry Cabot, 105

Logevall, Frederik, 99n55

London, England, 82n52, 219

Lon Nol, 145

Los Angeles, California: 80, 81, 95, 133, 218. *See also under* Democratic National Convention. *See also Los Angeles Times*

*Los Angeles Times*, 106n60, 222

Lowenstein, Allard, 156–157

Luce, Don, 171n108

Lynd, Staughton, 22n20, 35, 100, 102, 216

Lyons, Mack, 186

239

MacArthur, Douglas, 154, 172
Madison, Wisconsin, 9, 218, 223
Magruder, Jeb Stuart, 128
Malcolm X, 202, 215
Malloy, Bernard, 171
Mao Tse-tung (Mao Zedong), 63, 121, 149
March Against Death, 221
March on the Pentagon, 70n47, 109–112, 217, 218
Marcus, Marin, 136, 139
Marcuse, Herbert, 77, 80
Martinique, 47n37
Marxism, 37, 97, 119n70
mass organization, 25n22, 121, 197
Mayday, 38n28, 126, 127, 129, 222
McCarthy, Eugene, 4, 8, 49, 50, 167, 219; in Chicago, 61, 116–119; Hayden view of, 51; origin of campaign, 107, 114, 157
McCarthy, Joseph, 5n4
McCloskey, Pete, 168
McCord, James, 128, 175
McDew, Chuck, 16
McGovern, George: 1972 campaign, 4, 8, 9, 45, 52, 83–91, 130, 131; and Vietnam War, 14; IPC strategy, 1, 136, 142
McNamara, Robert, 47, 55, 105, 154, 155, 158, 163, 169, 217
McNaughton, John, 155, 169
McWilliams, Carey, 181
Meany, George, 11
Medical Aid to Indochina, 137, 138
Mendes-France, Pierre, 88, 89
Menras, Andre, 141n85
Mexico City, Mexico, 101n56
Miami Beach, Florida. *See* Democratic National Convention: Miami Beach 1972, Republican National Convention: Miami Beach 1972
*Michigan Daily*, 2, 3, 9
Michigan State University Vietnam Advisory Group, 106n60
Midwest Academy, 206
Mills, C. Wright, 151n93, 160
Mills, Herb, 2
Minh, Duong Van, 156
Minh, Ho Chi, 80, 111, 184, 201, 202, 213, 214
Mississippi, 16, 26, 48n38, 97, 221; as focal point, 98; McComb, 20–21,

216; Mississippi Freedom Democratic Party, 12, 21, 22, 26; Mississippi Sovereignty Commission, 17. *See also* Stokely Carmichael, Fannie Lou Hamer, Charles McDew, Bob Moses.

Moratorium, 58, 68, 104, 120, 157, 164, 166, 175, 220, 222. *See also* Chicano: Moratorium.

Morrison, Norman, 216

Moses, Bob, 16, 18, 22, 36

movements, 10–14, 67–73, 75, 76; electoral work and, 90–92; achievements of, 80–83. *See also* Chicano movement; civil rights movement, Free Speech Movement, leaders, New Left, nonviolence, old left, peace movement; populism, Resistance, student movement, women's movement

Muskie, Edmund, 168, 171

Muste, A.J., 100, 104

mutiny, 168n104, 220, 221

Myers, Barbara, 81n50

My Lai massacre, 79, 83, 219

napalm, 43n31, 86, 213, 214, 217, 221; Dow Chemical production of, 120n71, 217, 218

NASA, 3n1

National Committee for New Politics (NCNP), 107, 108

National Coordinating Committee, 104

National Liberation Front of South Vietnam. *See* NLF

National Peace Action Coalition (NPAC), 120, 133, 138

National Student Association (NSA), 8–10, 16, 18, 42, 156, 157

National Women's Political Caucus, 26n23

Near, Holly, 136, 141, 224, 225

Neshoba County, Mississippi, 21

Newark, New Jersey, 20–39 passim, 59, 76, 92, 104

New Brunswick, New Jersey, 223

New Deal, 11, 33, 48, 199

New Frontier, 3, 45, 83, 96, 198

New Hampshire primary, 157, 219

# INDEX

New Haven, Connecticut. *See* Yale University

New Left: defined, 22n20, 85, 86, 96, 97; initiative at Columbia and Chicago, 115–120; problems, 65, 111–113, 126–128; as a put-down, 119. *See also* old left, draft, leaders, pacifists, new politics, SDS, SNCC

New Mobilization, 120

New York, New York, 11, 50, 115, 122, 160, 214, 215, 218, 219, 223, 225. *See also New York Times*

*New York Times*, 115, 155, 159, 168, 169, 171, 177, 222

new politics, 4, 107, 114

Newton, Huey, 6n6, 47

Ngo Dinh Diem. *See* Diem, Ngo Dinh

Ngo Din Nhu, 215

Nguyen Cao Ky. *See* Ky, Nguyen Cao

Nitze, Paul, 160

Nixon, Richard, 95, 220-224; 1960 presidential campaign, 3, 4; 1968 presidential campaign, 51, 116, 118; 1972 presidential campaign, 1, 84–91, 136, 137, 142; Nixon Doctrine, 60, 150, 163, 164. *See also* Cambodia, détente, Kissinger, Pentagon Papers, Watergate

NLF (National Liberation Front of South Vietnam), 43, 101, 156n96, 219; achievement, 8, 149; founding of, 7, 96, 214; identification with, 40; Tony Russo interviews, 80–81; "Viet Cong," 8

Nonviolence, 7, 64, 125, 186–190, 192, 211, 212, 225

*North from Mexico: The Spanish-Speaking People of the United States* (McWilliams), 181

North Vietnam, 164, 174, 214, 219; Communist Party position, 101; Jane Fonda 1972 trip, 81, 223; Hayden 1965 trip, 35; Hayden 1967 trip, 38, 59; Trotskyist position, 103; U.S. bombing of, 37, 129, 219. *See also* dikes, Gulf of Tonkin incident, Haiphong, Ho Chi Minh

NSA. *See* National Student Association

nuclear weapons, 2, 37, 59n42, 166n103, 216, 221; in Operation Duck Hook, 166n103

# INDEX

Nuremberg Tribunal, 170n106

Oakland, California, 6n6, 109, 111, 114, 198n119
October League, 119, 121
Oglesby, Carl, 104, 108, 118, 216
OLAS (Latin American Organization of Solidarity), 48, 110, 112
old left, 10–14, 61, 78, 97, 100–103, 121, 202
*One Man Against the World* (Weiner), 166n103
*Operation Abolition*, 5
Operation Duck Hook, 166n103, 221
Organization of the Solidarity of the Peoples of Africa, Asia, and Latin America (Tricontinental), 46n33
orphans, 226
Oswald, Lee Harvey, 15
*Other America, The* (Harrington), 10n9
Oughton, Diana, 64

pacifism, 36, 40, 85, 100, 102, 107, 120, 133, 211; and Weather Underground, 64. *See also* Staughton Lynd, David Dellinger.

Paine, Tom, 106
Panthers. *See* Black Panther Party for Self–Defense
Paris, France, 50; peace talks, 44, 110n64, 116. *See also* Peace Agreement
Peace Agreement (Agreement on Ending the War and Restoring Peace in Vietnam), 130, 131, 137, 137–140, 175, 224, 225
Peace Corps, 3, 4, 6, 7, 83, 96
peace movement, 95–150
Pearson, Drew, 113
Pentagon Papers, 22, 43; origins, 79, 81, 155, 156, 159, 160; *Pentagon Papers Digest*, 136; tone, 45; domestic role of military, 58, 156; McGovern and, 89; release and trial, 106n60, 167, 171, 172n110, 175, 222, 224.
Pentagon Papers *(continued)* *See also* Daniel Ellsberg, Anthony Russo, Wise Men
People's Blockade, 223
People's Coalition for Peace and Justice (PCPJ), 133, 137, 139
*People's History of the United States, A* (Zinn), 43n31

243

# INDEX

Philadelphia, Mississippi, 21n18
Phnom Penh, Cambodia, 144n88, 145, 147, 177
pluralism, 151, 160
populism, 147–150, 209
Port Huron, Michigan; Conference, 9, 10, 30, 57, 86, 108n61; *Statement*, 1, 10, 84, 90.
Potter, Paul, 10, 16, 104
POWs (prisoners of war), 141n85, 175, 216, 224
power elite, 151–153
*Power Elite, The* (Mills), 151n93
Prague Spring, 46n35
Prairie Populism, 209
Praxis Axis, 117
Presidio Mutiny, 220
prisoners of war. *See* POWs
Progressive Labor Party, 61, 121
Project Air War, 142n86
public opinion, 19n17, 73, 86, 131, 153, 155; in France, 88; Gallup poll, 217; Harris poll, 147; Operation Duck Hook, 166n103; after Tet Offensive, 159, 165

Quakers, 38n29. *See also* American Friends Service Committee
Quang Ngai Province, Vietnam, 146n90
Quang Tri Province, Vietnam, 81
Quinn-Judge, Sophie, 156n96

racism, 8, 13, 14, 20, 30, 47n37, 52, 75, 143, 144
Ram Dass. *See* Richard Alpert
RAND Corporation, 80, 81, 155
Reagan, Ronald, 128
realignment, 12, 64, 114
Rebozo, Charles "Bebe," 174
Reconstruction, 102n57, 211n127
redbaiting, 6
reform, 195–201
refugees, 226
Reich, Charles, 76
repression, 47, 93, 113, 129, 158, 181, 182, 187, 188, 200; Chicago, 49, 91, 116, 118; cycle of, 13, 31, 34, 190; function of, 31, 152, 173; Weather Underground view, 62, 63
Republican National Convention: Miami

244

Beach 1972, 127–129, 223
Republican Party, 165, 177. *See also* Republican National Convention
Resistance, The, 218. *See also* draft
*Rethinking Camelot: JFK, the Vietnam War, and U.S. Political Culture* (Chomsky), 99n55
Rettig, Richard, 9, 10
revolution, 6, 10, 28, 37, 52, 73, 76, 90, 195, 196; John Kennedy view, 7; within New Left, 108, 112–128 passim; Vietnamese, 40, 47, 62, 96, 144, 145; SDS split-offs, 121, 122. *See also* Regis Debray, China, Cuba, old left, SNCC, Soviet Union, repression, Weather Underground.
Revolutionary Communist Party, 121n73
Revolutionary Union, 121n73
Revolutionary Youth Movement (RYM), 121
*Revolution in the Revolution?* (Debray), 45n32
Ridgeway, Matthew, 160
Ring Around Congress, 223
Robbins, Terry, 63

Rockefeller interest group, 160, 161
Rockefeller, Nelson, 3, 144, 153, 177
Roosevelt, Franklin Delano, 171n107
Ross, Fred, 181
rotation in office, 201
ROTC, 223
Rubin, Jerry, 70, 71
Rudd, Mark, 59, 115, 117
Rusk, Dean, 98, 105, 160
Russell, Bertrand International War Crimes Tribunal, 217
Russia. *See* Soviet Union.
Russo, Anthony, 80, 86, 170; indictment and trial of, 107n60, 222, 224
Ryder, Paul, 161, 171

Saigon, Vietnam: city (now Ho Chi Minh City), 43, 86; "fall" of, 145, 147, 177; political prisoners, 139, 142; protests in, 141n85, 214, 225; U.S.
Salazar, Ruben, 222
San Clemente, California, 224
San Francisco, California, 13n14, 68n46, 102; protests, 218, 220, 221, 222, 224, 225. *See also* HUAC

245

# INDEX

SANE (Committee for a Sane Nuclear Policy), 216
Santa Barbara, California, 107n60, 223; Bank of America burned, 122
Santa Cruz, California, 184n116
San Diego, California, 109n63, 125; Republican National Convention 1972, 127–129
Santa Monica, California, 109n63, 137n84, 138, 155n95, 161n101
Savio, Mario, 115
Scheer, Robert, 107n60
Schlesinger, Arthur, Jr., 171n108
Schwerner, Michael, 21–22
SCLC (Southern Christian Leadership Council), 38n29, 134, 211
Scott, Peter Dale, 99n55
SDS: 1; 1965 national Vietnam demonstration, 10n8, 36–38; founding, 4, 9–13 passim, 78. *See also* civil rights, Chicago, Columbia, Newark, New Left, Weather Underground
Seale, Bobby, 6n6, 71, 123

sect (sectarianism), 13, 24, 61, 67, 68, 75, 102, 119, 133, 165
segregation, 22n21, 98, 99
Sheehan, Neil, 159
Sheinbaum, Stanley, 106
Shero, Jeff (now Jeff Shero Nightbyrd), 209
Shriver, Sargent, 44
Sihanouk, Norodom, 145n89
Silone, Ignazio, 40n30
Sirica, John, 175n113
sit-in, 3, 4, 5n3, 6, 11, 216. 223, 224
Sitting Bull, 83, 87
Smith, George, 136
SNCC (Student Nonviolent Coordinating Committee), 16, 26n23, 35n25, 48n38, 75, 97, 112n66, 156, 206n123; and ERAP, 19–21; founding, 5, 214; nonviolence, 211; and Vietnam, 38n29, 107. *See also* Mississippi
socialism, 65, 97, 211; transition to, 195, 196, 199, 202
Socialist Party, 197
Socialist Workers Party, 102
social movement. *See* movement

246

# INDEX

Sorenson, Theodore, 171n108
South. *See* civil rights, SNCC, Mississippi
South Bend, Indiana, 216
Southern Christian Leadership Council. *See* SCLC
South Vietnam, government. *See* Saigon
South Yemen (now Republic of Yemen), 145
Soviet Union, 96, 104, 146, 171, 173, 204n122; SDS view, 22, 36; CPUSA and, 101; Trotskyist view, 103. *See also* détente, Cuba, China
Speer, Albert, 170
Spock, Benjamin, 114, 131, 216, 220
Spender, Stephen, 40n30
spontaneity, 73, 78, 112, 122, 125, 180, 203–205
Stalin, Joseph, 101n56; Stalinist, 103
Starkey, Tom, 184
State Department, 42–43, 45, 171n107; *See also* U.S. AID
Stennis, John, 22
Stone, I.F., 19, 37
Stone, Oliver, 99n55
Stop the Draft Week, 109, 111, 114, 219

student movement, 3–12 passim, 19, 20, 23, 47, 62, 67, 68, 73, 75: national student strike, 124, 221
Students for a Democratic Society. *See* SDS
Student Mobilization Committee, 120, 135
Student Nonviolent Coordinating Committee. *See* SNCC
Sunflower County, Mississippi, 26n23
Sutherland, Donald, 136n83, 222
Sweden, 140, 217, 219
Symington, Stuart, 154, 159
Syracuse, New York, 219, 223
Syria, 111

Taiwan, 82n52
Taylor, Maxwell, 160
teach-in, 38, 39, 78, 106n60, 133, 215, 216
Tet Offensive, 42, 158–159, 165, 187, 219
Thieu, Nguyen Van, 82, 145, 158, 163, 224, 225
Thompson, Gabriel, 181n115
Times Square Vigil, New York, New York, 215
*Tinker v. Des Moines*, 216

247

# INDEX

Thich Quang Duc, 214
Third Force, 156, 214
*Third Force in the Vietnam Wars: The Elusive Search for Peace 1954–1975, The* (Quinn-Judge), 156n96
Thoen, Erik, 218
tiger cage, 225
torture, 81n50
*Trampling Out the Vintage: Cesar Chavez and the Two Souls of the United Farm Workers* (Bardacke), 210n126
Tricontinental. *See* Organization of the Solidarity of the Peoples of Africa, Asia, and Latin America
Trotskyism, 101–104, 107, 120, 133, 135, 138
Truman, Harry, 105, 154, 158, 161, 163n102, 213; split with MacArthur, 154n94, 172
Truskier, Andy, 109, 137
Tunisia, 47n37
Tunney, John, 179
Turkey, 5, 7
"Two, Three, Many Vietnams", 45, 48, 111

U.S. AID, 80

*UFO* GI coffeehouse, 219
unexploded ordnance, 226
Unitarian Church, 80
United Campaign for Peace in Indochina, 140, 142
United Farm Workers, 179, 180, 187n117, 190, 210n126, 211. *See also* Chavez, Cesar
United Nations, 93, 111, 214, 225
unity, 118, 119, 143, 190, 191, 206, 207
University of Michigan: 154, 195, 215. *See also* Ann Arbor, *Michigan Daily*
*Michigan Daily*, 2–3, 9
University of Maryland, 223

Vance, Cyrus, 160, 166
veterans, 81–82. *See also* VVAW
Viet Cong. *See* NLF
Vietnam Day Committee (VDC), 70n47, 100, 106
Vietnam Overseas Procurement Office, 225
Vietnam Summer, 107, 108, 218
*Vietnam Times*, 38n29
Vietnam Veterans Against the War. *See* VVAW

# INDEX

Vietnam War: *See* decent interval, Haiphong, Ho Chi Minh, Indochina, napalm, Ngo Dinh Diem, NLF, North Vietnam, Operation Duck Hook, Peace Agreement, political prisoners, POWs, refugees, Saigon, Tet, tiger cages, torture, Vietnamization

Vietnamization, 162, 163n102, 167

vital center, 151

*Voices of 1960s Midwestern Student Protest* (Lieberman), 209n125

voter registration, 5n3, 16–17

VVAW (Vietnam Veterans Against the War), 125, 218, 222, 224, 225

Vy, Nguyen Minh, 110n64


Waldorf Astoria Hotel, New York, New York, 215

Walinsky, Adam, 53

Wallace, George, 30

Warnke, Paul, 158, 168

Warren Commission, 15

War Resisters League, 214

*Washington Post*, 113n67, 168, 171, 177

Watergate scandal, 129, 151, 153, 166, 168, 175; as opportunity for peace movement, 139, 140, 143, 146

Westmoreland, William, 159

Weather Underground (Weatherman, Weatherpeople), 59, 61–67, 117, 118, 120, 121, 122

Weiner, Tim, 166n103

W.E.B. Du Bois Club, 102

Wheeler, Earle, 158, 160, 219

Whitehead Lawson, Shari 109

*Who Rules America?* (Domhoff), 151n93

Winne, George, Jr., 124, 221

Winter Soldier Investigation, 125n77, 222

Wise Men, 159–163, 169

women's movement, 26n23, 28, 69, 72, 75, 88, 126–127, 223. *See also* Women's International League for Peace and Freedom, Women Strike for Peace

Women's International League for Peace and Freedom, 217

Women Strike for Peace, 214, 215, 217

Woolworth, F.W., 5

249

INDEX

World Bank, 45
World War I, 198n120
World War II, 11, 13n14, 43n31, 132, 154, 163, 165, 213; Ho Chi Minh declares independence, 111n65, 213
World War III, 176
*Wretched of the Earth, The* (Fanon), 47n37
Wright, Richard, 40n30

Yale University, 123, 124, 160
Yankees, 152
Yippies (Youth International Party), 57, 69, 70n47, 71, 209n124
Young Lords, 134
Ylvisaker, Paul, 33
Youth International Party. *See* Yippies

Zimmerman, Bill, 137
Zinn, Howard, 43, 171n108

# Acknowledgments

For their help in preparing this book, we are grateful to Al Haber and to Julie Herrada, Curator, and the staff of the Joseph A. Labadie Collection, Special Collections Research Center, University of Michigan Library in Ann Arbor.

For permission to use the *Rolling Stone* interview, we thank Maureen Lamberti at Wenner Media LLC in New York City. For permission to use the back-cover photograph, thanks to Marie Koltchak of the *Seattle Times*.

Printed in Great Britain
by Amazon